"It's not the way I intended to live my life.

It's a dangerous, tough, dirty job but someone's got to

do it. It would be nice if society didn't need

people like me, but while it does... I'll be there."

The late Rick Cook telling Brian Byfield, his art director, why he became a copywriter.

Published by RotoVision SA
7 Rue du Bugnon
1299 Crans Switzerland
Tel: +41 22 776 0511
Fax: +41 22 776 0889

RotoVision Sales and Production Office
Sheridan House
112/116A, Western Road
Hove BN3 1DD
England
Tel: +44 1273 72 72 68
Fax: +44 1273 72 72 69

First published 1995
Reprinted 1996
2nd Reprint 1996
3rd Reprint 1997
Production and Separation in Singapore by ProVision Pte Ltd
Tel: (65) 334-7720
Fax: (65) 334-7721

Printed in Singapore
ISBN No 2 — 88046 — 258 — 4

Tania Guha

THE DESIGNERS AND ART DIRECTORS ASSOCIATION
OF THE UNITED KINGDOM
IN COLLABORATION WITH ROTOVISION SA

It is difficult to know where great ideas come from but, in the case of this book, it's easy. Alastair Crompton came to D&AD in the summer of 1994 with the proposition that we should publish a book in which the world's top copywriters explain how they work – because, quite simply, it hadn't been done before. As a large part of our remit is to educate and inspire the next creative generation, we jumped at the chance.

The origins of some of advertising's most memorable copy lines will always be shrouded in mystery and mythology but this book unveils the approaches and methods of thirty–two top class copywriters and provides an invaluable insight into their thought processes.

Asking copywriters to write a specific number of words about how they write isn't easy. It quickly became apparent that, of those who were willing to contribute, many had clear and specific ideas as to how their copy should be presented and how long it should be.

In an industry where the 'look' of a piece of copy is designed to enhance what it says, this seemed appropriate. So we have made no attempt to standardise their submissions – their work is shown here exactly as it arrived at our offices.

While many contributors reveal highly individual approaches to their work, there is also a remarkable degree of commonality. Aspiring writers are urged to forget about clever puns and wordplays, for example, and to listen instead to the sound of their words when read in a phoney American accent. We have David Abbott to thank for that advice, and indeed I would like to thank all the contributors for turning this book from a great idea into a reality. I would also like to add my personal thanks to the Newspaper Publishers Association for sponsoring it and Lowe Howard–Spink for offering its talent and services in putting the book together.

Ranging from the serious to the seemingly glib and flippant, this book is a treasure chest of wisdom, hints and tips. I hope you will find it both enjoyable and highly informative.

Anthony Simonds – Gooding.

D&AD would like to thank all the copywriters who so generously contributed articles,

artwork and photographs for this book. Also deserving of special thanks are Lowe Howard–Spink,

David Christensen, Mark Cooke, Theresa Dauncey, Jasvir Singh Garcha,

Alfredo Marcantonio, Ian White and all the staff at the Newspaper Publishers Association whose

unstinting efforts turned Alastair Crompton's bright ideas into a reality.

Alastair Crompton – Commissioning Editor
Ian White – Editor
Jasvir Singh Garcha – Designer
David Christensen – Art Director
Theresa Dauncey – Project Co–ordinator
Mark Cooke – Production Manager
Michael Brooks – Artwork Co–ordinator
Darren Sugrue – Artwork Manager
Leonard Currie – Cover Calligraphy
Alex Buckingham – Cover Photography
Visual Network – Imaging
David Kester – Director, D&AD
Anthony Simonds–Gooding – Chairman, D&AD

CONTENTS

"THE TRADE OF ADVERTISING IS NOW SO NEAR TO PERFECTION THAT IT IS NOT EASY TO PROPOSE ANY IMPROVEMENT."

Dr Samuel Johnson
writing in the Idler, 1759.

First I want to make the apology without which this book is an impertinence. By no means are all the world's best copywriters to be found in these pages.

The fact is, the highest number it is possible to bring together at the same time and in the same place (even if that place is a book) is precisely 32, from Britain, the United States, Asia and Australia. If there are any questions about this, D&AD has the research to prove it.

We looked for, and spoke to, more top writers from these countries as well as from South Africa, but for good reasons they could not join us.

Even some a stone's throw away from the D&AD offices were not able to contribute. We should have taken out warrants for their arrest and held them in the cells while they wrote for us. Maybe some other time.

The apology is to all the superb copywriters we did not know about, could not reach or inadvertently (and unforgivably) overlooked. I'm sure you are out there, and sooner or later will pick up this book. Sorry we missed you, we would prefer to have had you along.

Several of the 32 who contributed asked, when we told them about the book, whether it might become repetitive. Was there a danger that too many of the contributors would have very similar things to say?

No danger at all, for as each writer's piece arrived it became clear we might equally have asked 32 painters how they went about their business, or 32 authors how to conjure up a best-seller, so diverse were the ideas we received.

What then, the aspiring copywriter might ask, should you take away from this book if great minds do not think alike?

The answer must be, as much gold as you can usefully carry. Test what you read and see if it works.

You may find that advice which is worthless when you work on some briefs is spot-on to solve others. Even if every one of our 32 is right, why should they all be right for you? Three thoughts come quite clearly out of everything we have been told. A copywriter shouldn't start to write the instant the brief hits the desk (who am I kidding?).

Instead start to think. At the same time feed the mind. The more you know about the product or service the easier ideas come, the less expected they are and, more often than not, the better they work. The converse is also true: working without facts means the work can only be fiction.

Never write to the target audience carefully delineated in the brief. Words like: 'All C1C2 housewives with children 5ft 2ins and under' are worse than useless. Instead, write to one person, the archetypal customer.

Maybe you'll know her personally, maybe you must create her before you create anything else.

Keep a mental picture of her, get under her skin and into her mind. Only then is it time to begin a dialogue.

Finally I'd like to touch on an intangible quality that permeates these pages which heartens and encourages me.

You will recognise it early on, and remember it after you put the book down.

There are no cynics writing here. The image of the copywriter that emerges at the end is a far cry from the heartless, manipulating huckster of films and pulp fiction.

Our 32 writers honour their reader's good sense and try to pull wool over nobody's eyes. A lifetime honing copy has taught them that any sentence written merely to please the author is worthless and that, once they ignore the intelligent reader, the intelligent reader will deservedly ignore them.

Alastair Crompton – Commissioning Editor
Alastair Crompton is leader of the Higher National Diploma Course in
Creative Advertising at Falmouth College of Arts.

I have written copy for Kodak; Mather & Crowther which became Ogilvy & Mather; Doyle Dane Bernbach which became DDB Needham; French Gold Abbott which became defunct and Abbott Mead Vickers which became Abbott Mead Vickers·BBDO. In the process, I became ancient.

I write with an Artline 200 Fine 0.4 Pentel — blue ink, never black. I generally work on A3 layout pads but will sometimes switch to an A4. Definitely low tech stuff.

Paradoxically, I do have a PowerBook on my desk but I haven't yet learnt how to use it. (To show how little I understood the PowerBook concept, I originally requisitioned two – one for the office and one for home). However, one day I know that I will be computer literate – probably the same day that I'm fluent in French and win the lottery.

In the meantime, the action picture you see of me at work is accurate. I write with my office door open — more often than not I keep my jacket on and in defiance of my mother's instructions, my feet are usually on the table.

Whatever the size of the layout pad, I write body copy in column widths. This habit goes back to my days on the VW account in the sixties. I knew how many words to the line were needed and how many lines to the ad. Writing in columns made it easier to get the word count right.

Alongside the column I jot down thoughts or phrases that come to mind before I need them. They stay there in the sidings until there's a place for them. I also write down in the margins all the clichés and purple bits that clutter my head. I find that only by writing them down do I exorcise them. If I simply try to forget them they keep coming back like spots on a teenage chin.

I rarely plan the shape of a piece of copy. By the time I come to write, the structure of the argument is somehow in my brain. I spend a lot of time fact–finding and I don't start writing until I have too much to say. I don't believe you can write fluent copy if you have to interrupt yourself with research. Dig first, then write.

Like many other copywriters, I read my copy out aloud as I write. It helps me check the rhythm of the line and ultimately the flow of the whole piece. I often adopt the appropriate accent or tone, though my general 'reading–copy' voice is laughably mid–Atlantic (I read silently if there are other people in the room).

I am a fast writer and in a sense I am not interested in words. I don't own a Thesaurus, I don't do crosswords and my dictionary has pictures in it. Words, for me, are the servants of the argument and on the whole I like them to be plain, simple and familiar. I believe that I'm paid to be an advocate and though I get pleasure from the bon mot, the bon motivater thrills me more. Word–play is fine if it helps the cause but I use it sparingly, or not at all. This wasn't always the case; I used to pun for England.

When I'm working on concepts, I draw the shape of the ad space and write the headline (or scribble the picture) within its borders. It's odd but I can't judge an Economist headline until I've drawn a line around it. When I was younger I used big Pentels and large pads and swashbuckled my way to fertility. An ad a page. Now my would–be ads are much smaller and I might cover a page with six or seven thoughts — though sometimes when I'm stuck I go back to the big pad and the big pen. A change in procedure is often a good idea when you're not getting one.

I've been writing copy since 1960 and by now I'm comfortable with the job. I don't panic and I know that the best thing for me to do when tired or thwarted is to walk away from the ad and do something else. The job still surprises me and for every easy problem, there's a stubborn sister. I might rework a headline fifty or sixty times to get the thought and balance exactly right. If I think there's an ad in there somewhere, I nag at it until it comes out. I'm often surprised how quickly time passes when I'm doing this. I look up and discover that I've been fiddling with the words for three hours.

Agency life rarely allows for this level of concentration so I also write copy at home, late at night, or I'll book a hotel room and work from there. (This piece, for example, is being written at the kitchen table). I couldn't work in an open–plan creative department, but I'm sure there are brilliant copywriters who do. Great copy has been written in cafés, on trains, on beaches, on planes, in cars — even occasionally at a desk. How you do it is less important than what you do.

I've never been much of a theoriser about copywriting, but here are five things that I think are more or less true:

1. *Put yourself into your work. Use your life to animate your copy. If something moves you, chances are, it will touch someone else, too.*

2. *Think visually. Ask someone to describe a spiral staircase and they'll use their hands as well as words. Sometimes the best copy is no copy.*

3. *If you believe that facts persuade (as I do) you'd better learn how to write a list so that it doesn't read like a list.*

4. *Confession is good for the soul and for copy, too. Bill Bernbach used to say 'a small admission gains a large acceptance'. I still think he was right.*

5. *Don't be boring.*

If he can make it, so can Volkswagen.

No disrespect intended, Mr Feldman.
But no-one would ever mistake you for Gregory Peck. Yet you've made it right to the top.
On talent.
And that's kind of reassuring when you make a car that looks like ours.
The Volkswagen isn't pretty, Mr Feldman. But it's got talent.
It has an air-cooled engine that can't boil over in the summer.
Or freeze up in the winter.
It's the kind of engine that can go on and on and on.
We know one person who went right on for 248,000 miles.
And for a little car it's got a great talent for fitting people in.
There's more headroom than you'd expect (Over 37½" from seat to roof).
If you were 6′ 7″ Mr Feldman you still wouldn't hit the roof.
And because there's no engine in the front, there's room to stretch your legs in the front.
We've even got a space behind the back seat where you can sleep a baby. In a carrycot.
So you see, Mr Feldman, looks aren't everything are they?

VOLKSWAGEN MOTORS LIMITED. VOLKSWAGEN HOUSE, PURLEY, SURREY. TELEPHONE: 01 668 4100.

Before Ron Brown and I created this ad, I had written in countless pieces of Volvo body copy that each weld on a Volvo is capable of supporting the entire weight of the car. As a fact it's impressive, but as a picture, as a testimonial, as a demonstration, it's a stopper. Don't just repeat facts, dramatise them.

IF THE WELDING ISN'T STRONG ENOUGH, THE CAR WILL FALL ON THE WRITER.

That's me, lying rather nervously under the new Volvo 740.

For years I've been writing in advertisements that each spot weld in a Volvo is strong enough to support the weight of the entire car.

Someone decided I should put my body where my mouth is. So we suspended the car and I crawled underneath.

Of course the Volvo lived up to its reputation and I lived to tell the tale.

But the real point of the story is this; the Volvo 740 may have a different body shape, a fast and frugal new engine, a new interior and a new suspension system, but in one respect it's just like the Volvos of yore.

It's so well built you can bet your life on it.

I know I just did.

To: Volvo, Springfield House, Mill Ave, Bristol BS1 4SA. Please send me details.

Mr/Mrs/Miss

Address

Postcode

THE NEW VOLVO 740. FROM £9249.

"I never read The Economist."

Management trainee. Aged 42.

The Economist campaign not only has its own look, it has its own tone of voice. What is potentially a banal positioning ('read this and be successful') is made acceptable and convincing by wit and charm. Directness has its place in advertising but so do subtlety and obliqueness. Things you can't say literally can often be said laterally.

I like headlines that draw the reader into the ad – a question is an obvious way to do it. In this case the question is partly answered by a witty visual and the copy does the rest. I was tempted to use 'uncannily like fresh fruit' as the headline but resisted. However, you'll often read ads where the body copy contains a better headline than the one the writer chose. Remember to check your copy for buried treasure.

SAINSBURY'S FLAVOUR SEAL UNSWEETENED GRAPEFRUIT SEGMENTS *in natural juice* Vacuum-packed for A BETTER, FRESHER TASTE 25% MORE FRUIT PER CAN 100 gram 14.1 oz

Guess what Sainsbury's new canned grapefruit tastes like?

In its own little way our new canned grapefruit is something of a milestone.

It's vacuum-packed. (As far as we know, the first on sale in Britain.)

The outcome is grapefruit that tastes uncannily like the fresh fruit.

But taste isn't the only advantage. With vacuum-packing, we're able to put much more

grapefruit into the can.

On average, 25% more fruit than with traditional canning methods.

You can buy our new 'flavour seal' grape-

fruit, unsweetened in pure juice or in a syrup.

Either way you get more flavour and more fruit.

Good food costs less at Sainsbury's.

Because I've known you all my life.

Because a red Rudge bicycle once made me the happiest boy on the street.

Because you let me play cricket on the lawn.

Because you used to dance in the kitchen with a tea-towel round your waist.

Because your cheque book was always busy on my behalf.

Because our house was always full of books and laughter.

Because of countless Saturday mornings you gave up to watch a small boy play rugby.

Because you never expected too much of me or let me get away with too little.

Because of all the nights you sat working at your desk while I lay sleeping in my bed.

Because you never embarrassed me by talking about the birds and the bees.

Because I know there's a faded newspaper clipping in your wallet about my scholarship.

Because you always made me polish the heels of my shoes as brightly as the toes.

Because you've remembered my birthday 38 times out of 38.

Because you still hug me when we meet.

Because you still buy my mother flowers.

Because you've more than your fair share of grey hairs and I know who helped put them there.

Because you're a marvellous grandfather.

Because you made my wife feel one of the family.

Because you wanted to go to McDonalds the last time I bought you lunch.

Because you've always been there when I've needed you.

Because you let me make my own mistakes and never once said "I told you so."

Because you still pretend you only need glasses for reading.

Because I don't say thank you as often as I should.

Because it's Father's Day.

Because if you don't deserve Chivas Regal, who does?

This ad is about Chivas Regal but it's also about me and my father. (I really did have a red Rudge bicycle). It's a risky ad and, for some people, it's sentimental but I know others who say that it vividly echoes their own experience. Incidentally, if you try to write a headline for this ad, you'll discover why it doesn't have one.

When the Government killed the dog licence they left us to kill the dogs.

One thousand dogs are killed in Britain every day.

For the most part, healthy dogs and puppies with years of life left in them.

The killings take place at local vets, in RSPCA centres and other animal charities throughout the country.

The dogs are given an overdose of anaesthetic and die within seconds.

A van makes regular collections and the dead dogs are taken to the local incinerator.

It doesn't take long to turn a Jock, Spot or Sandy into a small pile of ashes.

This daily slaughter is strange work for a society founded to prevent cruelty to animals.

We hate the killing.

We are sick of doing the Government's dirty work behind closed doors.

We want you to help us force through a dog registration scheme.

The dogs we kill are homeless dogs. Unwanted, or strays left to roam the streets and parks, often in packs.

There are at least 500,000 of them out there right now.

Left to themselves, the figure would be close to 4 million in ten years' time.

Homeless dogs cause road accidents, attack livestock and foul our parks and pavements.

And yet we can't blame the dogs, for we live in a society that makes it more difficult to own a television than a living, breathing creature.

There is no licence required. The Government abolished the licence last year and we are now seeing the consequences.

The RSPCA want to see a dog registration scheme introduced.

And so it seems do most of you. In a recent poll, 92% of you said "yes" to registration.

If there was a registration fee it would encourage responsible dog-ownership.

Each dog could be identified with a number so that its owner could be traced and held responsible for the dog's actions.

The money raised would finance a national dog warden scheme, more efficient clean-up operations and more education for dog-owners.

These measures seem so sensible you wonder why they haven't been tried before.

Well, many of them have.

Sweden, America, Germany, Australia, Russia, France and Ireland all have a more enlightened policy than Britain.

Help us catch up.

Write to your MP and press for dog registration.

If you're not sure how to go about it, call free on 0800 400478 and we'll give you an action-pack and add your name to our petition.

Do it now, for every day that goes by sees another 1,000 dogs put down.

And what kind of society kills healthy dogs?

(RSPCA)

Registration, not extermination.

In long copy ads, the trick is to make the construction invisible. Most copywriters have their favourite linking words or phrases — they're particularly useful when the client demands a lot of information in one ad. (Another useful word is no). In this case, however, the facts all supported the argument and I don't think the copy is longer than it needs to be.

John Bevins began his advertising career as a despatch boy at Hansen-Rubensohn-McCann-Erickson in Sydney in 1963. He joined Ogilvy & Mather as a junior copywriter in 1968. In 1972, at 26, he was made Creative Director of O&M Sydney. In 1982 he started his own agency. John Bevins Pty. Limited was named B&T Agency of the Year in 1991. Last year, a Campaign Brief poll among the nation's top advertising agency CEO's and Creative Directors named him Australia's Advertising Person of the Year and Creative Person of the Year.

Also in 1993 his long-copy, all-copy, press work for Bankers Trust was voted B&T Advertisement of the Year, edging out big budget TV commercials.

Is copywriting about sitting around trying to think up ideas? I don't think so.

Had I sat around trying to think up ideas for New Zealand Tourism, diligently following the flawed brief from the market researcher ("Australians think New Zealand is 'sickeningly wholesome', so make it a ' little bit wicked' "), I'd never have gone over to New Zealand and wandered aimlessly around the quiet back streets of Queenstown looking for ... *what*? I had no idea. But I found it nailed to a gate. It inspired the Paranoia ad.

Had I sat around trying to think up ideas for the Medical Benefits Fund of Australia, I'd never have gone over to meet the inspiringly dedicated Dr Joan Kroll who runs MBF's mammogram screening clinic, and who kindly gave me an hour of her precious time; plus this even more precious oh-by-the-way gem: "There's a painting that shows breast cancer long before medicine discovered it, I think it's by Da Vinci, or Van Gogh. Professor Michael Baum from London uses it in his lectures". A phone call that night to the Professor at the Reyne Institute revealed that the painting was Rembrandt's *Bathsheba at her Toilet*. "You know it, of course?", the Professor said. (I didn't.) But the next morning, the second I saw it, I knew that here was the campaign. Bathsheba's look said, with great dignity, everything that could be said about a controversial and vital issue that was being less-than-addressed by the government of the day. Further investigation revealed two compelling stories, many centuries apart, behind Bathsheba's — and especially Heindrickje Stoffel's — sorrowful look. And it all connected with a surprising fact filed away in the back of my head: that more Australians visit art galleries than (even) The Footie. To boot, it complied with a belief — too earnest? — that advertising should enrich people, not impoverish them. Damn it, it should.

Had I sat around trying to think up ideas for Bankers Trust to meet the television brief they'd given us in the pitch for their account, I'd never have gone over to try and persuade them that this shouldn't be a TV campaign at all but a newspaper campaign. Sure, I had no idea what the words would be about, just that there'd be a lot of them (and no pictures). But if they'd just let me inside their unusual organisation, past all their security doors, so I could interrogate their unusual people, if they would let me search their corridors for the *genius loci*, maybe I could write something people would really want to read. Okay, they said. And so I discovered What It Is about Bankers Trust, fund manager of the decade, and I discovered the magic of Compounding Interest and exactly what Dollar Cost Averaging is. And later, by compulsively dialling up the Associated Press news service on my Macintosh instead of trying to think up ideas, I discovered a chimpanzee in Sweden who had just made more money on the stock market than a bunch of stock analysts competing against him.

Had I sat around trying to think up ideas for Peugeot, I'd never have got to chat with all those Peugeot owners, and Peugeot mechanics, and Peugeot engineers and designers at Peugeot's plants and design centres in France — where, remarkably, Peugeot flew the Australian flag to welcome the agency even though Australia accounted for just a half-a-day-a-year's production — and I'd never have discovered that there is a *passion* at Peugeot that runs deep, a passion to do with one thing: making cars go exactly where you point them.

For me, it *is* about discovery, first and foremost, about following your instincts rather than following a brief. Sacrilegious?

It's also about collecting useless things you know sooner or later will come in handy and, with words as flux, about welding prospects and products together with those things. And it's about remembering that understanding the prospect is far, far more important than understanding the product, even though understanding the product is extremely important.

And, as for when you do sit down, finally, for all those hours, for the writing part of copywriting, for the drafting and then the crafting, what's important above all else, then, is this:

"If you don't enjoy writing it, no-one will enjoy reading it." It's one of the mottoes I trot out to myself and, together with other corny-but-nourishing mottoes like "Spell it out and it's out with the spell" and "There's no future in writing a great ad if it's not what the client wants and there's no future in writing what the client wants if it's not a great ad", it helps me get closer to figuring out this strange way of earning a living.

"If you don't enjoy writing it, no-one will enjoy reading it" I find helpful because it reminds me that all writing, unless you write things like instruction manuals, is more about putting something in than putting information out. That 'something' I can't explain.

But when a writer puts something in there's the chance of an unintentional gift for the reader. This makes writing writing and reading reading. While putting something in is no guaran-tee that a piece will get read, just putting information out is a guarantee it won't, unless it's irresistible information. Who reads instruction manuals?

I therefore think, and if it's true it's a juicy irony, that good copywriters don't really do it for the client or for the agency or even for the reader... they do it for themselves. Which suggests that as vitally important to your work as the craft is, the craft is not the work. It is not the art. Not the expression. The journey-man copywriter, even when he is the most masterful craftsman, fails to take us with him.

And you can't fake expression. You do have to be in the mood to write. Copywriters — unlike bookwriters or songwriters — only get days or weeks to produce the inspiration to produce their work, and are expected to be constantly productive. Being constantly in the right mood so that it's always more a joy than a job is a prerequisite. Fun's fundamental.

The best way I know how to get in the mood to write is to start writing. That said, it's vital to surround yourself with the right people, the right workmates and the right clients, those whose response to your work you respect and trust.

This means finding the right agency, at all costs.

Or starting your own.

Expressive copy—putting "something" in rather than just putting information out— connects writer and reader.

THE SWEDISH CHIMPANZEE METHOD (PLUS A SOUNDER WAY TO GET RICH).

Nº 6· IF YOU PERSEVERE with this wall-to-wall text, you will be rewarded with an introduction to Dollar Cost Averaging, the minor marvel that could help make you rich. But first, to Stockholm, and a chimpanzee named Ola.

Last August, a Swedish newspaper gave five stock analysts and Ola 1,250 kronor each. The idea was to see who'd make the most money on the Stockholm stockmarket. Ola won. After just one month, Ola's portfolio went up by 190 kronor. While each of the five experts expertly considered What Exactly To Do, Ola tossed darts at names of listed companies. One dart hit Forsheda, a small diversified company whose share price went up 44 per cent over the month.

Easy.

Except, of course, such a method is rather risky. And not just because you might hit someone in the eye with your dart (or get hit yourself if you commission a chimpanzee).

Every bit as risky is that other 'hit or miss' method. You know, the one where the 'investor' lets his heart, rather than a dart, decide for him. Mark Twain said *all emotion is involuntary when genuine.* Genuine emotion – as in "I didn't mean to buy the shares when they were priced high, and I didn't mean to panic and sell them when the price fell"– drives the demise of most mug investors.

So what *drives the rise* of the successful investor?

Sometimes it's sheer brilliance. Mostly, it's sheer discipline. Yerk. Discipline? Hold on, and read on. Even dull old discipline becomes exciting when it's combined with something called Dollar Cost Averaging.

Dollar Cost Averaging?

Dollar Cost Averaging is an investment strategy that requires no thinking, no decision making, no analysis, no will-I-or-won't-I hankie wringing. All you do is invest the same number of dollars at regular intervals, no matter what. You invest, say, $100 every month in a unit trust ... no *matter what.* No matter whether the share markets are up or down, soaring or crashing, bear weather or bull. You simply grit your teeth and, Nike*-like, Just Do It.

This very simple strategy works. For this very simple reason: your regular, set-amount investment buys less when the market's up, and more when the market's down. It does this *automatically.* And therefore frees you from the worry of trying to time the market, something not even the world's most sophisticated analysts can do well enough to guarantee a profit. Sure, Dollar Cost Averaging doesn't guarantee a profit either. If you have to sell at the bottom of a falling market you will lose money – just like anyone who's forced to sell at the bottom. But when you stick to a disciplined Dollar Cost Averaging plan, you are forced *to buy ... not sell.* That's the whole point. And fortune does favour the brave.

Sounds good in theory, doesn't it? But what about in practice?

Introducing Lucile Tomlinson.

For sophisticated investors the defiantly simple discipline of Dollar Cost Averaging has been around at least since the early fifties. Way back then analyst and author Lucile Tomlinson tested Dollar Cost Averaging on Wall Street share prices, as part of a comprehensive study she did of formula investing plans†.

Benjamin Graham, in his classic text, *The Intelligent Investor,* tells of Tomlinson's study: "Tests were made covering 23 ten-year purchase periods, the first ending in 1929, the last in 1952. Every test showed a profit either at the close of the purchase period or within five years thereafter. The average indicated profit at the end of the 23 buying periods was 21.5%, exclusive of dividends received. Needless to say, in some instances there was a substantial temporary depreciation at market value."

Of course, Dollar Cost Averaging is no Get Rich Quick scheme. Just a Get Rich Slow scheme. And it's a scheme that's even better than forced saving, because *it's forced investing.*

You see, you can't eeny, meeny, miny, mow your way to greener pastures. And you can't really follow the herd there ... because even the most bullish, especially the most bullish, herds get lost. Or turn out to be lemmings. You must have a plan.

Dollar Cost Averaging could be such a plan for you. If you are interested in finding out more about it, interested in seeing an example of how it works in rising markets, falling markets and fluctuating markets, you might like to read a leaflet BT has prepared on the subject: *How you can benefit from investing in the downs as well as the ups.*

You also might like to examine at the same time the prospectus on the BT Lifetime Trust because it offers a simple savings plan that is ideal for a Dollar Cost Averaging strategy. The BT Lifetime Trust, incidentally, is an investment that is spread by experts across, primarily, *a range* of BT unit trusts. Trusts that have proven long-term performance.

For reading all this ... *tack."*

Bankers Trust Australia Group

For additional information on Dollar Cost Averaging or on the BT Lifetime Trust, speak to a financial adviser or call 008 022 555. Or cut and post this coupon to: Reply Paid No. 13, Bankers Trust Australia, PO Box H184, Australia Square, Sydney NSW 2000.

Mr/Mrs/Ms_____

Address_____

_____P/code_____

006PWA

Phone (BH)_____(AH)_____

BT Financial Services Limited and member companies of the Bankers Trust Australia Group do not guarantee the repayment of capital or the future performance of the Trust.

A copy of the current BT Lifetime Prospectus has been lodged and is dated 21 December 1993 and is available upon request from any BT office. Applications for investment may only be made on the form contained therein. BT Financial Services Limited is the Manager of the Trust. John Bevins BT117012PWA

Nº.6 IN A SERIES 'INSIGHTS FOR INVESTORS', BROUGHT TO YOU BY BT FINANCIAL SERVICES.

*Nike is a registered trademark of BRS Inc. †Practical Formulas for Successful Investing, Wilfred Funk, Inc., 1953. **Tack means thank you in Swedish.*

The prospect is more important than the product.

THIS IS PERHAPS THE MOST INFURIATING AD YOU WILL EVER READ. UNLESS YOU ARE 21.

Nº 5. WHAT YOU ARE about to read will fascinate you, or infuriate you, or both. It will also present you with a delicious paradox, by proving that a person who decides to stop saving can save considerably more than someone who decides to save diligently all the way to 65. Come again? Let's put it another way. This insight is about the saving ethic and as with its cousin, the work ethic, the underlying truth is that saving smarter beats saving harder. Disciplined saving is the ethic's essence. Discipline is even more important than dollars when it comes to producing a result.

You will probably wish someone had explained all this to you when you were young enough to really learn and profit from it. Still — and this is your consolation — you can be the someone who explains it to someone else; to a young person who still has the time to profit from it. It? "It" is the "magic of compound interest", and it isn't really magic at all — it's simple mathematics. But magic for most is more intriguing than maths, so let's think of it as magic.

Imagine you are 21 again. You decide, because someone explained this magic to you, to save $2,000 a year — until you turn just 30. Then you stop saving altogether and leave your nest egg alone until you turn 65. Let's say, for the sake of the exercise, that you earn an average return of 8% p.a. (after fees and taxes) which you always reinvest. Let's say, again for the sake of the exercise, that inflation is 0% (so your *real* return is a healthy 8%).

Now imagine an alternative scenario. Again, you are 21 but decide to do nothing about saving until you turn 31. At 31, you begin saving $2,000 a year and you continue to do so *every* year until you turn 65, again reinvesting the 8% p.a. average return. You figure you will more than make up for lost time by saving harder — i.e. for 35 years rather than 10 years.

Which is the better strategy?

The 10-year plan, in which you will have invested $20,000 will reap $428,378. The 35-year plan, in which you will have invested $70,000, will reap considerably less: $344,634. Here are the basic calculations for you to check. The bold type represents those years when you contribute $2,000.

Age	Plan A	Plan B
21 years old	**$2,000**	
22 years old	**$4,160**	
23 years old	**$6,493**	
24 years old	**$9,012**	
25 years old	**$11,733**	
26 years old	**$14,672**	
27 years old	**$17,846**	
28 years old	**$21,273**	
29 years old	**$24,975**	
30 years old	**$28,973**	
31 years old	$31,291	**$2,000**
32 years old	$33,794	**$4,160**
33 years old	$36,498	**$6,493**
34 years old	$39,418	**$9,012**
35 years old	$42,571	**$11,733**
36 years old	$45,977	**$14,672**
37 years old	$49,655	**$17,846**
38 years old	$53,627	**$21,273**
39 years old	'$57,917	**$24,975**
40 years old	$62,551	**$28,973**
41 years old	$67,555	**$33,291**
42 years old	$72,959	**$37,954**
43 years old	$78,796	**$42,991**
44 years old	$85,100	**$48,430**
45 years old	$91,908	**$54,304**
46 years old	$99,260	**$60,649**
47 years old	$107,201	**$67,500**
48 years old	$115,777	**$74,900**
49 years old	$125,039	**$82,893**
50 years old	$135,042	**$91,524**
51 years old	$145,846	**$100,846**
52 years old	$157,514	**$110,914**
53 years old	$170,115	**$121,787**
54 years old	$183,724	**$133,530**
55 years old	$198,422	**$146,212**
56 years old	$214,295	**$159,909**
57 years old	$231,439	**$174,702**
58 years old	$249,954	**$190,678**
59 years old	$269,951	**$207,932**
60 years old	$291,547	**$226,566**
61 years old	$314,870	**$246,692**
62 years old	$340,060	**$268,427**
63 years old	$367,265	**$291,901**
64 years old	$396,646	**$317,253**
65 years old	$428,378	**$344,634**

The table shows the dramatic effect that compound interest can have on a disciplined saving plan, even when you decidedly stop saving. Imagine now a savings plan that goes beyond regular saving into regular investment:

Discipline pays dividends.

A plan that teaches the essence of sound, balanced investment. Imagine getting that kind of opportunity, that kind of education, that initiation to the magic, when you were just 21.

The BT Lifetime Trust is a unique managed unit trust with such a savings plan. $1,000 and $100 a month can get an investor started. It cannot guarantee, it does not promise, the minimum 8% essential to the example given earlier (what can these days?) but it has earned, through its Future Goals Fund, 37.1% net of management fees over the year to 1 Sept, 1993.

If you are a parent or a grandparent who would like to get a young investor started, or if you are someone who believes it's never too late to start saving yourself, you might like to investigate the BT Lifetime Trust.

BT will be happy to send you full details …

Bankers Trust Australia Group

For more information, see your financial adviser, call BT toll-free 008 022 555 or send this coupon to: Reply Paid No. 13, Bankers Trust Australia, PO Box H184 Australia Square, Sydney NSW 2000.

Mr/Mrs/Ms_____

Address_____

_____ P/code_____
122012PWA
Phone (BH)_____ (AH)_____

BT Financial Services Limited and member companies of the Bankers Trust Australia Group do not guarantee the repayment of capital or the future performance of the Trust.

A copy of the current BT Lifetime Trust Prospectus has been lodged and is dated 21 June 1993 and is available upon request from any BT office. Applications for investment may only be made on the form contained therein. BT Financial Services Limited is the Manager of the Trust. Performance returns are quoted in accordance with IFA Performance Standards. John Bevins BT122012PWA

Nº 5 IN A SERIES 'INSIGHTS FOR INVESTORS', BROUGHT TO YOU BY BT FINANCIAL SERVICES.

If you don't enjoy writing it, no-one will enjoy reading it.

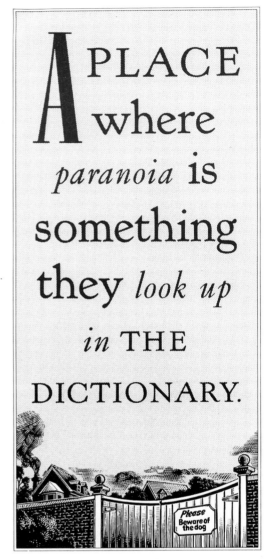

A PLACE where *paranoia* is something they *look up* *in* THE DICTIONARY.

THERE IS A SIGN on the gate of a house in Queenstown, New Zealand.

This is what it says:

Please beware of the dog.

That's right, *please* beware of the dog.

What kind of a threat is that? *Please* beware of the dog?

Why doesn't New Zealand have the kinds of signs we have here in Sydney? You know, signs like: "Trespassers will be shot. Survivors will be prosecuted." *

Well, there's a very good reason.

A reason that will dawn on you after you've spent your first few days in this haven from a hostile world.

"You know what," you might say to your companion, "the people here *trust each other*."

Wonder of wonders.

There you are in country crammed with all kinds of wonders — geysers, glaciers, even a whole new kind of *green* — yet the wonder of wonders is that The People Trust Each Other.

TRUST NEVER SLEEPS

A good example of this trust is honesty stalls.

Driving down the Central Otago Road to Queenstown, for instance, between Millers Flat and Roxburgh, you'll find lots of honesty stalls.

Indeed, one that's not so much an honesty stall as an honesty emporium. A huge shed packed with huge bags of walnuts, peaches, dried apricots, plums and apples — apples that still have their leaves on. *Leaves.* Instead of sticky, little labels. To buy something, you simply drop some money into a jar that's temptingly — nay, trustingly — full of notes and coins. You help yourself to the change, and then leave with your bounty. Feeling, well, enriched.

A RETREAT, NOT A RESORT.

Clearly, New Zealand is different.

A place where you can be reminded of what life should be about, what life used to be about, so that when you return to what life is about you are equipped to deal with it.

Accordingly, it is the best holiday you can have.

A holiday for the heart and the head, a holiday for the soul and spirit.

Good God (not blasphemy, He was the architect), the scenery alone will replenish you. If you simply hopped over and stood on any square metre of countryside, turned 360°, and returned home immediately, you'd still feel replenished.

But the real replenishment comes from collecting experiences — a pastime far more rewarding than collecting, say, souvenirs. Experiences like the five-course lunch they serve at the Onetangi Pub. (Four pints and a pie.) Or a few days spent bunking aboard Cliff Barnes' fishing boat on Dusky Sound.

Cliff'll cook you dinner, but he expects you to catch it. (You'll never go hungry, mind you. The waters are *rich* with fish.)

The islands of the sunset – Dusky Sound

OH, SOMETHING ELSE THAT WILL DAWN ON YOU IN NEW ZEALAND.

At last count, there were five thousand one hundred and twenty-eight million people on this little planet.

Most of them don't trust each other. A good place to ponder this peculiarity of "progress" is at Mt. Hikurangi, East Cape, as you watch the sun rise.

The new dawn – East Cape

This enlightening place is where the first rays of each new day tickle the earth. So you and your companion will have the goose-bump-inducing privilege of seeing the new day dawn well before any of the other 5,127,999,998 people.

And what will also dawn on you is that New Zealand isn't

Roadside fruit stall – Central Otago.

behind the rest of the world. It's actually ahead.

Not just several hours ahead. Several decades.

Real progress, it will dawn on you, is preserving what we have that's of value. And the most valuable things that we have are those that, ironically, cost nothing.

Until we lose them.

Trust. Clean air. Clean water. Stuff like that.

The North American Indians said that we don't inherit the earth from our parents, we borrow it from our children. It seems the only place anyone heard them was way down there in New Zealand.

Did you know, for instance, that the largest body of un-polluted water in the world is in New Zealand?

It's called Lake Taupo.

Lake Taupo is so unpolluted, the locals will encourage you to drink from its shores.

"Go on", they'll say, "have a sup."

The big question is, can they be trusted?

Well … finding out is one of the great pleasures of visiting New Zealand.

— — — — — — — —

I am trusting you to send me the 70-page New Zealand Book. Please deliver it, post haste, to:

Name _____

Address _____

_____

_____

_____ Postcode _____

Send this coupon to NZTP, G.P.O. Box 614, Clarence Street, Sydney, NSW 2001 or, better still, call the nice people at the New Zealand Tourist Office direct on — (02) 233 6633, (03) 650 5133, (07) 221 3722, or (008) 331 106.

— — — — — — — —

"Stay where you are, New Zealand. I'm coming over."

*On the gate of a house in Terrey Hills, Sydney.

John Bevins NZ05005

Following your instincts might be more productive than following the brief.

YOU WILL NEVER forget this masterpiece. It tells the story of Bathsheba and King David. It was painted by REMBRANDT in 1654. A fateful detail is the letter being read by Bathsheba. It is from King David. ▦ ⬚ ⬚ ⬚ ⬚ ⬚ ▦

▦ It asks that she meet him in secret. The consequences for Bathsheba – already wed – can only be tragic. But there is an even more fateful detail, discovered only recently. It gives new meaning to the brooding poignancy of "BATHSHEBA."

▦ Look closely at the model's left breast. Can you see the dimpling? This detail, recorded unknowingly by Rembrandt, is advanced breast cancer. ▦ ⬚ ▦

▦ The consequences for the model? Well, she died several years later. ▦ ⬚ ⬚ ⬚ ⬚ ⬚ ⬚ ▦

▦ She was *Hendrickje Stoffels*. She was also Rembrandt's common-law wife and, within a year of the painting, mother of his daughter. (Was she pregnant as she posed?)

▦ In those days, neither model nor artist, nor anyone, had heard of breast cancer. Expert medical opinion now is that, almost certainly, she died of breast cancer. ▦ ⬚ ⬚ ⬚ ⬚ ⬚ ⬚ ⬚ ▦

A WOMAN'S BEST PROTECTION IS EARLY DETECTION.

Breast cancer is the most common cancer in women. ▦▦

▦ These days, doctors can detect breast cancer long before it becomes even an unseen, unfelt lump. And long, long before it becomes the classic *"orange peel dimpling"* recorded by Rembrandt. For many women early detection can mean a complete cure. ▦▦

▦ Early DETECTION is your best PROTECTION from the consequences of breast cancer. It can save your life, often without the need for a mastectomy.

THE ONLY EARLY DETECTION THAT WORKS IS REGULAR SCREENING MAMMOGRAMS.

Regular screening mammograms are recommended for women over 40 and for younger women where there is a

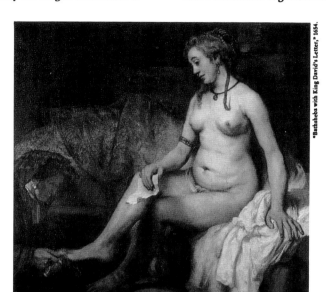

"Bathsheba with King David's Letter," 1654.

family history of breast cancer. ▦ ⬚ ⬚ ⬚ ⬚ ⬚ ⬚ ⬚ ⬚ ⬚ ⬚ ▦

▦ *Screening mammograms* are not covered by Medicare unless symptoms are present or unless there is that family history.

▦ If you are under 40, with no family history of breast cancer, your doctor is the best person to talk to about breast health and a detection regimen most appropriate for you. ▦ ⬚ ⬚ ▦

TO AN ART LOVER,
THIS IS A CLASSIC REMBRANDT.
TO A DOCTOR,
IT'S CLASSIC BREAST CANCER.

THE MBF SYDNEY SQUARE BREAST CLINIC.

MBF is determined to provide for its members what Medicare does not. For this reason, MBF recently acquired the respected Sydney Square Diagnostic Breast Clinic, now the MBF SYDNEY SQUARE BREAST CLINIC. Subsidised screening mammograms for MBF members, according to the medical guidelines above, are now available. ▦ ⬚ ⬚ ⬚ ⬚ ⬚ ⬚ ▦

▦ The fee is JUST $20. (Screening mammograms are available to non-members for the standard $60 fee.) ▦ ⬚ ⬚ ⬚ ⬚ ⬚ ▦

ADVANCE BOOKING ESSENTIAL. CALL (02) 285 9999.

There is a limit to the number of screening mammograms that can be carried out. ▦ ⬚ ⬚ ⬚ ▦

▦ Not because of the equipment – MBF can always buy more equipment to meet the demand of its members. The limiting factor is the *highly-skilled personnel* essential to perform and interpret the X-rays. ▦ ⬚ ⬚ ⬚ ⬚ ⬚ ⬚ ⬚ ▦

▦ MBF acquired the Clinic for its members because it is run by some of Australia's most skilled and experienced breast health experts and *specialist radiologists*. ▦ ⬚ ⬚ ⬚ ⬚ ⬚ ⬚ ⬚ ⬚ ▦

▦ The Clinic views more than 10,000 X-rays each year. The MBF Sydney Square Breast Clinic can currently handle 100 screening mammograms a week, so naturally, advance booking is essential. For more information, call the Clinic on (02) 285 9999. ▦ ⬚ ⬚ ⬚ ⬚ ⬚ ⬚ ▦

▦ If you are an MBF member, please have your membership number handy.

John Bevins MBN 00511/1   Medical Benefits Fund of Australia. Incorporated in NSW. A non-profit, registered health benefits organisation.

Enriching the reader enhances the readership. This ad showed the value of talking up, not down.

I have been a copywriter for 35 years. Sometimes it feels longer. Though I have written some well known commercials — Cinzano (with Rossiter and Collins) Shredded Wheat (bet you can't eat three) Clarks Shoes (foot drawing) and Volkswagen (casino) — people keep telling me I'm a press writer and I've come to believe them. It was my good fortune to work at DDB and CDP when both were at their height. With them I won eighteen D&AD silvers and three golds (I have hopes for more) for which I owe thanks to the fine art directors I've worked with, most notably, of course, my great friend Neil Godfrey who was responsible for four of the six ads shown here. Freedom Food was art directed by Stu Baker and Chivas by Martin Walsh.

Who wrote this?

'An 80-year-old man contacted me.

He said 'I'm having trouble satisfying me wife. What do you advise?'

I wrote back, 'Get a lodger'.

Three months later he got in touch again. Your advice has worked, my wife's pregnant.'

'How's the lodger?' I replied.

'Fine,' he said. 'She's pregnant too.'

Now this isn't just a good joke, it's good writing. There isn't one redundant word. Each sentence leads inevitably to the next and onwards to the punch line.

I think it's good for another reason, too: you can work out who wrote it, George Burns. Without a headline or a logo (and far less a corporate statement beneath a logo) older people, take it from me, would recognise his tone of voice.

In a similar way I believe each company should have its own individual voice, and that the way we write copy can help.

Clearly this means you have to know your clients pretty well, so take the time to see them (cut through the protective screen account directors and planners throw around them) and ask some tricky questions:

What do they stand for? Where are they going? What would and wouldn't they do for money? How do they treat their employees? And their customers? What do they value most — profit, reputation or professional ethics?

Gradually a picture, or rather a voice, will emerge and if you are quiet when you write, you'll convey it to your readers.

From my portfolio I've chosen ads where people tell me I succeeded in doing this.

Because Albany Life was a new insurance company (and who wants one of those?) I tried to make a virtue of their energy and fresh ideas.

Instead of 'blue-skying' potential customers with sunny prospects of wealth in the distant future, I addressed the real anxieties of white collar workers when their lives begin to fray.

I asked what happens when they get over the hill, get fired and get under their wife's feet, then offered savings schemes for the foreseeable future. It gave Albany Life the authority to discuss people's real lives rather than their dreams, which the company's youth would otherwise have denied them.

On the other hand, when I visited Dunn & Co, the men's outfitters that dressed the over-fifties, I found that employees who'd shared an office for twenty years still called each other 'Mister'. In my copy for them I referred to their customers as 'gentlemen' and tended to use words that were current when they were boys: 'jolly good', 'old man', 'splendid'.

It goes without saying, I hope, that I try to show all clients at their best and enthuse about their products.

For Parker I extolled the joys of writing (with a fountain pen) and sometimes used literary quotes. I suggested that ball-points were anonymous and told how your own nib style transcribing 'gleaming wet words' would express your individuality.

Recently, for the RSPCA's new venture 'Freedom Food' which guarantees farm animals basic freedoms, I tried to capture a sense of quiet reasonableness rather than righteous anger.

(Generally speaking, the hotter I feel, the more I look at my writing with the cold eyes of an assassin).

I said earlier how vital it is to meet clients. I'd never have written recruitment ads for army officers the way I did if I hadn't spent so much time with them.

I found them surprisingly cultured and, dare I say it, sensitive.

They felt their career had a higher purpose (than killing people) and wanted their peers in civilian life to know this.

Thus in the ads I stressed the peace–keeping nature of the job, the importance of defending personal freedom and, at a time when the communist threat was real, democracy itself.

Finally I'd like to mention one of my early Chivas ads. I didn't create the tone of voice and for purely egotistical reasons, I wanted to change it. It took Bill Bernbach just 60 seconds to persuade me that I shouldn't. He was right, of course. The Chivas voice was unique and valuable. It lasted for 25 years or so until some other idiot changed it.

I hope these few tips help you with your writing. If so, it will be part repayment to all those who helped me hugely with mine.

Freedom Food. The voice of quiet reason not righteous anger.

Answer these ten questions and work out the date of your own death.

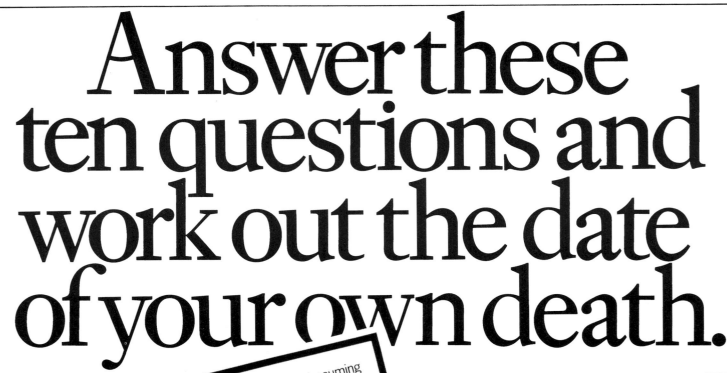

Start with the age of 77 for a man and 81 for a woman (assuming you are over twenty years old now) and add or subtract according to your answers.

1. How old are you now?
Up to 50 no score.
51 – 55 add one year.
56 – 60 add two years.
61 – 65 add three years.
66 – 70 add four years.

2. Do you smoke?
Over 40 a day subtract 9 years.
Over 20 a day subtract 6 years.
Up to 20 a day no score.

3. Do you drink?
Heavily (more than 5 drinks a day) subtract 10 years.
Moderately, no score.
Teetotal, subtract 2 years.

4. Sex?
If you enjoy sex once a week, add 1 year.

5. Family History?
If any close relative has died of heart disease before 50, subtract 4 years.
Between ages 51–65, subtract 2 years.
If any close relative has suffered from diabetes or mental disorder, subtract 3 years.

6. Overweight?
If your problem is measured in stones rather than pounds, subtract 6 years.

7. Your job?
Professional, technical or management, add 1 year.
Semi-skilled, subtract 1 year.
Labourer, subtract 4 years.
But: active, add 2 years, desk-bound, subtract 2 years.

8. Exercise?
Proper exercise (heavy breathing) at least twice a week, add 3 years.

9. Life-Style?
Single, living alone, subtract 1 year.
Widow, or separated within past 2 years, subtract 4 years.

10. Health?
If you have an annual check-up, add 2 years.
Any serious illness or disease requiring hospital treatment in the last 5 years subtract 10 years.

These are the sort of questions actuaries ask before they insure you.

Answered honestly, they will give you a rough idea of your life expectancy, no more.

They won't tell you if you are going to plough your car into a lamp-post. Or jump out of a window. Or choke on a fishbone.

They are just statistics based on the lives and deaths of hundreds of thousands of people.

And we are raising this chilling topic on a Sunday morning for two reasons.

First, to make you think of providing for those you couldn't bear to leave unprovided for.

Secondly, and more unusually, to make you consider the last half of your life.

What are you going to do with it?

More than likely (according again to statistics) you are going to have a second career.

But whether it will be absorbing and challenging or boring and time-serving, is not just a question of your ability.

It will also depend on how much money you have to set up a business or supplement your salary.

And if after twenty years of screamingly high taxation you haven't a bean, don't worry, we can help you.

If you can put by something every month for the next ten years or so, we will invest it for you.

In this respect we are uniquely advised by no less than Warburg Investment Management Ltd., a subsidiary of S.G. Warburg & Co. Ltd.

We are also aided by the Inland Revenue. The taxman allows us to retrieve a certain amount of your income tax which we also invest on your behalf.

This way we can eventually give you a tax-free income or lump sum.

If you have read this far you are obviously of a fearless and enquiring mind. Let us tell you more about our savings plans.

This coupon will bring our brochures speeding to you.

Albany Life. A young company which understood a young man's anxieties.

Russian armour entering Kabul.

Next?

Will Russian tanks roar across the plains of Germany?

Will crises erupt somewhere so remote we all have to scour maps to find out where it is?

Will one of our NATO allies call for moral support on its borders?

Will we be asked to join an international peace-keeping force to separate the sides in a civil war?

Frankly, your guess is as good as ours.

The world is so unstable it could go critical at any time without so much as a warning light.

This is why we have made the Army much more mobile.

And why we always try to recruit the type of young man who can add calmness and good humour to a tense situation.

Now we need another 900 young Officers whom these men will follow, if necessary, to the ends of the earth.

A job with no guarantee of success.

You may well argue that your joining the Army would not have saved one life in Afghanistan.

We would go further, it might not save anyone's life, including your own.

On the other hand, it might.

It might, if enough like-minded men join with you, help to prevent a nuclear war.

And it might, just might, hold the world together long enough for the powers of freedom and sweet reasonableness to prevail.

Some hopes?

Perhaps. But the alternative is no hope at all.

Hoping for the best, preparing for the worst.

Your part in this will be to prepare for a war everyone prays will never happen.

Depending on the job you choose, you will rehearse battle tactics in Germany.

Confront heat in Cyprus, Belize or Hong Kong.

And heat of a different sort in Northern Ireland.

You will practise, repair, train and try to forge links with your men that will withstand fire.

Occasionally, you may be asked to clamber into a VC10 on the way to, well, somewhere like monitoring a cease-fire in Rhodesia.

But more often, the worst enemy your men will face will be boredom, when it will take all your skills as a teacher and manager to motivate them.

Then it will be difficult to remember that you are still protecting your country and all you love most.

An easy question to dodge.

The question is, are you prepared to take the job on for three years or longer?

No one will accuse you if you don't.

Women won't send you white feathers and children won't ask what you did in the war.

All we ask is that every young man at least takes the question seriously and answers it to the satisfaction of his own conscience.

This way we are bound to get our 900 new Officers.

If you are undecided but want to take the matter a stage further without committing yourself in any way, write to Major John Floyd, Army Officer Entry, Department A7, Lansdowne House, Berkeley Square, London W1X 6AA.

Tell him your date of birth, your educational qualifications and why you want to join us.

He will send you booklets to give you a far larger picture of the life and, if you like, put you in touch with people who can tell you more about the career.

 **Army Officer**

Army Officer. Not the prospects offered by civilian jobs.

Rediscover the lost art of the insult.

Do you know plumbers who never turn-up?

Hairdressers who missed their vocations as butchers?

Drycleaners who make your stains disappear–and your clothes with them?

Today, we at Parker give you the chance to get your own back.

Not only are we offering a beautiful new pen called the Laque which owes its deep lustre to a Chinese technique 2000 years old, but we are attempting to revive something that went out when the telephone came in:

The well-aimed, witty, malicious dart.

Imagine yourself, for example, in a quiet room, a sheet of pristine notepaper before you and your Parker Laque poised like a javelin.

How about this to the dustman who keeps spilling litter down your steps:

May the curse of Mary Malone and her nine, blind, illegitimate children chase you so far over the hills of Damnation that the Lord himself can't find you with a telescope.

A good, old Irish curse and already you're feeling better. Now for the book club that won't stop sending you junk mail.

With gleaming wet words you see the Laque effortlessly transcribe your wrath into a death blow:

You louse in the locks of literature.

A nice bit of alliteration borrowed from Tennyson but they won't know that.

While you're at it, how about a post card to an airline that's lost your bags.

You have delusions of adequacy.

Or to a chef who nearly poisoned you:

Two partridges, ill trussed and worse roasted . . . an old hare newly killed and poorly stuffed; celery and some other trash; in short, a very poor performance. A.G. Hunter

You might say with some justification that you don't need a gold nibbed pen costing £34 to write a decent insult, even if the nib is so symmetrical you can use both sides of it.

We can only answer that just as a beautifully made car tempts you to drive so a perfectly engineered pen tempts you to write.

Try this on the old bore who keeps asking you your opinion of his literary works:

Your manuscript is both good and original; but the part that is good is not original and the part that is original is not good. Dr. Samuel Johnson

But you can knock spots off these hacks, surely.

Come on, get yourself a Parker Laque and let rip.

Someone, somewhere deserves a real stinker from you.

♦PARKER

An ABC of helpful words:

Amateur.	Goatbrained.	Meat-head.	Oik.	Unprofessional.
Bodger.	Has-been.	Noisome.	Pusillanimous.	Verminous.
Cretin.	Idiot.		Quack.	Wally.
Dunderhead.	Jumped-up.		Rip-off.	Xantippe.
Egomaniac.	Know-nothing.		Sycophant.	Yes-man.
Feckless.	Lemming.		Toady.	Zombie.

THE PARKER LAQUE 180 SHOWN HERE   RECOMMENDED PRICE £34.07 INC. V.A.T.

Rediscover the lost art

Parker. The joy of writing with a fountain pen.

"When."

When you're pouring Chivas Regal, it's unwise to let your guests draw the line.

So often they seem to find themselves with a mouthful of peanuts.

Or they decide to lose their voice.

The only consolation is that while they're drinking your Chivas, they're developing a taste for the 12 year old Glenlivet whiskies we blend.

(They're at least twice as old and smooth as most.)

So you shouldn't have long to wait before they buy themselves a bottle of Chivas.

And give you the chance to lose your own voice.

Chivas Regal. A voice that should never have changed.

Success doesn't always go to your head.

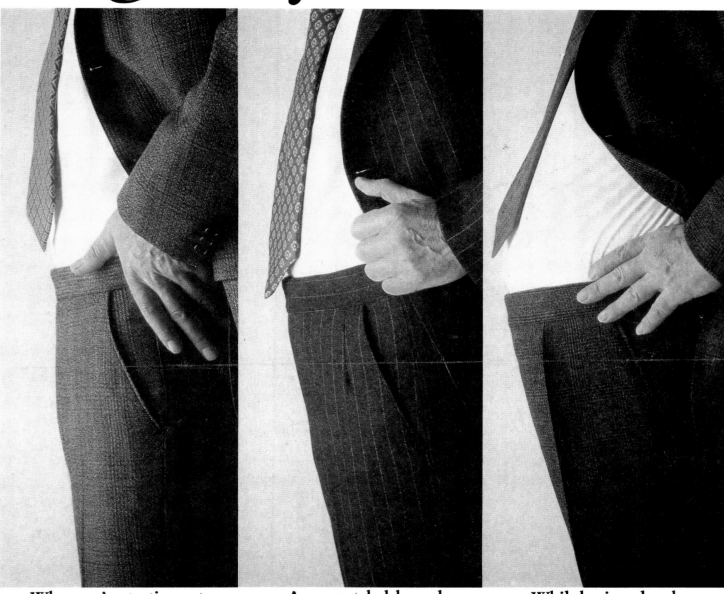

When you're starting out you can probably wear our suits with flat-fronted trousers.

As you get desk bound you might need a couple of darts at the waist.

While business lunches usually mean you need two pleats.

A gentleman's waistline is nobody's business but his own.

For this reason we thought long and seriously about publishing the above photographs.

Are they indiscreet? we asked ourselves. Are we in the slightest way opening our customers to such smirking remarks as:

"You don't need a couple of darts at the waist, old man, you need a grapefruit diet."

But consider our predicament.

There are still some men who just won't believe a ready-to-wear suit will ever fit them.

Even though we have related countless times that we have different fittings for slim, portly, short portly, stout and short stout men.

Not to mention how many times we've mentioned that we also cater for men with long arms or short arms, and men with long legs or short legs.

So we decided to release our waistband secrets and tell the world how we can soften the ravages of time and the business lunch.

Hoping that you will be persuaded to walk into Dunns and try on every suit in the shop.

Safe in the knowledge that even if you hate them all, it won't have cost you a penny.

Dunn & Co

Dunn & Co. Addressing middle aged men in language they used themselves.

Place of birth: Columbia, Tennessee.
Current position: Creative Director, Chiat /
Day New York.
Toughest Boss: Ed McCabe & Jay Chiat (tie)
Most influential partner: Helmut Krone.

Most hated (by others) campaign: Reeboks Let
U.B.U.
Most sceptical of: advertising award shows.
Most proud of: people breaking glass to steal my
posters.

IN PRAISE OF THE WRITER BEHIND
THE MARLBORO MAN.

I don't know his name. Somebody thinks he died.

In my professional youth, I had made fun of him. All of us hungry young copywriters in Chicago laughed that he must have the cushiest job in town. We, who laboured long into the night trying to come up with ever more clever headlines, didn't appreciate his genius. While we struggled to put a pun into every line of body copy, he elegantly cut to the core of the idea.

The writer of the original Marlboro Man campaign understood the simple truth that a picture is worth a thousand words. It needed no verbal adornment. Headlines, taglines, they come and go. The craggy-faced Marlboro Man simply changes his hat.

My adornment comes naturally. When I was a kid, I was always drawing. Civil War battle scenes. Cutaways of the Mercury space capsules. But I never got it quite as right as my pal Rodney Henmi. He became an architect.

I became a copywriter. Not so much because I was an avid reader and had studied journalism in college, but because there was always a Rodney around who could draw better than me. By rights they got to be the art director.

But do not mistake me for a frustrated art director. I am simply a realist. Times have changed. We are finally breaking the hegemony of the picture/clever headline school of advertising.

We don't have readers anymore. We have thumbers, browsers, window shoppers through printed media. The image stops the thumber. The words seduce him to stay.

No, I repeat, I am not a frustrated art director. I am a misunderstood copywriter. How many times have I had to suffer the age-old putdown of the competing copywriter:

"Congratulations, that's a great looking ad?" Sneering between the lines, what they mean is "You obviously had nothing whatsoever to do with that ad." Once it cost me a job. The man who was thinking about hiring me didn't because he decided my Reebok campaign was an art director's campaign. I don't think we would have gotten on very well.

Other copywriters have also been misunderstood for thinking visually. A good friend of mine, Jeff Gorman, had won every medal the American advertising industry can bestow upon it's copywriters, several times over. Finally, while he was working at Chiat/Day in Los Angeles, he did the famous original Nike athlete campaign. Heresy of heresies, it featured wonderful photographs of athletes, not a word in sight. Just a tiny Nike logo up in the corner. It won everything there was to win. And Jeff retired from copywriting. "How could I top that?" he moaned. Now he's a successful commercials director.

Oh, what slings and arrows the Marlboro writer must have suffered in his day. But who's to say what copy is anyway? In the Nikon campaign, the photograph is the body copy. We reasoned that most photographers are more eloquent with images than with words. We just gave them their voice.

I like finding other keys on the keyboard. The "" keys worked well for Nikon. I remember a wonderful ad that Ed McCabe did for Perdue chickens that used most of the keys on the top row (!*@%?) to great effect.

I have also toyed with the spelling of words as in "Reeboks let U.B.U." and with using icons as typography as in the Fruitopia "tagline." I once did ƨıɥʇ to illustrate what wouldn't happen to your slides in a Bell & Howell slide projector.

Anything to make the words more visual.

I've chosen the ads you see here in homage to the man behind the Marlboro Man. And to make sure there are at least a few pictures in a book on copywriters. And because I'm still sensitive to the accusation of being too art director-y, I've included a Nissan ad that's got a whole bunch of words in it.

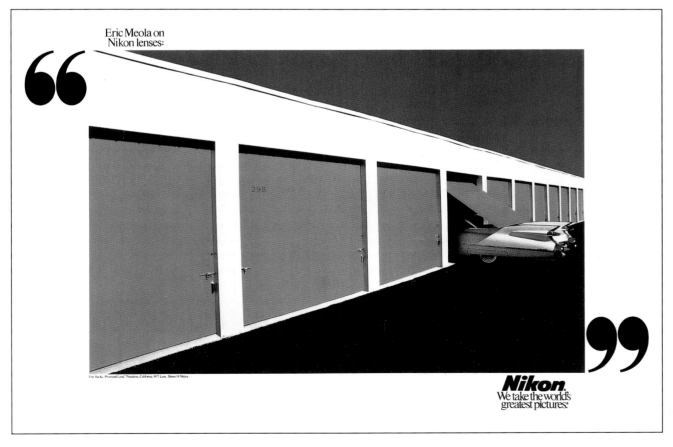

The pictures speak for themselves.

IF WE CAN'T FIND A WAY TO LIVE WITHOUT THE CAR, WE'D BETTER FIND A CAR WE CAN LIVE WITH.

A CAR COMPANY WITH A CONSCIENCE?

After years of trumpeting its virtues, it's time a car company faced up to the car's darker side.

Cars have been involved in 4,221 fatalities this year alone. (Of course, drunk drivers must take much of the blame.) Cars, along with many other products, threaten the future of the planet. And despite the fact that they cost more each year, cars still break down.

But admitting the problems isn't solving the problems.

Let's take safety first. Last year alone, Nissan invested over $2 billion in research and development. From airbags to air conditioning. (An uncomfortable driver is an unsafe driver.)

In addition, no other import offers Anti-Lock Brakes (ABS) on a broader range of cars. Not just on our high-end sedans, but our compact economy cars as well.

We believe that you shouldn't have to be rich to be safe.

We also believe automobile manufacturers must be environmentally responsible.

Every Nissan dealer in Canada now recycles 100% of the freon (CFC-12) in our air conditioners.

Nissan is introducing the world's first mass-production electric car.

And this year's Nissans burn less fuel than ever before. But herein lies the typical Nissan paradox: while this year's Sentra uses 4.2% less fuel than the 1990 Sentra, it delivers 22% more horsepower.

Responsibility can be fun. Lots of fun.

But problems are no fun. So we're introducing the Nissan Satisfaction Commitment.™ It's the most comprehensive full-line customer care program in Canada.

Six-year warranties against major component failure, rust perforation and harmful emissions.

Three-year complete vehicle warranty and emergency roadside assistance. And a 24-hour toll-free Helpline.

We believe it's about time companies took responsibility for the products they sell. This may be why the Nissan Sentra is the only car ever to win the CAA' Pyramid two years in a row for reliability and customer satisfaction.

In terms of sales, Nissan is number four in the world. But in terms of automotive awards collected this decade, Nissan is number one.

Maybe the old moralists were right after all: having a conscience does have its rewards.

NISSAN

BUILT FOR THE HUMAN RACE

For product literature call 1-800-387-0122 (9am to 7pm EST). "CAA is a registered trademark of the Canadian Automobile Association.

"A whole bunch of words"

"THE MAN WHO GOES ALONE CAN START 2-DAY; BUT HE WHO TRAVELS WITH ANOTHER MUST WAIT TILL THAT OTHER IS READY." -HENRY DAVID THOREAU

Photography by Max Vadukul. ©1988 Reebok International Ltd. All Rights Reserved. Reebok is a registered trademark of Reebok International Limited.

REEBOKS LET U.B.U.

Spelling games

Tony graduated with a Masters Degree from Edinburgh University. After spells at CDP, Davidson Pearce and Hall's, he became creative director of DDB in 1986 and continues in that capacity at BMP DDB. Tony has won D&AD Silver Awards for radio, poster and television. He has also won the Gold Award at Campaign Press, the Creative Circle Honours Award and the Creative Circle President's Award.

"Christ!" said the duchess, "I'm pregnant. Who dunnit?"

The best stories usually hook you with their intro. They start as they mean to go on, rather than clearing their throat before getting down to business. As the Editor in "The Front Page" asks, with more realism than sensitivity to a hack's vanity: "Who the hell ever reads the second paragraph?" When it comes to an attention–grabbing form of scribbling like advertising the copywriter had better let the reader know what's going on early. Or he may be left with no reader.

But the copywriter does not work alone. He works with an art director whose job is to come up with the picture. And one picture, they say, is worth a thousand words. That sentence is ten words long. I still have 990 words left over. Think how much I can say with a few of them: "I love you." "Form follows function." "Less is more."

But however succinct, words like these do not make a great press ad because the thoughts are, in themselves, complete. And a good advertisement requires the reader to complete the communication on his own behalf.

It stands to reason, doesn't it? An advertisement is made up of two elements. The words and the picture. Together, they make a whole. In isolation, they don't. Take the headlines on these Volkswagen advertisements. The pictures don't make complete sense without the words. And the words don't make complete sense without the pictures. The reader has to decipher both to work out what the advertisement is saying. Only when the penny's dropped is communication complete.

What this implies, of course, is that the copywriter has to think visually. He has to 'see' what goes into the space occupied by the picture because otherwise the words he writes will be misconstrued.

The same is true of the art director. His picture, unless it is qualified by the words, is equally likely to be misconstrued. Which is why it is so hard to do a half–way decent ad of any kind, let alone one for Volkswagen.

And that brings us to the one unalterable fact that differentiates copywriting from all other forms of writing. An ad is never an end in itself. It always refers to something beyond it, the product. And just as there are only half a dozen stories of any kind, there are only half a dozen car product stories.

Speed. Economy. Engineering. Style. Ecology. Handling.

These stories have been told countless times before. David Abbott worked on the Volkswagen business. So did Tony Brignull. And Tim Mellors. And Dawson Yeoman. And several other copywriters who have had to take their salaries home in an armoured car. On the way, they left a legacy of advertising that has built a reservoir of goodwill towards Volkswagen.

Most people have, after all, chuckled over a Volkswagen ad at some time in their lives. At the very least, they have appreciated its wit and style. Or enjoyed the honesty that treats the reader like an intelligent friend. The copy is self–deprecating rather than self–congratulatory, the tone irreverent and disarming.

All the press ads shown here were created with Mark Reddy. "The only squeaks and rattles you'll ever hear in a Volkswagen" was written to the brief of engineering solidity. Several dozen other headlines had been greeted with a storm of apathy. The instant Mark heard this one, however, he drew an exact pencil sketch of what was to become the photograph.

The second ad, "We put people in front of cars", was our attempt at extolling Volkswagen's care for the environment. About six teams worked on the brief for several weeks and, in the end, ours was the best of the bunch. I'm still not quite sure though whether the visual is as apt as it might be. Shouldn't the car be coming towards the camera with the child facing us in front of the car? I don't know.

I do know, however, that the psychiatrist ad was a piece of total serendipity. By one of those quirks of amazing good fortune, I found a cartoon in The New Yorker of a car mechanic lying under a psychiatrist's couch. The very same morning a brief arrived on my desk for a Volkswagen service ad. I wrote the headline first–time off and showed the result to Mark who asked Andreas Heumann if he'd take the photograph of a reconstruction of Freud's consulting room. Most of the body copy is culled from an old American ad but I'm very pleased with the way it fell together, almost as if it were some kind of reward for all the wasted effort that's ended up in my rubbish bin.

What have I learned over the years? That instinct discounts superlatives. That adjectives stretch credulity. That blatancy does not command respect. That overstatement creates resistance. And that inside every fat ad there's a thinner and better one trying to get out. In short, the less said the better.

Do we drive our mechanics too hard?

For most people, going under a car is the end of their career.

For a Volkswagen mechanic, it's just the beginning.

He starts with the humble spark plug.

And works his way up to the digitant electronic system.

He takes every part apart. And puts it back together again.

Over and over and over again.

Until he can show us where every bolt, every washer and every nut goes.

What every part does.

And how to service every single one of them.

Then we really turn the screws on him.

Because, when he's not working on a Volkswagen, Volkswagen are working on him.

At one of our training schools.

There he spends seven hours a day study-ing the mechanics of the car.

So, by the end of his apprenticeship, he knows his Volkswagen bumper to bumper and sill to sill.

All this is part of the quaint Volkswagen notion that the service has to be as good as the car itself.

It's the kind of madness that makes us make our cars the way we do.

The sanest things on wheels.

The only squeaks and rattles you'll ever hear in a Volkswagen.

Who objects to decibels of delight coming from the back of their car?

Or to being able to actually hear a conversation, or the radio?

What is objectionable, is listening to the irritating results of shoddy workmanship and lazy engineering.

Which is why we at Volkswagen are so dedicated to building the soundest cars on the road.

To Volkswagen, silence isn't golden, it's dull grey, high tensile steel that we form into a rigid safety cell.

Inside, underneath, and around that rigid cell our engineers, robots and computers quietly set to work.

We make sure 10,000 times over, that a door shuts with a reassuring thud, not a hollow slam.

We torture bodywork.

We torment axles and wheel mountings. And if something squeals in less than 300 hours of merciless testing, we dispose of it.

Why go to such great lengths?

Because there's something that's very important you ought to know when you buy a family car.

That it's a lot more than just sound. **Golf**

FOR PRICES AND BROCHURES CONTACT VOLKSWAGEN INFORMATION SERVICE (55) YEOMANS DRIVE BLAKELANDS, MILTON KEYNES MK14 5AN. TEL: 0908 6040 HA FLEET SALES: 0908 2040 FAX FLEET SALES 0 486 845

We put people in front of cars.

At Volkswagen, we've always worried our little heads about even littler heads.

We were among the first major car manufacturers to make all our models capable of running on unleaded fuel.

The first to produce a range of small cars, the Polo, with a catalytic converter as standard.

The first to produce the world's cleanest production car, the Umwelt Diesel. And one of the first to replace toxic paints with water-based paints.

That said, we can hardly expect you to buy a Volkswagen out of the goodness of your heart.

Nor, heaven forbid, should you buy one simply because we've been named Environmental Manufacturer of the Year.*

We were, after all, among the first to introduce a reinforced safety cell with crumple zones front and rear.

The first to include rear seat belts as standard across the range.

And one of the first to make self-stabilising steering a standard feature.

When it comes to protecting your family, it seems, we rarely let anything get in our way.

*SOURCE: AUTOCAR & MOTOR   FOR BUSINESS AND PRIVATE PURCHASE INFORMATION CONTACT VOLKSWAGEN INFORMATION SERVICES (DEPT E3/88), YEOMANS DRIVE, BLAKELANDS, MILTON KEYNES MK14 5AN. TEL (0908) 60169I TAX FREE SALES: 071-486 8411

Tim Delaney started his career in advertising in the mail room at the age of 15. He founded Leagas Delaney in 1980, aged 34. He currently works with clients such as Harrods, The Guardian, Porsche, Talking Pages and Adidas for whom he has won numerous awards both here and in America. In 1992 he was president of D&AD. He was an adviser to Prime Minister James Callaghan and his chari‑table works include The Royal Marsden Appeal and Special Olympics. He is a frequent speaker at seminars in this country and abroad.

How I write copy:

- *in longhand*
- *with every available fact about product and category to hand*
- *on Sunday afternoons or late at night*
- *past the deadline.*

FROM THE DAYS WHEN MEN WERE MEN. AND SO WERE THE WOMEN.

The old West was definitely no place for wimps and faint hearts.

Those foolhardy enough to go in search of Eldorado were hard-bitten, unfeeling brutes who often had to wrestle with wild animals for their food, build entire cabins with the most rudimentary of tools and had to dispatch Apaches with their bare hands on a daily basis.

The men were pretty tough too.

Yes, as the history books show, it was women who were America's true pioneers.

While the menfolk went buffalo hunting and killing, gold-mining and killing or sometimes just shooting and wounding, the girls were left to fend for themselves in the wilderness for months on end.

And exactly what kind of fending was involved?

Well, they made almost everything they stood up in except, ironically, their boots.

This particular item of clothing proved beyond even their resourcefulness. Which is totally understandable.

In these circumstances, footwear needed to be tough and long-lasting, though not so heavy that it could be thought unlady-like. Most important of all, these boots had to keep out the rain and snow of the appalling prairie winters.

A tall order. One that even today would be hard to fill.

And while those intrepid womenfolk had to trek for days to their local trading post to obtain such a pair of boots, their descendants are more fortunate. All they have to do is buy a pair of boots made by Timberland.

For enshrined in all our boots are the very same qualities that helped those brave women slog gamely across America.

Naturally, the materials we use today are a little less, shall we say, rustic than in those days.

You only have to compare the leathers we have at our disposal today with the rather limited choice they had.

Their rawhide was often just that, with an odour which was not at all helpful to relationships with menfolk.

Our hides, on the other hand, are hand-picked from tanneries across the country who pride themselves on making strong, durable leathers soft and supple.

Understandably, a woman abandoned in un-charted Indian territory would not have been overly concerned about the colour scuffing or flaking off her boots.

Or whether, indeed, the degree of water repellency was all it was cracked up to be.

(When women were out pioneering, such things were not exactly top of the agenda.)

Way up in the wilds of Hampton, New Hampshire, however, this is precisely the kind of thing our craftsmen worry about constantly.

Which is why immediately the leathers are brought to the workshops, we dye them right through, then impregnate them with silicone oils.

Not only does this preserve the colour of the boot after years of wear, it also acts as a seal against the elements.

Looking back, it is difficult to understand why the early settlers didn't stop a passing Red Indian and enquire as to the precise method employed in the making of their footwear.

Certainly, it is now acknowledged that the original moccasin design was uniquely comfortable.

Which is exactly the reason we utilise the wraparound construction, using one piece of leather, for all our boots and shoes.

Of course, however warm and comfortable we make the actual boot, if water gets in all our painstaking handiwork counts for nothing.

Let us put your mind (and feet) at ease. Unlike the womenfolk who blazed the Oregon Trail, you won't have to worry about the occasional deluge or ten foot snowdrift.

The boot in our picture is, for example, guaranteed 100% waterproof.

First, we sew each boot with a high strength nylon yarn, using a double knot, pearl stitch. Then, we seal each seam with not one but two coats of latex. Add a Gore-Tex inner bootie, glove leather lining and a soft padded collar and the boot becomes posit-ively luxurious.

Although just to make absolutely certain your feet never have to encounter the kind of hardship that caused many a pioneer woman to die with her boots on, we didn't stop there.

The midsole is stitched to a lightweight polyurethane mini-lug outsole after which it is bonded to the upper.

No doubt all those hardy travel-weary females who opened up the West could have done with a pair or two of our boots.

Or some clothes from our new womens' Weathergear outdoor collection.

But then they might have looked like women, the men would have stayed home and the wild West would still be wild to this day.

Timberland (UK) Limited, Unit Five, St. Anthony's Way, Feltham, Middlesex. TW14 0NH.

Timberland ⊛

YOUR EYES ARE FROZEN. YOUR SKIN HAS TURNED BLACK. YOU'RE TECHNICALLY DEAD. LET'S TALK BOOTS.

The retina begins to freeze at minus 2·2°C. The skin on your body has a freezing point of minus 0·53°C.

It goes red, then starts to blister when it's exposed for relatively short periods at minus 1·9°C.

Even unexposed areas, like gloved hands, can turn black from frostbite within minutes.

And according to the eminent doctors who wrote a book called High Altitude Medicine and Physiology, someone with profound hyperthermia can be indistinguish-able from someone who is dead.

At Timberland, we make boots and shoes for people who love spending time outdoors in conditions like these.

People who, while not exactly Arctic explorers, are nonetheless willing to push their bodies to the limit of human endurance.

People, in fact, who quite often find themselves in situations where the only thing between survival and the alternative is the clothing they stand up in.

Naturally, this puts a heavy responsibility on their clothing and our boots.

But we're used to it.

Timberland does, after all, sponsor the Iditarod, generally acknowledged to be the last great race on earth.

This 1049 mile dog sled race is run from Anchorage to Nome in the Alaskan wilderness.

A little exercise that also serves as a testing ground for boots like our Super Guide Boot, pictured right. A boot that will protect your feet all the way down to minus 40°F.

And just what do we do to our boots to be able to make a claim like that?

Well, we certainly don't do what everyone else does.

Our hides, for instance, aren't picked up from any old bulk wholesaler.

Instead, we scour the entire United States for tanneries who find no contradiction in our demand for full grain leathers that are strong yet supple, rough but soft.

When we get the leathers back to our workshops in Hampton, New Hampshire we impregnate them with silicone to keep water and snow out.

To ensure your feet are comfortable from the moment you try our boots on, we employ our famous moccasin construction.

This entails using one piece of leather,

pre-stretched on a special geometric last, then sewn by hand into a kind of cradle for the foot. Making the uppers in this way is expensive and time-consuming but we figure the Arctic Circle is no place to discover that your boots are rubbing you up the wrong way.

At sub-zero temperatures, moisture inside the boot is as dangerous as water on the outside.

The Super Guide Boot solves this problem by utilising a Gore-Tex lining.

This remarkable man-made fabric has 9 billion pores per square inch, each one 20,000 times smaller than a raindrop, but 700 times larger than a molecule of perspiration.

As a result, we can guarantee to keep water away from your feet yet still allow them to breathe normally.

Of course, keeping your feet warm isn't just a matter of thwarting the cold.

On the Super Guide Boot, we augment your body's natural warmth by using Ensolite in the toes and Thinsulate in the shaft, tongue and quarter.

Having built an upper that can withstand the worst conditions known to Man, we then attach the lightest, most slip-resistant sole known to Timberland.

Made from an exclusive triple density polyurethane, the sole is injection-moulded and then permanently bonded to the upper using one of the many patented processes we employ at Timberland. Apart from being more flexible than a traditional rubber sole, it also provides higher insulation.

The Lug design is even self-cleaning to prevent ice getting trapped in the tread and conducting cold through to your feet.

At sub-zero temperatures you can't afford anything that's sub-standard.

Not even seemingly insignificant things. Take stitching. Other boot-makers are content to sew up their boots using one or maybe two rows of thread. Not Timberland.

Call us old-fashioned but we like four rows of high-strength nylon yarn on all the important seams.

These seams are then tape sealed with latex to make sure that water can't sneak in.

The lacing system may not strike you as something that could mean the difference between life and death, but we're not prepared to take that chance.

Our quick-acting system lets you get in and out of the boots in no time, even though it runs right down to the toe.

The D-rings are made from toughened stainless steel for the simple reason that they won't rust or rot with time. While the laces themselves are made from premium grade nylon for extra strength.

We could go on but we've talked boots enough.

Your eyes are still frozen. Your skin is still black. You're still technically dead.

Maybe we should just sell you a pair.

Timberland ⊛

WE STOLE THEIR LAND, THEIR BUFFALO AND THEIR WOMEN.

THEN WE WENT BACK FOR THEIR SHOES.

The Red Indians were an ungrateful lot.

Far from thanking the whiteman for bringing them civilisation (guns, whisky, disease, that kind of thing), they spent years making very bad medicine.

Naturally, during the course of their disputes, the whiteman found it necessary to relieve the Red Indians of certain items.

Thousands of square miles of land, for instance, which they didn't seem to be using.

The odd buffalo, which provided some interesting culinary experiences for the folks heading West.

And of course the squaws, who were often invited along to soothe the fevered brows of conscience-stricken gun-runners and bounty hunters.

But perhaps the most lasting testament to this cultural exchange programme is the humble moccasin.

A shoe of quite ingenious construction. And remarkably comfortable to boot.

Even now, nearly two centuries after the first whiteman tried a pair on, they have yet to be bettered.

Which is why at Timberland, all of our loafers, boat shoes and walking shoes are based on the original Red Indian design.

How is this possible? Surely a shoemaker of our standing is capable of showing a clean pair of heels to a few pesky injuns?

Not really.

Although over the years, we have managed to make some modest improvements.

Rather than use any old buffalo hide, we always insist on premium full-grain leathers. And when we find a tannery that can supply them, we buy its entire output.

We then dye the leathers all the way through so you can't scuff the colour off and impregnate them with silicone oils to prevent the leather going dry.

It is at this point that we employ the wraparound construction of the moccasin to create the classic Timberland shoe.

Using a single piece of softened leather, our craftsmen mould and stretch the upper

around a specially-developed geometric last.

This has the effect of breaking the shoes in before you've even set foot in them.

It also extends the life of the shoe for many, many moons.

Our hand sewn shoes also hark back to the days before the whiteman came.

No machines. No mass production. No deadlines.

Just a pair of nimble hands making shoes in the time-honoured way.

With just a little help from the twentieth century.

Like the high-strength nylon thread, double-knotted and pearl stitched to prevent it coming undone even if it's cut or in the unlikely event that it breaks.

The two coats of latex sealant, added to stop even tiny droplets of water sneaking in through the needle holes.

And the patented process which permanently bonds the uppers to the soles.

(If the Indians had only known how to cobble soles onto their moccasins, we probably wouldn't be in business today.)

As you would expect, the result of all our

labours is a shoe which comes with a heap big price tag.

For which we make absolutely no excuses.

After all, who else uses solid brass eyelets? Or self-oiling rawhide laces? Or glove leather linings?

Come to that, what other shoemaker shows such concern for your feet when big rains come?

For example, as well as utilising all our traditional methods, our new Ultra Light range uses new technology to keep your feet dry.

They're lined with Gore-Tex to make them completely waterproof while allowing your feet to breathe. (Gore-Tex has 9 billion holes per square inch. We didn't believe it either but it works, so now we believe it.)

The soles are made from an incredibly lightweight and highly resistant, dual-density polyurethane.

And, in an uncharacteristic concession to fashion, some models even sport tightly woven waxed cotton cloth.

LEFT: TIMBERLAND UPPERS. RIGHT: THE ORIGINAL MOCCASIN.

A far cry from the Red Indian moccasin? We certainly hope not.

Because if we ever forget our origins, or change our old-fashioned way of making boots and shoes, one thing's for sure.

A lot of people are going to be on the warpath.

Timberland Shoes and Boots, 23 Pembridge Square, London W2 4DR. Telephone 01:727 2519.

THIS ST. VALENTINE'S DAY,
MAKE SOMEONE CRY.

IT IS HARD TO BELIEVE THAT ONLY ONE DAY A YEAR IS SET ASIDE FOR THE EXPRESSION OF FEELINGS WHICH WE ARE TOLD MAKE THE WORLD GO ROUND.

PERHAPS FOR THIS VERY REASON, ST. VALENTINE'S DAY HAS DEVELOPED AN ATMOSPHERE AKIN TO A MEDIEVAL FEAST DAY.

PROCLAMATIONS ARE MADE. DARK SECRETS DIVULGED. PRANKS AND DECEPTIONS ARE DE RIGUEUR. WHY, YOU CAN EVEN GET BALLOONS TO TRANSPORT YOUR TRUE LOVE'S NAME TO THE HEAVENS. (WHERE ELSE?)

AMIDST ALL THE REVELRY, MAPPIN & WEBB, SILVERSMITHS AND JEWELLERS TO GENTLE FOLK SINCE 1774, OFFER LOVERS OF AN ALTOGETHER MORE SERIOUS DISPOSITION THE CHANCE TO EXPRESS THEMSELVES A LITTLE LESS FRIVOLOUSLY.

THIS IS ONLY TO BE EXPECTED.

THE MATERIALS WE WORK WITH AND THE SKILLS WE SO PAINSTAKINGLY EMPLOY ARE AS TIMELESS AS LOVE ITSELF.

AND JUST AS DEMANDING.

YOU CANNOT DALLY WITH SILVER. OR TRIFLE WITH GOLD. OR, HEAVEN FORBID, PLAY FAST AND LOOSE WITH DIAMONDS.

WHICH IS WHY ON OCCASIONS LIKE ST. VALENTINE'S DAY THEY ARE SO APPROPRIATE.

TAKE, FOR INSTANCE, THE DELICATE ROSEBUD IN OUR PICTURE.

SCULPTED IN PORCELAIN BY BOEHM, IT COMES WITH ITS OWN SILVER-PLATED VASE, PRICED £75.

AND WHILE IT MAY BE A LITTLE MORE EXPENSIVE THAN ITS NATURAL COUNTERPART, IT WILL NOT WILT OR FADE COME THE DAWN.

A METAPHOR WHICH WE ARE SURE WILL NOT BE LOST ON THE FORTUNATE RECIPIENT.

BUT SUPPOSING YOUR HEART'S DESIRE IS ALLERGIC TO ROSES?

OR, HER BEAUTY IS SUCH THAT A ROSE WOULD PALE BESIDE IT?

THEN YOU HAVE NO CHOICE BUT TO PRESENT HER WITH AN 18 CARAT GOLD NECKLACE WITH A SINGLE DIAMOND PENDANT, PRICED £1,450.

IF YOU WISH TO BE MORE DISCREET AND SPEND LESS MONEY, MAY WE SUGGEST A STERLING SILVER PHOTOGRAPH FRAME, HEART-SHAPED OF COURSE, PRICED £18 AND UPWARDS DEPENDING ON THE SIZE.

(SHOULD YOU DECIDE TO CONCEAL YOUR IDENTITY, A PHOTOGRAPH OF YOURSELF AS A BABY INSERTED IN THE FRAME COULD PROVE AN AMUSING DIVERSIONARY TACTIC.)

INCORRIGIBLE ROMANTICS MIGHT WELL

WANT TO MAKE THIS ST. VALENTINE'S DAY PARTICULARLY MEMORABLE.

IN WHICH CASE, THE THIRD FINGER OF HER LEFT HAND SHOULD BE ADORNED WITH OUR HEART-SHAPED SINGLE DIAMOND ENGAGEMENT RING, PRICED £2,500.

AS YOU MAY HAVE GATHERED, OVER THE YEARS MAPPIN & WEBB HAS GAINED VALUABLE INSIGHTS INTO THE ART OF GIVING.

HEREND, DRESDEN, SPODE, BACCARAT, LALIQUE, WATERFORD. THE VERY NAMES ARE CAPABLE OF PRODUCING A SHIVER OF JOYOUS EXPECTATION.

AND WHILE ON THE SUBJECT OF NAMES, A CERTAIN SILVER PLATE MAKER CALLED MAPPIN IS REGARDED BY THOSE WHO KNOW AS BEING THE FINEST IN THE WORLD.

SO WHEN NEXT YOU WISH TO CELEBRATE A BIRTHDAY, A WEDDING, AN ANNIVERSARY OR SIMPLY TO SAY 'I LOVE YOU' PAY US A VISIT.

YOU WILL FIND A WORLD WHERE THE TRADITIONAL STILL TAKES PRECEDENCE OVER THE FADDISH. WHERE PERMANENCE DEFEATS TRANSIENCE. WHERE BEAUTY HOLDS SWAY OVER ORDINARINESS.

IN FACT, WE CAN'T THINK OF A MORE APPROPRIATE PLACE TO BUY A PRESENT FOR YOUR VALENTINE. CAN YOU?

SAPPHIRE AND DIAMOND CLUSTER RING £3,220.

18 CT. GOLD NECKLACE WITH DIAMOND PENDANT £1,450.

HEART-SHAPED SINGLE DIAMOND ENGAGEMENT RING £2,500.

STERLING SILVER PHOTOGRAPH FRAMES FROM £18.

ART DECO STYLE SAPPHIRE AND DIAMOND RING £875.

Mappin & Webb

170 REGENT STREET, LONDON W1. TEL (01) 734 5842.   65 BROMPTON ROAD, LONDON SW3. TEL (01) 584 9361.   2 QUEEN VICTORIA STREET, LONDON EC4. TEL (01) 248 6661.   125-6 FENCHURCH STREET, LONDON EC3. TEL (01) 626 2171.
88 GEORGE STREET, EDINBURGH EH2 3DF. TEL (031) 225 5502.   67 ST. VINCENT STREET, GLASGOW G2 5TB. TEL (041) 221 7683.   12-14 ST ANN STREET, MANCHESTER M60 2LJ. TEL (061) 832 3331.

Whose countryside
would you rather see?
Thomas Hardy's?
Or John McAdam's?

Can you imagine curling up with a novel entitled 'Tess of the M4'?

Or how about 'Far from the Madding Service Station'?

Perhaps 'The Mayor of Motorbridge' would have you digging into your wallet next time you're in the bookshop in eager anticipation of a thundering good read? No? We thought not.

Yet sadly, these titles are probably an accurate reflection of the way most of us experience the landscapes that Nature so generously gave our great writers, composers and painters for inspiration.

Why is this? Why do more and more people seem content to limit their enjoyment of our wondrously beautiful countryside to a sort of high-speed slide show, conveniently framed by a car window?

A show where no sounds are allowed. They might, after all, clash with the pop music coming from the hi-tech dash board.

A show devoid of smells. Own up. Don't your own children turn up their noses at the unusual scents and pungent aromas which characterise the countryside?

Yet this sorry state of affairs needn't exist. The glorious, undulating landscape described in Thomas Hardy's books is there still. And it is waiting for you to discover it in the very same way he did.

Not at 70 miles per hour. Not cushioned in velour. Not protected from the sounds of the first cuckoo and the smell of newly-mown hay by shatterproof glass.

But by leisurely strolling or cycling along the lanes and by-ways of the Dorset countryside he loved.

The only difference between you and Thomas Hardy is that while he knew the area well, you might have to call on the services of an experienced and trusted guide. *Ordnance Survey.*

The subject of our Touring Map and Guide number 15, for example, is *Wessex*, the Anglo-Saxon kingdom used as a backcloth to Hardy's lyrical stories of rural intrigue.

Like all Ordnance Survey maps, this particular guide is both friend and tutor.

Do you need a telephone? A picnic spot? A camp site? Allow us to give you their precise location.

Are you interested in old battlesites? Historic houses? Or what about those caves you've heard tell are in the area?

Once again, an Ordnance Survey map can show you the way. [We will even furnish you with the date that battle took place].

And though our maps are invaluable in assisting you in getting from the proverbial A to B, they can also greatly enrich the journey.

On the reverse side of most Ordnance Survey Touring Maps is a heading: Where to go and what to see.

This masterpiece of English understatement conceals deep and expert knowledge of the area, its history, geography, crafts, even local curiosities and follies.

Map 15, for instance, will direct you to the smallest pub in Britain. Or to a monument shaped as a pyramid in honour of a horse that saved its owner's life.

It reveals the whereabouts of the local vineyard that is open to the public. Pin-points the lesser-known Elizabethan manor which has interesting additions by John Nash and gardens landscaped by Capability Brown.

It will also take you on a guided tour of Thomas Hardy's old haunts. The church where Tess was married. The cottage where he wrote Far from the Madding Crowd. The graveyard which, rather gruesomely, contains the author's heart. [*His ashes are interred at Westminster Abbey*].

You will also learn which particular roads Hardy liked to travel and why.

But how, you may be wondering, does Ordnance Survey unearth these little nuggets of information? What drives us to leave no stone, cobble or pebble unturned to bring you these insights into our countryside and its famous inhabitants?

It's quite simple. This year is our two hundredth anniversary.

We drew our first map at the end of the eighteenth century when Britain was faced with invasion by Napoleon. The British Army desperately needed accurate maps of the South Coast and this was duly carried out by the Board of Ordnance.

And while Napoleon failed to show up, the age of the map certainly arrived.

So you see, map-making has been in our blood for a very long time.

To the extent that Ordnance Survey originated practically all the maps of Britain that are around today.

[Indeed most of the maps with other brand names on were originally drawn by us. But don't tell them we told you].

Of course, nowadays our maps are used less for the defence of the realm and more by those people who wish to appreciate it.

If you like going for regular jaunts into the countryside, you might like to take one of our Landranger maps with you next time you head off.

Usually more detailed than our Touring Maps, a Landranger will show you what kind of trees populate your local forests or woodlands, point out particular rock formations in the region and, perhaps most important of all when you're walking in the countryside, where to find a public convenience.

If Landranger maps are for people who like a little information on their rambles, our Pathfinder Series is for those who like a little rambling with their information.

Thomas Hardy enthusiasts following our Pathfinder 1318, for instance, will be able to amble around the outskirts of his beloved Dorchester certain in the knowledge that they are walking on the remains of an old Roman road, that ahead lies ground covered in bracken and that half a mile in front of them there's a natural spring still burbling away.

Coming into the main part of town, the same narrow streets Hardy meandered along are drawn up in such detail that even houses and their boundaries are clearly marked.

Do we really need to provide you with this degree of accuracy? We think so.

Every day the face of our towns, villages and countryside changes. Sometimes it is imperceptible. At other times, when property boundaries are moved or roads are added, the changes actually reshape our country.

The better your knowledge of these changes, the greater your appreciation will be of what the British countryside in its many guises has to offer.

Then, who knows? Perhaps one day, with the guidance of Ordnance Survey, you may get to know Wessex almost as well as Thomas Hardy did.

Even see it through his eyes. Feel what he felt when he wrote *'Wessex Heights'*.

'There are some heights in Wessex, shaped as if by kindly hand

For thinking, dreaming, dying on, and at crises when I stand,

Say, on Ingpen Beacon eastward, or on Wylls-Neck westwardly,

I seem where I was before my birth, and after death may be."

Now, isn't that the kind of countryside you want to see?

Ordnance Survey.
The most detailed maps in the land.

Woolbridge Manor, with its three prominent chimneys and mullioned windows, was Thomas Hardy's Wellbridge Manor, where Tess of the d'Urbevilles spent her honeymoon. Her name was taken from a historical family called Turberville who were once owners of the house. Further up the road, is a small village with the quaint name of Wool.

Many of the rivers, brooks and streams of Wessex run off the high ground of Salisbury Plain and the Mendip Hills and through the chalk soils. Rich in fish such as brown trout, they also house vast aquatic insect populations providing food for waterside birds like the dipper and the grey wagtail. Look out for marigolds and ladies smock.

Dorset's most famous literary figure Thomas Hardy is commemorated by this statue in the main area of Dorchester, which is otherwise known as the Casterbridge of his novel. Nearly all the locations used for his stories still exist today although you will need help in finding them as he gave them fictional names to avoid offending the local populace.

OS 200 YEARS 1791

'A table for two? Certainly you old trout.'

Have you ever doubted the sincerity of an Italian waiter's smile? Wondered what it was you said that made those Spanish shop assistants giggle? Or questioned why that French doctor gave you headache pills for food poisoning? Haven't we all?

But imagine, for a moment, how different these situations might be if you could understand and talk to people when you're abroad.

At Linguaphone, we've spent the last 60 years helping people talk to each other. In fact since we began, Linguaphone has enabled over 5 million people to learn another language. And along the way, we have also learned some very important lessons.

Number one is that people learn faster if they're enjoying themselves. Number two is that people learn more easily when they listen to languages before they start reading about them.

Which sounds simple enough. And indeed it is. It's the very same way babies learn to talk.

Using a method developed by some of the most eminent linguists of our time, Linguaphone have taken this most elementary form of learning and speeded things up a little.

We use native speakers in life-like situations. The text book (you didn't think you'd get away without one did you?) is illustrated throughout with familiar objects with new names. Very quickly, you start imitating. Then conversing.

We use the same method to teach 30 different languages in 101 different countries.

Japanese use it to learn English. (Why don't more English businessmen learn Japanese?

Maybe we would still have a motorcycle industry.) Welsh people use it to learn Welsh. Someone somewhere uses it to learn Icelandic.

In this country, Linguaphone has helped men, women and children to further their education and advance their careers.

No fewer than 27 British universities use it. As do many of the biggest companies in the world. Ford, Unilever, BP, American Express and British Airways among them.

If you want to know more about our language courses, just fill in the coupon.

And then the next time a waiter says something disagreeable, you won't have to smile graciously and agree with him.

LINGUAPHONE

Dear Linguaphone, I would like to enjoy civilised conversations when I am abroad. (Even with uncivilised waiters.) Please specify language. _____ Mr/Mrs/Miss Ms _____ Address _____ Postcode _____ Language _____ Linguaphone, Freepost, Linguaphone House, London W6 9BR. Call 0800-400405 anytime (no charge).

Hats stretched to fit more comfortably. Shirt sleeves adjusted. Umbrella spokes straightened. Who, in this disposable and throwaway age, would provide services such as these? Who else but Harrods?

Yes, it is a world famous store. Certainly the existence of its 300 departments is an irrefutable fact. Yet in many ways Harrods still behaves as if it were a small Victorian emporium. In keeping with the spirit of that particular age, we believe that a timely repair is often better than an impulsive and expensive replacement. (Provided, of course, that the repair is to an item originally purchased in the store.)

Which is why we are happy to replace the locks and trims on your trusty briefcase. Re-grip and re-string your favourite tennis racquet. And, if your radio or television suddenly goes on the blink, we'll help resume normal service.

We will be delighted to repair your watch, your shoes, your Timberland boots, your lighter, even items from the Les Must de Cartier range.

Garment alterations are also something of a speciality. Carried out with great skill, particular attention is paid to the integrity and detail of the original design.

This service covers both men's and women's fashions, and includes the fitting and alteration of maternity bras. Even the life of your favourite riding boots can be extended by the intervention of one of our equestrian cobblers. And should your beloved Barbour become porous, we'll re-wax it, or give the jacket a complete overhaul.

And as you would expect, Harrods is quite capable of relieving you of even the most important and time-consuming of chores.

For example, our Design Studio can dream up imaginative interior designs for anything, from

one room to a whole mansion. They can help with fitted cupboards, fitted carpets or perhaps a fitted kitchen. All fitted to your particular budget.

Having furnished you with a new wardrobe, another service can provide the clothes to fill it.

The Executive Suite, based on the First Floor, is a shopping service for those who do not have the time to browse and select the looks and colours that suit them best. After a personal consultation, an Executive Suite consultant shops in the store for you and presents a small selection of clothes, accessories or other items in a private fitting room.

UMBRELLAS REPAIRED, SHIRT SLEEVES SHORTENED, HATS STRETCHED. 87 BROMPTON ROAD SW1. EST. 1849.

Harrods Bank also prides itself on its discreet personal service. To this end, the bank is open the same hours as the store. Until 6pm on Saturday and until 7pm on Wednesday, Thursday and Friday.

And you'll find the same attention to customers' needs is evident in every department.

We'll make a celebratory cake. Find theatre tickets for all the best shows in London, Paris and New York. Deliver a hamper anywhere in the world. You can have a full eye test. And have a new pair of spectacles fitted within one hour. Or you can have a golf club tailored to your height and grip. The list is endless. Which is hardly surprising. Of the hundreds of thousands of customers who come to the store, each one has different requirements.

Call us old-fashioned, but we believe that it is Harrods' role to match those needs with an appropriate service. So please, keep bringing your broken umbrellas, your tight hats and your over-length shirt sleeves to 87 Brompton Road, London SW1. Should you ever stop, Harrods will surely cease to be Harrods.

Harrods
KNIGHTSBRIDGE

Harrods Ltd., Knightsbridge, SW1X 7XL. Tel: 071-730 1234.

FOR A YORKSHIRE WOMAN THE JOURNEY TO THE MATERNITY WARD CAN OFTEN BE A LONG ONE.

Fate has not been kind to the Yorkshire woman.

It is as though upon entering life's theatre, she is immediately shown to a seat behind a pillar, allowed only a restricted view of what life has on offer.

This situation has come about not as a result of any inherent defects but simply because being a Yorkshire woman automatically precludes her from being a Yorkshireman.

Which, as the whole world knows, is still the only officially-recognised and accepted gender in that county.

Thus it is that the unfortunate female finds herself some way down the pecking order in established Yorkshire society.

Or seventh, to be absolutely accurate.

Coming after, in no particular order: fishing, rugby league, insulting Lancashire, football, household pets, cricket and, of course, Tetley bitter.

It is to escape this somewhat relegated status that many a woman

S.S. DISHFORTH

has fled her homeland in search of a community that values her at least above rugby league. (This has often proved difficult.)

Yet however far they may wander, however remote their final destination, there is one occasion when every self-respecting Yorkshire woman is impelled to return.

The birth of another Yorkshireman.

(In common with many primitive societies, it is always assumed in Yorkshire that the expectant mother will bear a son unless she has transgressed in some manner during the pregnancy i.e. burning the Sunday joint or forgetting to get in a six pack of Tetley's from the local high street supermarket.)

Stories of these perilous return journeys are, of course, legend in drawing rooms and parlours across the length and breadth of the county. Though for the sake of credibility only those verified by witnesses are re-told here.

Above: The GRINTON GRIP. Traditional welcome given to fathers-to-be in North Yorks. Below: The view that inspired the celebrated 'Lament for Yorkshire' by Yorkshire's much-maligned POET LAUREATE William WORDSWORTH Wigglesworth.

Nora Pilkington's tale is typical of many.

In late 1893, she left Slingsby and went as a missionary to Papua New Guinea. Within two days she got

'over-involved' in her job, and married the Chief of the tribe.

After a brief honeymoon spent on the outskirts of the village, they settled down to a life consisting mainly of whittling small sticks and twigs.

When Nora declared that she was with child and intended to return to Yorkshire in order that her son might qualify to play cricket for the county, her husband flew into an uncontrollable rage.

Not even the offer of her last can of Tetley's, kept as a reminder of her carefree youth, would console him.

He threatened to kill her with a poison dart then shrink her head.

Finding this idea entirely unacceptable, she negotiated a 27/6d return to Slingsby, although secretly she knew she would never go back to Papua Nora, as she had come to call her adopted home. She later settled down with William Wigglesworth, her childhood sweetheart who dedicated his famous

An obstetrician wearing the regulation head-gear for Yorkshire births.

poem 'Lament for Yorkshire' to her:
'For years I wandered far and wide
'cross very big moor and valley wide
e'er hill and dale so awfully wide
with lots and lots of chimney pots.'

A different fate was to befall a group of fifty three Barnsley couples on their way back from Wollongong, New South Wales in 1936.

By a strange coincidence all of the emigrant wives were expecting their sons on the same day.

Indeed, a new wing was built on the local hospital to commemorate the event.

They were never to set eyes on it.

Somewhere in the Caribbean, their ship disappeared completely in an area that came to be known as 'The Barnsley Triangle.' (This name was later changed to one which was deemed to be more fashionable.)

Some weeks after the tragedy, several barrels of Tetley bitter were washed up on a beach in Uruguay

Above left: 1 Chief Big Cloud and his squaw, (a former MISS RIBBLESDALE) shortly before her return home to have their eighth child. Above: 1 TANGANYIKA, 1892. Members of staff at the British Consulate celebrate the birth of the Ambassador's son back in Huddersfield.

but as the beer had not been drunk, experts concluded that it could not possibly have come from the ship's saloon.

Another story concerns a Yorkshire woman who lived in Finchley between the wars and was actually in labour when she set off for the Sheffield Infirmary.

The 165 mile journey up the A1, undertaken in a 500cc Norton, with sidecar, took 57 minutes and has yet to be bettered.

The noise emitting from the sidecar during the record-breaking run is also said to have prompted the idea for the sirens later used on police vehicles throughout the world.

And while his wife was giving free rein to her emotions in Maternity, eye-witnesses claim that her husband was carried shoulder-high into a local hostelry.

Once inside, he slaked his thirst with a pint of Tetley bitter, an ale whose strong, mellow flavour and creamy head has always represented a perfectly valid reason for a Yorkshireman to return home, with or without the wife.

Tetley bitter has been brewed in Yorkshire since 1822 and is now being exported to selected pubs in the South of England. Keep an eye out for it.

After all, so many women have made sacrifices for Yorkshire, the very least a man can do is sample the county's premier ale.

TETLEY BITTER

A MAN CAN GET ATTACHED TO A TETLEY'S.

If you want to find out how banks became the richest, most powerful institutions in the world, go into the red one day.

Banks have not always been as big and profitable as they are today.

Believe it or not, all the big boys on the High Street were small businesses once.

(In 1955, Barclays only made just over £2½ million profit.)

How then, did the High Street banks achieve the status they enjoy today?

COMMISSION
OVERDRAFT ADMIN
****   £26.00

Innovative ideas? Hardly. The first cheque was issued in 1659.

Dynamic management? You have called your bank manager a lot of things in your time, we bet 'dynamic' isn't one of them.

Customer satisfaction, then? No comment. No.

Quite simply, it is you, dear reader, who have made the banks so rich and powerful.

You, and millions of people like you, who over the years have put your hard earned money into their coffers and received little in return.

Indeed, when you have had the temerity to go into the red, you have paid dearly for it.

Thankfully, there is now an alternative to a bank current account.

Nationwide Anglia's FlexAccount.

An account based on a very simple idea: that it is your money and we should not forget the fact.

So if you go into the red with a FlexAccount you don't start attracting mysterious 'service charges.'

You won't suddenly find yourself having to pay for standing orders and direct debits for a whole three month period when you have only slipped into the red for one day. And we won't slap in a bill, sorry, 'arrangement fee' just for discussing and sorting out an overdraft.

All we ask of you is interest on the money you borrow until you're in the black.

We think this is reasonable, straightforward

and, most important of all, easily understood.

Of course, the reverse is true with most bank current accounts.

Which is no doubt why they have Hollywood-style adverts telling customers how much they care for them.

At Nationwide Anglia, we believe in deeds not words.

So we pay FlexAccount holders interest on the money in their current account.

Not just to people with lots of money in their account, mind.

Every FlexAccount holder gets 2% net per annum on anything up to £99. 3% interest on sums between £100 and £499. And 4% when you're £500 or more in credit.

(Both the higher rates are paid on the whole balance, not just the amount over £100 or £500.)

All calculated daily and paid into your account annually.

This is the interest the High Street banks have traditionally believed is theirs.

Somewhat strange logic as it is your money that earns it.

Isn't there anything good about a bank current account?

Of course there is.

Cheque books, cheque guarantee cards and cash cards. Not forgetting other services like standing orders and direct debits.

All excellent facilities.

Which is why they are all available to FlexAccount holders.

But that's not all.

Being rather keen on new ideas, we also offer our customers something called a Home Banking Unit.

Which works like an unusually helpful, round-the-clock counter clerk.

You simply ring one phone number and punch in your personal code. Then, by pressing a few more buttons, you can pay your bills.

Or, just as easily, get instant confirmation of your balance or order a full statement.

From any telephone in the world, at any time day or night. And all in return for a £10 deposit, which is refundable.

Not everyone will want one, we know. But that's not the point.

It's another expression of our philosophy. Another way of helping people manage their money and, ultimately, get more from it.

Does all this sound too good to be true? It shouldn't. It is, after all, common sense.

Which is no doubt why Channel Four television's 'Money Spinner' programme singled it out as being a service "which High Street banks would do well to take notice of."

So far they haven't. Just check your last statement.

If you went into the red, you'll find a deduction has been duly made.

No information about how it's computed. No breakdown. No nothing.

Is it really the best way to treat a customer?

We don't think so. Maybe that's because we are not one of the richest, most powerful institutions in the world.

For further information, just call into your local Nationwide Anglia branch.

Or write now to Claire Adams, Nationwide Anglia Building Society, Chesterfield House, Bloomsbury Way, London WC1V 6PW.

FlexAccount

We always remember whose money it is.

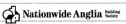
Nationwide Anglia Building Society

Simon worked as a copywriter at Saatchi & Saatchi, where he was made Joint Creative Director. He has consistently won industry awards for outstanding press, television and cinema work for clients such as British Airways, Carlsberg-Tetley, Pilkington, The Independent, ICI, The Conservative Party and the Samaritans. He is a founding partner of the New Saatchi Agency.

A LESSON LEARNT.

I suppose we all experience turning points in our careers. I'm not just talking about the usual landmarks like your first offer of a job or the first ad you write that actually gets into print and your mother sees, but moments in the game when you learn something that changes the way you approach things for ever.

One such moment sticks in my mind and this seems to be a good place to tell you about it. It goes something like this.

In the run-up to the 1984 election I was working on the Conservative Party campaign. (Whoops ... I've lost my audience already ... rule of copywriting, don't begin by alienating your readers, never mind, here goes ...)

The Conservatives were already in power and seeking re-election. They were worried that people would have forgotten what life was like under Labour — naturally this was something that they thought was beyond the pale.

The brief was to produce an advertisement that would warn people what they would be letting themselves in for under a Labour Government.

Fergus Fleming and myself had been slaving away to this end in a sweaty little outpost of a God-forsaken area of the creative department dubbed "Milton Keynes" and as far as we were concerned we had cracked it.

Our headline read: "Putting a cross in the Labour box is the same as signing this piece of paper." There then followed a series of ghastly facts and to top it all at the bottom of the page was a dotted line challenging the reader to put his or her name to it as if it were some dreadful hire-purchase agreement.

We were thrilled.

I had spent some hours researching and writing the copy and to cap it all the client had bought it.

Time to put the feet up and bask in the undoubted glory that would follow as the nation went to polls to vote Conservative.

No. Time to learn something.

The door opened and there stood Charles Saatchi.

"You did this ad?" he asked, brandishing the aforementioned article.

"Yes", we replied, rising to our feet as lesser mortals tend to when they unexpectedly find themselves in the society of a 'Demi-God'.

"It's great", he said.

"Oh ... well ...thanks", we said as we sat down.

"Fergus" he elaborated, "it looks fantastic."

Fergus went a pretty colour which I was only subsequently to witness when he announced the birth of his first son.

"Now," he continued, "I need to have a word with Simon."

That's when he let me have it.

"Every ad is an opportunity. This could be a great ad. Every word you write now will be with you forever. Find the right tone and stick with it. Don't just write it as a series of facts, but find an attitude. And remember, once it's printed you can't change a thing. You want to be able to read this ad in years to come and be proud of it."

I followed his advice and the bugger was right. I read it today and I'm glad I did.

ASTRONAUT WANTED
NO EXPERIENCE NECESSARY.

GLAVCOSMOS, the Soviet Space Administration, has offered a place to a British astronaut on a space flight in 1991.

Whoever is chosen will have had no experience because no Briton has ever flown in space ■ He or she will automatically write themselves into the history books ■ It is fitting that the flight is scheduled to take off on the 30th anniversary of Yuri Gagarin's historic first manned space flight on the 12th April 1991. It will be called the 'Juno' Mission.

The flight touches down eight days later.

The First ANGLO-SOVIET Space Mission. The eight days in space will be spent on the Soviet Space Station MIR from which the British astronaut will conduct scientific experiments ■ The MIR Orbital Space Station is a permanently operating 'laboratory in space' which has been orbiting earth since it first became fully operational in February 1988.

The British astronaut will become a full member of the Anglo-Soviet flight team fulfilling the tasks of an astronaut as well as conducting a series of scientific experiments ■ The mission is carrying no passengers.

The PURPOSE of the Mission. The aim is to conduct a series of scientific experiments in space which exploit the virtual absence of effective gravity in an orbiting spacecraft.

Most of the microgravity experiments will be carried out in order to advance our knowledge in basic science, others will demonstrate important principles in education and a few will test advances in space technology ■ The work will encompass biological experiments involving plants, cells, bacteria, and the astronaut.

Experiments in material science will include the growing of crystals, particularly of proteins, possibly the development of alloys, and the study of fluids under conditions which it is not possible to replicate on Earth.

The First COMMERCIAL Space Flight. The mission is the first commercial joint venture between the Soviet Space Administration and British industry.

In fact it's the first ever commercially supported manned space mission of its kind anywhere in this world. (Up until now commercial opportunities in space have been limited to unmanned satellite launches) ■ The mission will be funded by companies paying for the research capabilities of the mission as well as by sponsorship ■ (Previous flights from both East and West have been funded by their governments or space agencies and although it will be the first private enterprise space mission, it is operating with the full knowledge and consent of the respective governments).

This will without doubt be just the first of many commercial flights into space, as space becomes an increasingly viable product both academically and commercially.

How is The Mission FINANCED? The catalyst behind the mission is the Moscow Narodny Bank ■ This is a City of London bank which this year celebrates its 70th birthday as an established British incorporated bank.

It specialises in joint ventures and project finance and has provided the seed finance for the marketing and sponsorship raising campaigns ■ By co-operating closely with Licensintorg (foreign trade agents for Glavcosmos), the bank helped Glavcosmos enter commercial markets, internationally, for the first time ■ The Russian word for it is Perestroika.

The mission will raise £16M in revenue from the research capability and sponsorship ■ Commercial organisations will be able to sponsor the flight, the astronaut, or even supply products or services for the mission.

There will naturally be a programme of media events providing coverage of the mission around the world and it will also generate educational programmes, exhibitions and lectures.

Who's at The Mission CONTROLS? The selection process for the British astronaut, and the design and construction of much of the equipment which will be used to carry out the experiments devised by industry and universities, will be carried out at Brunel University.

The Brunel Institute for Bioengineering is one of the very few organisations in the UK with experience in the microgravity field and will act as the focus for this work.

Your OPPORTUNITY to Make History. The chance to become the first Briton in space is open to both men and women.

Applicants will be aged 21-40 and possess a formal scientific training in either biology, applied physics, engineering or medicine, combined with good manual dexterity.

Successful applicants will have proven ability to learn a foreign language and have a high standard of medical fitness ■ They will also have the ability to work as a member of a team and communicate easily with people from a different background and culture.

The SELECTION Process. Candidate assessment starts this month and at later stages will include a series of demanding medical, psychological, aptitude and stress tests.

These will be completed by November 1989 when two final candidates will be selected to undergo a full schedule of training in the Soviet Union at the Gagarin Centre, Star City ■ One candidate will fly on the mission, whilst the other acts as back-up with duties in the running of control experiments at ground level which will be based at a laboratory close to the launch site.

How to APPLY. There is no coupon to clip and send.

The Mission has employed MSL International (UK) Limited as recruitment consultants. They are at 32 Aybrook Street, London W1M 3JL ■ To obtain an application form please phone 01-224 2211 (16 lines) between 9am and 7pm on weekdays and 10am and 5pm at weekends ■ The line will remain open until Friday 14th July 1989.

The application closing date is Monday 24th July. Only applications on the formal application form will be considered.

JUNO
ДЖЮНО
THE FIRST ANGLO-SOVIET SPACE MISSION ■

AS A PENSIONER HE'D BE BETTER OFF VOTING CONSERVATIVE.

As a pensioner in 1979 Michael Foot would have received £31.20 a week.

Now, under the Conservatives, he would receive £52.55 a week.

An increase of 68 per cent, way above any rise in prices over that period.

Under the Conservatives he would have received a Christmas bonus every year. A pleasant change after the cold Labour winters of '75 and '76.

As a pensioner he's better off voting Conservative.

Let's hope this time he puts his cross in the Conservative box.

It won't make him Prime Minister. But that's just as well for everybody.

Peter Smith reporting for the Daily Mail.

PUTTING A CROSS IN THE LABOUR BOX IS THE SAME AS SIGNING THIS PIECE OF PAPER.

1. I hereby give up the right to choose which school my children go to and agree to abide by any decision made by the State on my behalf.

2. I empower the Labour Party to take Britain out of Europe, even though my job may be one of the 2½ million which depend on Britain's trade with Europe.

3. I am prepared to see the Police Force placed under political control even though it could undermine their capability to keep law and order.

4. I agree that Britain should now abandon the nuclear deterrent which has preserved peace in Europe for nearly forty years. I fully understand that the Russians are not likely to follow suit.

5. I agree to have the value of my savings reduced immediately in accordance with Labour's wishes to devalue the pound.

6. I empower the government to borrow as much money as they wish from other countries and I agree to let my children pay the debt.

7. I fully agree to a massive expansion of nationalisation, whatever the cost to me in higher taxation.

8. I do not mind if I am forced to join a union. I do not expect to vote for the leaders of that union and do not mind if I am not consulted by secret ballot before being told to strike.

9. I sign away the right to buy my own council house.

10. I do not mind paying higher rates.

11. I am prepared to allow my pension fund to be used by the government to invest in any scheme that they see fit whether or not this shows a good enough return on my investment.

12. I understand that Labour's plans could mean that prices will double once more, as they did under the last Labour government.

13. I realise that the tax cuts from which I will have benefited under a Conservative government may be withdrawn at once.

14. I waive my right to choose any form of private medicine for my family.

15. I understand that if I sign this now I will not be able to change my mind for at least five years.

SIGNED.

CONSERVATIVE X

Why you should think more seriously about killing yourself.

We wouldn't want to alarm or shock unnecessarily.

But it is alarming that every year over 200,000 people in this country try to kill themselves.

And it is shocking because only a very few of them really want to die.

Over 95% of these people who try to kill themselves and survive are glad that they survived.

Out of those who didn't survive there will sadly be many who didn't really want to die because in most cases, an attempt at suicide is first and foremost a cry for help.

So is a call to the Samaritans.

The difference is that it's a cry that will always be answered.

That's exactly why a call to the Samaritans is a serious alternative.

This isn't to say that you have to be about to kill yourself to call the Samaritans.

We hope that people will call long before they reach that point.

The Samaritans are there to listen to anyone who needs someone to talk to, no reason for calling is ever too trivial.

A Samaritan will never censure, criticise or pass judgement.

All conversations, whether face to face or over the telephone are conducted in absolute confidence.

Samaritans are on call for 24 hours a day and 365 days a year. Anywhere in the country.

And there are daytime centres you can visit in nearly 200 cities and towns so there is bound to be one near you.

Anyone who does try to commit suicide and succeeds will never have the chance to change his or her mind.

That's why everyone should think more seriously about taking the easy way out and call the Samaritans.

Please.

The Samaritans.

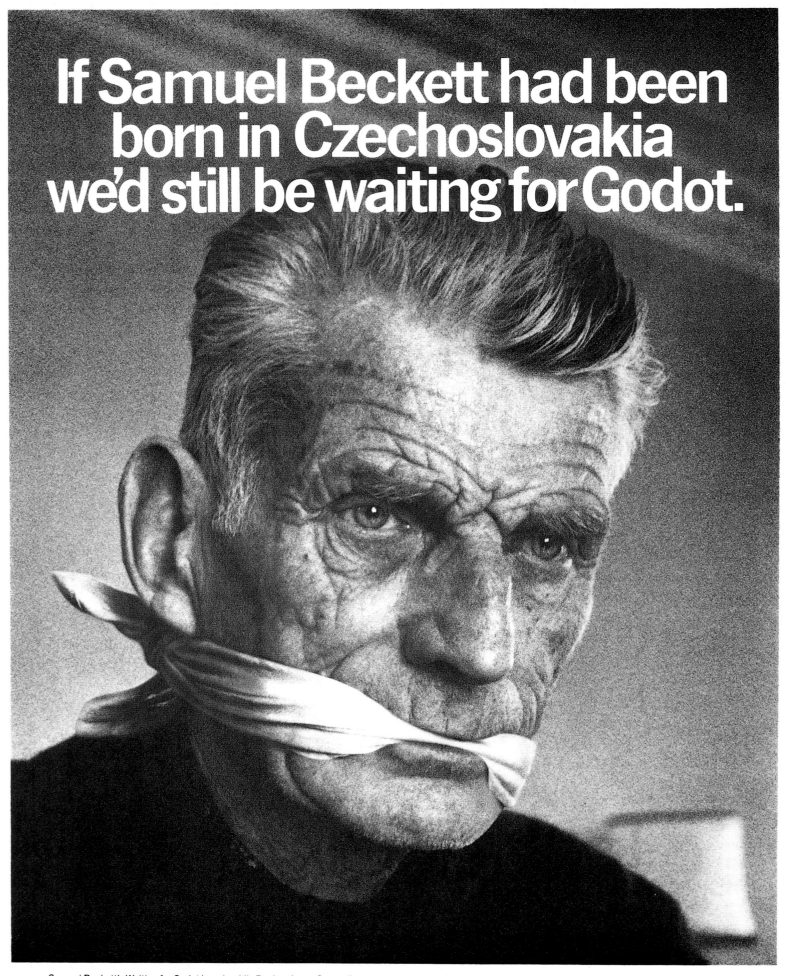

If Samuel Beckett had been born in Czechoslovakia we'd still be waiting for Godot.

Samuel Beckett's Waiting for Godot is banned in Czechoslovakia. In fact any writing that doesn't reflect the opinions of the Czech government is banned.

Luckily Beckett is not Czech. But what of those writers who are Czechs? Index on Censorship is a magazine that is committed to exposing censorship around the world and publishing the work of censored writers, film makers and photographers.

Work which you would otherwise not be able to enjoy. To subscribe please write to us at 39c Highbury Place, London N5 1QP or you can telephone us on 01-359 0161.

Support Index on Censorship for crying out loud.

Which one of these men do you think would be best at rape?

These men are solicitors.

One of them is better at Bankruptcy, one at Property and one at Crime.

You can't tell which is which just by looking at them and you wouldn't be able to tell simply by looking them up in the Yellow Pages.

That's why the Law Society has produced the Solicitors' Regional Directory.

It names solicitors in England and Wales and tells you broadly the experience of each.

It even tells you what languages they speak.

That way, when you take advice, you know you're getting the best advice.

The Solicitors' Regional Directory.

THE SOLICITORS' REGIONAL DIRECTORY IS AVAILABLE AT LOCAL LIBRARIES, ADVICE CENTRES AND SIMILAR OFFICES.

There was a time when advertising agencies were measured by the quality of their work rather than the number of their offices.

It was at this time Carl Ally, Amil Gargano and myself met. We opened Carl Ally, Inc. on July 2, 1962 and things began to happen. Oh boy, did things happen. The agency lit up the scoreboard with heroic wins, spectacular losses and headline controversies.

In your face creativity was the order of the day. Screaming and fighting and raging and laughing, and cheering went far into the night. Every night. Never before, or since, has a single agency been endowed with such a magnificent array of talent. David Altschiller, Ron Berger, Ed McCabe, Tom Messner, Steve Penchina, Martin Puris, Dick Raboy, to name but a few.

As copy chief I hired, taught, nurtured, mentored and learned from this crew. After 14 years a long-cherished fantasy became a reality and I left the advertising business to study at the Art Students League. A year of study showed I could paint. Which I still do. Not great. But good. Then came 10 years of running Durfee & Solow, Inc. with friend and fellow writer Martin Solow. Our plan to stay small succeeded beyond all expectations. Which led to a most stimulating three years as Vice Chairman, Corporate Creative Director of Della Femina McNamee Inc. Which led to a merger forming Messner Vetere Berger McNamee Schmetterer Euro/RSCG. I am again a partner, in an agency with one office and only one measure of success.

The quality of the work. Damn, it feels good!

"KILL ALL YOUR DARLINGS."

If a single commandment could be burned into the mind of each beginning writer, it should be this one. If a single mantra were to be chanted by every experienced writer, it should be this one.

Mark Twain wrote these words, and lived by them. Here's why I try to.

By shunning that darling of all darlings – the pun headline –I'm left with no-nonsense straight talk. Prospects can never get enough of that. By avoiding cutesy-clever copy phrases I eliminate the danger of show-off writing.

And when I'm writing long, flowing, beautiful, heart-pounding sentences (like this one) I know I'm in danger of spewing ego-garbage. Which endangers clear thinking. So I start over. Well, usually.

Copywriting, of course, is not a matter of rules and regulations. Hell, then anybody could do it.

Yet guidelines and checkpoints can be helpful. Here, in no particular order, are a few that work for me.

Believe, really believe, that every word you write will be read and you'll write better. And be read more. Never lecture. Remember how boring lectures were in college?

A headline that needs a subhead usually needs more work.

Don't fall into the trap of writing to a prospect profile. In fact, don't 'write' at all. Visualise the one person you want to influence, then sit that one person down across from you. Now talk to him or her through your pen, pencil, typewriter, word processor or whatever.

Every product has its own truth, its own believability zone. Stray and your readers will know. Oh yes, they'll know.

Don't rely on your art director to save you. A strong idea, simply presented, is far more effective than a weak idea strongly presented.

There is no such thing as long copy. There is only too-long copy. And that can be two words if they are not the right two words.

If you find yourself developing a creative philosophy, your growth is over. Stagnation has set in.

Write short sentences with small words and few adjectives. They are easier to read. And more interesting and believable.

Never write an ad a competitor can sign.

When you get your copy to the point where you're really, really happy with it, cut it by a third.

Take the embarrassment test. Imagine yourself standing before your family, reading your copy aloud. Still proud of it?

Listen hard as you write. Are you hearing the prospect say, "Yes! Yes! That's what I want to hear. More! More!"

Write for yourself. Never write for your creative director. Neither of you will be happy with the result.

Every writer needs an editor. If you find a good one, treasure the relationship. I have not only been blessed with a great editor, she consented to marry me 22 years ago.

And now about these ads.

Break a rule now and then. Enable was a new, sophisticated, multi-purpose software package. Rather than headline claims by an unknown company about an unknown product, I opted to let the reader write his own headline. It worked. The page turners we lost were more than replaced by the huge number of users who got into the ad, read every word, and bought.

Tilt the playing field to favour your client. AT&T represents size and tradition. MCI represents initiative and responsiveness. That's what this ad is all about. Tremendous growth through cultural and attitude differences that work in favour of the MCI customer. Attributes not open to competitive counter claim.

Sometimes an ad is stronger without copy. When you write a headline that induces the reader to become emotionally involved, he'll write his own copy. And it'll be better than yours.

If you're being attacked, don't defend. Attack back. In the great rent-a-car war, it took only 90 days, with ads like this, to demolish a powerhouse Avis underdog campaign that had been hurting Hertz for years. And "We're No. 1" became the cry of the land.

Drive it like you hate it.

When Volvo came to the U.S. from Sweden in 1956, Chevy was the "hot one," Ford was the "safe one" and Volkswagen was just catching on as the "funny one."

We'd like to say that Volvo immediately caught on as the "tough one." It didn't.

At first only the "car nuts" bought it. They figured that if a Volvo could hold up under Swedish driving (no speed limits), survive Swedish roads (80% unpaved), withstand Swedish winters (30° below), that a Volvo would hold up under anything.

They figured right. Volvos were driven right off showroom floors onto race tracks where they proceeded to win more races tʰ ·ny other compact ever made.

Volvos are still ⁄inning races. But that isn't why they're bought today. Volvos are now being used and misused as family cars. They're safe. And on the highway they run away from other popular-priced compacts in every speed range, yet get over 25 miles to the gallon like the little economy cars.

Volvo is now called the "tough one." And it's the biggest-selling imported compact in America today.

You can drive a Volvo like you hate it for as little as $2565. * Cheaper than psychiatry.

*Manufacturer's suggested retail price East Coast Port of Entry. Overseas delivery available. See the Yellow Pages for the Volvo dealer nearest you.

Always be listening for headlines. In a meeting Carl once growled, "You can take a Volvo out and drive it like you hate it." The very essence of Volvo. I wrote the copy, Amil did the rest. Some of the best headlines I ever got credit for came from others. Even clients.

The first four times Paul Fishlock changed jobs he also changed continents. From JWT London to BLG&K Johannesburg to CDP London to Saatchi's, Sydney. Along the way he rubbed shoulders with some of advertising's best and attributes any success he may have had to the fact that some of it must have rubbed off.

In 1993 he joined The Campaign Palace working with art director Warren Brown where they quickly became one of Australia's most awarded teams.

For years I lived in fear of being found out. I'm not a proper writer, see. There's no novel in me struggling to get out (I only read a couple of books a year). I've never had a letter published in a quality paper. I didn't even win the school essay competition.

Every time I had more than the baseline of a poster to write I became paralysed with fear, wishing I was a 'concept creator' instead of a copywriter and could send headlines down to the copy department for men with leather elbow patches and pipes to fill in the grey lines.

I loved everything about being a copywriter except writing copy and knew that if I didn't find a way around it, the best job in the world (that I had somehow stumbled into) would collapse in an untidy heap.

So I studied award-winning copy until I thought I knew all the tricks backwards. Start with your second choice headline (never waste it). Write absurdly short paragraphs.

Like this.

Use quirky brackets about writing ads (Still reading? Good, then I'll continue). Never begin your penultimate paragraph with "So..." and always end with a joke. (Even if it takes half a column to set up, and isn't very funny.)

I tried them all, but somehow my copy was still the same self-conscious drivel it had always been. So out came the annuals again, the only reasonable explanation being that I had some-how missed something.

Then, one day, faced with an agonisingly straightforward piece of copy I could put off no longer, I threw my hands in the air and officially gave up.

It was time to confront the horrible truth. I would never make the Copywriter's Hall of Fame. I simply wasn't cut out to be a proper writer and should cut my losses. From now on I would work out the absolute minimum required and write as simply and clearly as possible using common words and ordinary phrases anyone could understand.

Rejected headlines and clever word plays were banned unless they said something absolutely essential at least as quickly as the 'straight' equivalent. And as soon as I'd said everything that had to be said, I'd stop. Even if it meant finishing on a phone number instead of a joke.

Then I'd go back to the beginning to see if any smart-arse indulgencies had slipped through the net and whether any particularly hoary old clichés could be freshened up without forcing the reader to translate them back into what I'd just changed them from.

I imagined an editor with an irritating voice yelling in my ear: "I don't care if you're James Joyce — get to the point," and I took to reading "How to write clearly" books aimed at high school students.

It all felt like an embarrassing admission of defeat. Now I would have to work harder than ever on TV briefs if I was to become a famous adman.

Then something very strange happened. Suddenly, I started writing much better press ads. My copy-phobia disappeared. I got my first pieces in the copy section of the book. And, strangest of all, I was invited to contribute to a D&AD book on how to write copy in the company of proper writers.

HERE'S A DEAD DOG. WHERE'S MY AWARD?

THIS YEAR AWARD WILL BE GIVING LESS TO CHARITY.

Community service and charity advertising has always been a special case when it comes to awards.

It has its own categories in every major advertising festival around the world. AWARD is no exception. However, we've spotted a problem.

Not only have community service and charity ads been able to enter their own categories, they've also been able to enter the general ones. A small space charity ad, for example, gets three bites at the guernsey; the Community Service and Charity section, the Small Space section and the Newspaper section.

Hardly fair on a packet soup ad that only gets one go. And often resulting in a book that looks more like a Charity Awards Annual.

So we've made a few changes for AWARD'91. Community Service and Charity ads will now only be judged in their own categories. Likewise, Small Space ads.

A minimum size for posters has been introduced to stop press ads being entered on the grounds they were pinned to the wall.

And Christmas cards, wedding invites, birth announcements, etc get their own category and are no longer a direct threat to direct mail for proper clients.

Details of changes are in the 13th AWARD Call for Entries booklet. If you still don't have a copy, call Mary or Sandra on (02) 267 6907 or (02) 267 6916.

But get a move on, the deadline for entries is June 7th. And if you've been pinning all your hopes on getting several gongs for one charity ad, all is not lost.

Just think of the money you'll save only having to enter it once.

1991 CALL FOR ENTRIES.

AWARD appreciates the assistance of Saatchi and Saatchi: John Currow and the NSW RSPCA for production of this advertisement

The headline is so strong there's no need to refer back to it.

Your lungs are now full of air, the most important part of which is oxygen.

But it's not just your lungs that need oxygen, every cell in your body does.

So how do you get it to your toes, the tips of your fingers and your ear lobes?

By attaching it to the iron rich cells in your blood stream. Simple and efficient.

Unless like seven out of ten Australian women aged 25-54, you're not getting your recommended intake of iron.*

Or worse still, you're among the one in three running an increased risk of iron deficiency and quite possibly experiencing symptoms such as fatigue, lethargy and lack of concentration.*

You may also find yourself more prone to illness and infections.

And in severe cases, become anaemic.

All because you haven't got enough iron to carry oxygen to where it's needed.

The early warning signs of a possible iron problem are so familiar that many women dismiss them as 'normal'.

Others blame their tiredness on another aspect of their life: Stress, raising a family or lack of sleep, for instance.

All of which may be contributing factors. But lack of iron could be another.

So how can you tell if you're not getting enough iron?

And what can you do about it if you aren't?

Firstly, if you recognise any of the symptoms we've described, ask your doctor to check your ferritin level (iron stores).

If it's particularly low your doctor may prescribe an iron supplement in the short term.

However, nutrition experts agree that for most women a change of diet to include iron rich foods is by far the more natural and effective long term solution.

(Especially for those who can barely remember the last time they weren't on some kind of fad diet.)

One of the best iron rich foods readily available is lean beef.

As part of a balanced diet, the Australian Nutrition Foundation recognises it as one of the richest sources of iron.

It also helps you absorb up to four times the iron from other foods, like vegetables.

If you'd like more information on iron and how to make sure you're getting enough, please write to Nutrition Communications, PO Box 4129, Sydney 2001.

The good news is that lack of iron is one womens problem that's, more often than not, very easily solved.

Doesn't that make you breathe easier?

Are you getting your essential daily iron?

SUPPORTED BY AUSTRALIAN NUTRITION FOUNDATION

*Source. National Dietary Survey of Adults, 1983.

Telling women their health is at risk is no laughing matter, so no jokes.

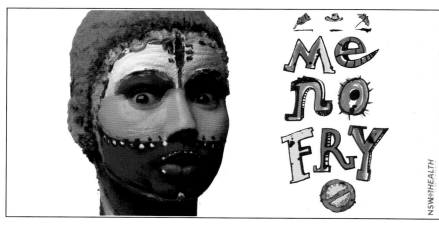

Me no fry. Only abuse grammar for the right reasons. 'I won't get sunburnt' just wasn't the same.

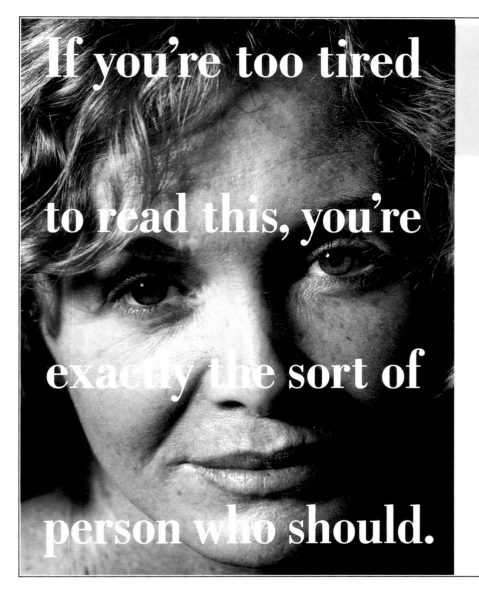

If you're too tired to read this, you're exactly the sort of person who should.

Do the words run down, listless, worn out, lethargic or sluggish ever describe you?

You are not alone.

A great many women feel exactly the same and lack of iron may be to blame.

Perhaps it's time you did something about it.

Reading this could be your first step.

You may be wondering why everyone is suddenly talking about iron.

Is it mineral of the month? Another dietary fad that will disappear as miraculously as it came to light?

Unfortunately not. The iron issue is very much a fact of modern life.

Seven out of every ten Australian women aged between 25-54 years aren't getting their recommended intake of iron.

With at least one in three running an increased risk of iron deficiency which may eventually progress to anaemia.

Most of us always knew we needed iron. But no one ever told us why. So let's start right at the beginning.

Iron is important for several reasons.

Maintaining a healthy immune system and energy production are two of them.

But by far its most vital function is carrying oxygen in our blood.

If we don't have enough iron, our muscles don't get enough oxygen and that's when we can start to feel tired and run down.

Unfortunately, this is so familiar to many women that they simply dismiss it as being, well, normal.

Others blame something else in their life.

A busy schedule, stress, not sleeping well, sometimes even the weather.

All of which may be contributing factors, but lack of iron may well be another.

So what can you do about it?

What sort of things should you be eating to top up your iron stores?

Are iron supplements the answer?

Not according to the nutritional experts who agree that for most women it is much better to obtain nutrients from natural food sources.

The Australian Nutrition Foundation recommends a balanced diet including foods rich in the two types of iron.

Haem iron (found in red meat, poultry and seafood) and non-haem iron (found in breads, vegetables, cereals etc).

Of the two, haem iron foods contain iron in a form that is much more easily absorbed by the body.

For instance, a moderate 125g grilled lean rump steak has about three times more iron than a regular 70g serving of cooked spinach.

On top of which, twelve times as much of the iron present is absorbed.

As a general rule, the redder the meat, the the higher the iron content.

Which is why lean beef is recognised as one of the best sources of daily iron.

If you think you might have an iron problem see your doctor and ask about your ferritin level (iron stores).

Or if you'd like more information why not call 008 675 898 right now.

And if you're too tired to pick up the phone? You guessed it.

You're exactly the sort of person who should.

Are you getting your essential daily iron?

Source: National Dietary Survey of Adults, 1983.

Look at the person sitting opposite you.

Just a quick glance. Try not to stare.

What do you think they do for a living? How much do you think they earn? More than you?

Could you do their job?

Think of five possible christian names for them. And one nickname.

Are they married? To what kind of person? Imagine their home. Their furniture.

What do they keep on their mantelpiece?

What colour bathroom do they have?

Consider the ANY DISTINGUISHING MARKS section of their passport.

We're not allowed to tell you about Winston cigarettes, so here's something to pass the time.

What does it say? What should it say?

Where are they heading now? And why? To meet somebody? Who? For what reason? Do they look as if they're late?

And if they suddenly leant forward and offered to buy you dinner, what would you do?

But before you pass too harsh a judgement on this poor, unsuspecting fellow-traveller, here's something else to think about. There's another Winston ad, just like this one, directly above your head.

WINSTON
FILTER CIGARETTES
KING SIZE
TWENTY CLASS K

LOW TO MIDDLE TAR As defined by H.M. Government

DANGER: Government Health WARNING: **CIGARETTES CAN SERIOUSLY DAMAGE YOUR HEALTH**

Written for a bored, captive audience on tube trains.

If only women could solve their iron problem as easily.

Popeye can take on the world after a quick hit of spinach. The same cannot be said of Olive Oyl.

If a woman tried The Popeye Diet she'd struggle to get through a normal day.

For one simple reason: women need over twice as much daily iron as men.

That's why it's so important for women to understand that there are two different types of iron in foods.

The iron in vegetables, cereals and grains is called non-haem iron and the iron in fish, chicken and red meat is called haem iron.

Haem iron is up to ten times easier for your body to absorb.

And the redder the meat the more haem iron it contains.

Which is why lean beef is recognised as the best source of daily iron.

Dietary experts recommend that women eat a balanced diet that includes a rich source of haem iron, such as lean beef.

If Olive Oyl took their advice she'd be more animated than ever.

Lean Beef
Your best source of essential daily iron.

Australian Meat and Live-stock Corporation.

If only women could solve their iron problem.

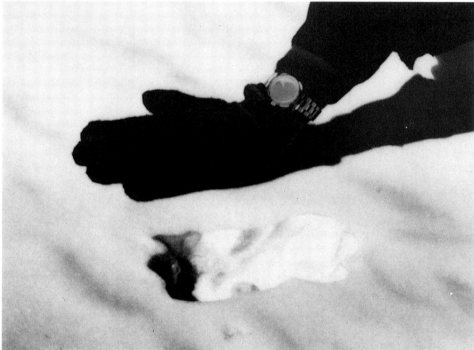

A rare sight indeed.
Abominable prints from an Olympus.

On April 14th 1987, a group of climbers in the Himalayas stumbled across mysterious footprints in the snow.

Could they be the tracks of an Abominable Snowman?

Fortunately, Chris Bonington's team were armed with a couple of our Olympus compact cameras at the time. So they clicked away, confident that the world would soon see clear evidence.

The tracks had been made by a two-legged creature moving fast across the snow in running bounds. Closer inspection proved that they were not those of man or any creature known to man.

The Tibetan porter had no doubt in his mind.

These were the marks of the 'Chuti' – the smaller of the two Yeti – said to live in the high mountain forests of the region.

"It was an extraordinary moment" said Jim Fotheringham, leader of the climbers at the time "four experienced mountaineers snapping away like wedding photographers".

Most of us are unlikely ever to be called upon to record the tracks of a Yeti half way up Mount Menlungtse.

But when it comes to your holiday snaps, it's reassuring to know that a small Olympus can take a great set of prints.

OLYMPUS CAMERAS

A gift of a job, sold short by too much copy, trying too hard to be clever.

Richard Foster started his advertising career at the very bottom – in the accounts department at Brunnings.

That was in 1968. The following year he got his first writing job at Dorlands, since when he has had the good fortune to have been hired by most of his heroes in the business – Tony Brignull (as a junior copy writer, Vernons 1970) Peter Mayle (as a copywriter, BBDO 1971) John Salmon (as a creative group head, CDP 1976) and David Abbott (as a senior writer/Board Director, Abbott Mead Vickers 1980).

His work has won awards at all the major creative competitions, including a gold and five silvers at D&AD.

Today I'm writing the copy for a Sainsbury's olives ad.

The rough is pinned on the wall in front of me. (I always have the rough in front of me when I'm writing a piece of copy. It helps get me started.) The visual is of a Sainsbury's Queen olive in a glass of martini. The Queen olive is a very big olive, so it's hogging the glass. The headline says: "Would you like a martini with your olive?"

The first thing I have to do is tell people that this is a big olive and not a small martini. I have a jar of Queen olives on my desk, together with a jar of ordinary olives. I take out an olive from each jar and put them side by side on a plate. As I'd hoped, the Queen olive looks about twice the size of the ordinary olive. So I write (in longhand, as always) "The Queen olive is twice as big as ordinary olives."

Before I finish the sentence I've already got the next line. "And twice as delicious." I immediately realise that "twice as delicious" is a matter of opinion, so I make it a matter of fact. "And, some would say, twice as delicious".

I need to expand on "delicious". I take the Queen olive from the plate and eat it. I write what I taste: "Its flesh is plump, but firm, with a luscious fruitiness that makes it the perfect appetiser..." It occurs to me that a martini is a kind of appetiser, so I add (in brackets, of course) "...with or without the martini."

As I said, this is an ad for Sainsbury's olives, which means Sainsbury's entire range of olives. There are nine olives in the range. All but one of these olives come from Spain. More than that, they come from Seville, the best olive-growing district in Spain. The odd one out, damn it, comes from Greece.

Of the eight Spanish olives, seven are green and one is black. The Greek olive is also black. Of the seven green olives, one is the Queen olive and the other six are Manzanilla olives. Of the six Manzanilla olives, one is whole, one is pitted, two are stuffed and two are marinated. Of the two black olives, the Spanish one has a strong flavour and the Greek one is just Greek.

How should I arrange all these different olives in the copy? I lead with the Seville story. I re-read my opening lines and continue: "Like all Sainsbury's Spanish olives, our Queen olives come from Seville, the most renowned olive-growing district in Spain".

Now I have to introduce all the other olives in the range. I decide to get the Manzanilla olives over with in one fell swoop. I write: "We also sell the more familiar Manzanilla olives, either whole, pitted, stuffed or marinated."

I then continue to explain that one of the stuffed olives is stuffed with pimiento and the other with almonds, and that one of the marinated olives is marinated in olive oil with garlic and chilli and the other in olive oil with herbs.

It's too long. I'm going to have to boil it down. So I rewrite the end of the paragraph as follows: "...stuffed (with pimiento or almonds) or marinated (in olive oil with garlic and chilli or with herbs)."

Now I'm on the home straight. All I have to do is talk about the two black olives, mention the fact that Sainsbury's have the widest range of olives, and then clinch the sale with a call to action.

I start to re-read the entire piece. I only get as far as the opening line. "The Queen olive is twice as big as ordinary olives." I don't like the word 'ordinary', it's too ordinary. Common-or-garden olives? No, I've seen common-or-garden too many times. The common olive? No, too derogatory. Wait a minute, Queen olive...royalty...commoner.

"The Queen olive is twice as big as commoner olives."
Time for lunch.

SAINSBURY'S OLIVES

Would you like a martini with your olive?

The Queen olive is twice as big as commoner olives.

And, some would say, twice as delicious.

Its flesh is plump, but firm, with a luscious fruitiness that makes it the perfect appetizer (with or without the martini).

Like all Sainsbury's Spanish olives, our Queen olives come from Seville, the most renowned olive-growing district in Spain.

We also sell the more familiar Manzanilla olives, either whole, pitted, stuffed (with pimiento or almonds) or marinated (in olive oil with garlic and chilli or with herbs).

All these olives are green olives, but our range would be incomplete without the black variety.

Hence Sainsbury's Calamata and Hojiblanca olives.

The Calamatas come from Greece, where they are usually to be found adorning the classic feta salad.

Hojiblancas are stronger in flavour than their green cousins, which makes them the perfect partner to paella or pizza.

As you may have guessed by now, Sainsbury's offer a wider range of olives than any other supermarket.

So if you want the choice of the choicest olives, choose Sainsbury's.

SAINSBURY S Where good food costs less.

Sainsbury's – Would you like a martini with your olive?

The Financial Times

AMOCO

Give us time, give us time.

Of the 38,000 petrol stations in Britain, something like 360 are ours.

Don't laugh.

It was only in December 1963 we opened our first.

Like nearly all the ones that followed, it was run by a tenant, not a manager.

The difference being that a tenant makes his money according to how much petrol he sells.

While a manager gets paid the same wage however well, or badly, he does.

We don't have to tell you who gives you the warmer welcome.

The trouble is, with so few Amoco stations around, there may not be one near you.

Take heart.

360 stations in seven years works out at about one new one a week.

Next week could be your week.

My first whole page broad sheet colour ad and less than a square inch of colour. Astonishingly, the client changed his logo a fortnight after the ad ran.

If only.

Nobody has ever smoked an entire cigarette.

In fact, about two-thirds of the smoke produced by a cigarette goes straight into the atmosphere.

Which in a room, pub, restaurant or cinema can create an extremely unpleasant atmosphere.

Breathing other people's cigarette smoke doesn't just get up non-smokers' noses.

It gets down their throats and into their lungs.

According to the British Medical Journal (and we quote) "substances released into the air from tobacco smoke can be assumed to cause at least some cases of lung cancer."

The article goes on to say that the children of parents who smoke have more chest infections than the children of non-smokers.

If you smoke, we hope you'll spare a thought for the majority who don't. And if you don't smoke, but live or work with people who do, we hope you'll put this advertisement where they can't miss it.

Right under their noses.

Don't force smoking down other people's throats.

FOR A FREE LEAFLET 'BREATHING OTHER PEOPLE'S TOBACCO SMOKE' WRITE TO THE HEALTH EDUCATION COUNCIL, DEPT 6H2, 22/24 CLARKE ROAD, MOUNT FARM, MILTON KEYNES MK1 1HQ

The copy exhorts the reader to put this ad under smokers' noses. I sincerely hope some of them did.

EVEN IN THE WET, A VOLVO STARTS FIRST TIME.

Landlubbers will not be acquainted with the Volvo Penta 6-cylinder 4-stroke direct-injected turbo-charged marine diesel engine.

But Venetian taxi-drivers are.

They hail it as one of the most reliable marine engines in the business. And when you're clocking up 50,000 nautical miles a year, reliability is all.

(If the engine conks out, you can't just pull in to the side of the road.)

All this will come as no surprise to drivers of Volvo motor cars.

Indeed, our car engines are designed to operate happily in extreme weather conditions.

(By extreme, we mean anything between minus 30°C and plus 40°C.)

As well as car engines and boat engines, we also make jet engines.

In fact, it's a Volvo engine that powers the new supersonic Gripen interceptor built by our compatriots at Saab.

But that's another advertisement. **VOLVO**

FOR DETAILS OF THE VOLVO RANGE WRITE TO: VOLVO, SPRINGFIELD HOUSE, PRINCESS STREET, BRISTOL BS3 4EF.

An ad suggested to me by our widely travelled head of television. The copy ends with a reference to another ad coming shortly. It did.

Lifelike, isn't it?

We really must hand it to our advertising boys.

They've achieved something we've always thought was impossible:

Demonstrate the lifelike qualities of Sony's unique Trinitron picture on the page of a newspaper.

(Excellent though colour printing is nowadays, it could never quite do justice to our colour picture.)

And if the demonstration is ingeniously simple, so is the Trinitron system.

Instead of the customary three small electron lenses, Trinitron uses just one large one.

By focusing the colour beams through the centre part of the lens, we can produce a picture of exceptional sharpness and clarity.

Another department in which Sony set a shining example, is brightness.

Which is where our Aperture Grille comes into its own.

It's made up of stripes, not holes, thereby allowing more of the colour beams to reach the screen.

But perhaps the real beauty of our television lies in its solid state circuitry and low running temperature.

For it is these things that make the Trinitron so reliable.

And there's only one thing better than a lifelike picture.

A lifelike picture that lasts.

SONY

SEE THE 13", 18" AND NEW 20" TRINITRONS* AT YOUR LOCAL SONY DEALER OR THE SONY SHOWROOM 134 REGENT ST., LONDON W1R 6DJ. *TUBE SIZE MEASURED DIAGONALLY.

I was so pleased with this ad I congratulated myself on it in the opening line of the copy.

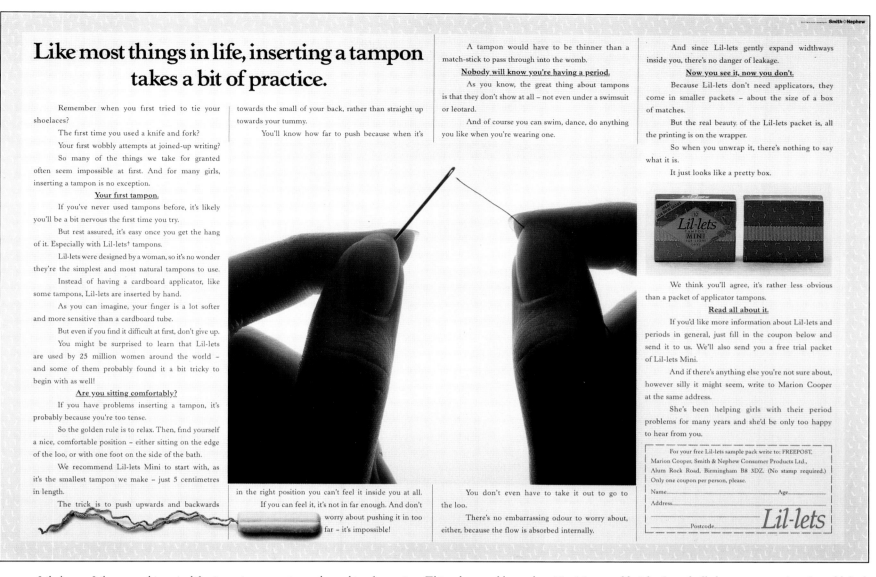

Like most things in life, inserting a tampon takes a bit of practice.

Remember when you first tried to tie your shoelaces?

The first time you used a knife and fork?

Your first wobbly attempts at joined-up writing?

So many of the things we take for granted often seem impossible at first. And for many girls, inserting a tampon is no exception.

Your first tampon.

If you've never used tampons before, it's likely you'll be a bit nervous the first time you try.

But rest assured, it's easy once you get the hang of it. Especially with Lil-lets† tampons.

Lil-lets were designed by a woman, so it's no wonder they're the simplest and most natural tampons to use.

Instead of having a cardboard applicator, like some tampons, Lil-lets are inserted by hand.

As you can imagine, your finger is a lot softer and more sensitive than a cardboard tube.

But even if you find it difficult at first, don't give up.

You might be surprised to learn that Lil-lets are used by 25 million women around the world – and some of them probably found it a bit tricky to begin with as well!

Are you sitting comfortably?

If you have problems inserting a tampon, it's probably because you're too tense.

So the golden rule is to relax. Then, find yourself a nice, comfortable position – either sitting on the edge of the loo, or with one foot on the side of the bath.

We recommend Lil-lets Mini to start with, as it's the smallest tampon we make – just 5 centimetres in length.

The trick is to push upwards and backwards towards the small of your back, rather than straight up towards your tummy.

You'll know how far to push because when it's in the right position you can't feel it inside you at all. If you can feel it, it's not in far enough. And don't worry about pushing it in too far – it's impossible!

A tampon would have to be thinner than a match-stick to pass through into the womb.

Nobody will know you're having a period.

As you know, the great thing about tampons is that they don't show at all – not even under a swimsuit or leotard.

And of course you can swim, dance, do anything you like when you're wearing one.

You don't even have to take it out to go to the loo.

There's no embarrassing odour to worry about, either, because the flow is absorbed internally.

And since Lil-lets gently expand widthways inside you, there's no danger of leakage.

Now you see it, now you don't.

Because Lil-lets don't need applicators, they come in smaller packets – about the size of a box of matches.

But the real beauty of the Lil-lets packet is, all the printing is on the wrapper.

So when you unwrap it, there's nothing to say what it is.

It just looks like a pretty box.

We think you'll agree, it's rather less obvious than a packet of applicator tampons.

Read all about it.

If you'd like more information about Lil-lets and periods in general, just fill in the coupon below and send it to us. We'll also send you a free trial packet of Lil-lets Mini.

And if there's anything else you're not sure about, however silly it might seem, write to Marion Cooper at the same address.

She's been helping girls with their period problems for many years and she'd be only too happy to hear from you.

For your free Lil-lets sample pack write to: FREEPOST, Marion Cooper, Smith & Nephew Consumer Products Ltd., Alum Rock Road, Birmingham B8 3DZ. (No stamp required.) Only one coupon per person, please.

Name.. Age......

Address..

.... Postcode....................

Lil-lets

Lil-lets – Like most things in life, inserting a tampon takes a bit of practice. This ad was addressed to 11–14 year old girls. I read all the teen magazines I could find to get into the right tone of voice.

Born 1944. Expelled from minor public school at 16. Rent-collector, account executive, bouncer, waiter, singer, matador, rock band manager, promoter, account executive again and copywriter. Started an agency: went spectacularly broke after seven years. Joined Holmes Knight Ritchie in London 1980. Joined and left Batey Ads in Singapore 1986. Joined Ball Partnership also in 1986 as Vice Chairman & Regional Creative Poohbah; got fired 1991.

Pottered about directing and consulting for a bit. Now Consultant Asian Regional Creative Thingy for O&M again.

'Straordinary, really.

Asking thirty-two blokes who spend their lives writing advertisements to tell people exactly how they do it. You'd think a simple apology'd suffice. But no. Apparently not.

So, since you've actually shelled-out good money for this scam of scams, I guess I'll have to make it sound difficult, or scientific, or something. If you're looking for folks who take all this seriously, there are conceivably one or two in here.

My advice is, if you come across 'em, think how much money they make, and ask yourself, did they get that stinking rich by handing out the real secret of success to every bozo capable of navigating his way to the "How To" section of an airport bookstore? Right? Quite so. Anyway. Here it is. *"My Way".* By Neil French. Aged 50 1/2.

First and foremost, avoid like genital warts the temptation to start writing. Once I've read the brief, I tend to waddle off and play pool, or hang about with unsuitable women for a while. On the one hand it allows the important bits of the brief to sink in, and the reams of dross to fade into richly-deserved obscurity, and on the other, it's a far more sensible way of spending the time than sitting in an office counting the number of times a junior account executive uses the word 'creative'.

When I can only remember one thing about the brief, and just before I forget there was a brief in the first place, and assuming I'm not on the black, I write that one thing down and get the account people to write a strategy round it. This is not, of course, the 'correct' way to go about things, but in my experience it's the only way to get the strategy to match the ads. In any case it keeps the account people out of the pool-halls and knocking shops. They do so lower the tone of a place.

Next, I look at every other ad in the category, so I know what my ads mustn't look like. This is quite possibly the most important part of the entire wossname, come to think of it.

I have this heartfelt theory that people hate ads. Ads interrupt TV programmes and bulk out newspapers and mags and are generally a waste of perfectly good trees. So I try to avoid writings 'ads'. Or at least I try to make my stuff look different, so that it doesn't scream off the page "Hi! I'm an ad! Ignore me!"

And at the very least I make sure that my stuff doesn't look like any competitors'. If you gather a wad of ads in a category, you'll often find they form a sort of genre. It becomes established over time, that 'car ads look like this' and 'bank ads look like that'. Stands to reason that if you can make a car ad that looks like a bank ad, you'll stand out in the category. Got it? OK.

Maybe I should say, right now, that I don't work with an art director. I do my own. And I do my own because I was tired of being disappointed when my concepts came back looking, somehow, 'wrong'. I realised then that, at the instant a writer has an idea, he usually has a glimpse of the finished 'look' of the piece, and that glimpse is part of the idea itself. So now, even if my ads are horrible, at least they're exactly how I saw them in the first place. I'm never disappointed. Everyone else may be, but I'm not.

At this point I decide what sort of an ad it's going to be. There are only two sorts; a copy ad or a picture ad. Anything half and half is wimpy, in my view.

If it's a copy ad, it's either going to be masses of words, with a nod in the general direction of the product, so we still get paid, or a single sentence of pithy prose writ large or little with a pack shot. In the latter case, you use the phrase because you can't think of a sufficiently jolly picture, and in the former the wodge of copy is, in itself, a design-element. It says "My, but these people have a lot to say for themselves", so even if the consumer shows the good sense not to read the whole sermon, he's left with an impression, at least. And we still get paid.

If it's a picture ad, it's a hugely-amusing snap with, if really necessary, some explanatory jotting beneath or within, for the benefit of the terminally bewildered. If it's this sort of ad, I do a little picture, write the line, and toddle off to the beach. No point in knocking yourself out for no good reason, what?

But if it's a long-copy job, it all gets jolly technical. Please concentrate, from here on.

Firstly, I get a good bottle of red; ideally, Rioja; possibly a Vega Sicilia or a Castillo Ygay, from the cellar, and remove the cork. Then I find a large expensive wine glass, of the type that goes 'ting' for a long time after you've tinged it, and I place that in close proximity to the bottle and myself. This takes years of practice to perfect, but persist; I think you'll find it worthwhile.

Then I pour some of the wine into the glass and I think about the ad. Snatches of sentence, natty little phrases, excellent words, all come to mind. But I never write them down. All this while I am simultaneously drinking the red, slowly, from the tingy glass, (I warned you this was the tricky part), but I'm withstanding the temptation to pick up a pen. When I've finished the wine there frequently doesn't seem a lot of point in thinking about bloody ads any more, so I have a little lie down.

When I wake up, I let rip. Anything that survives the little lie-down is obviously memorable, and goes in the ad. Anything I've forgotten obviously isn't and doesn't.

Now, I'm no good with slide-rules, and I can't type, so I do everything by hand. I take a sheet of tracing paper and in pencil draw the shape and design of the ad, very accurately. I then take an Extra-Fine Pilot Hi-Techpoint, stick my tongue out about half a centimetre between my lips and commence. I decide on a point-size for the type, and whether it's going to be serif or sans, and start in the top left-hand corner.

When I see the bottom right hand corner looming up in my periphery vision, I start to wrap up the argument, and waffle along till the space is full. Then I stop.

I rarely re-write, except to amend awkward typography; firstly because it's tedious and secondly because I can never seem to keep the flow, once I start to tinker.

I only have one rule and I recommend it to you. In any ad, most people will tell you, there is a minimum of four elements: headline, picture, copy, logo.

Forget captions, tag-lines, diagrams, - they're all optional add-ons. The minimum of elements in ninety percent of press ads is four.

If you can do an ad that really works, using only *one* of those elements, you've got a winner.

Two elements only, and it'll be pretty good. Three and it'll still look better than anything else in the paper. If you can't get below four, it's possible that the basic idea isn't strong enough, or you haven't expressed it well enough.

Reductio ad absurdum. Try it. It works.

Finally, I can't advise you how to write. There's a school of thought that tells you to submerge your own personality, and be the voice of the client. I can't do that. I'm always me, chatting away on *behalf* of the client. If I always sound like me, that's OK, because I am, and the public is nowhere near as gullible as they're made out to be. They can tell if it's bullshit.

I wish I could show more ads, and more variety. But since this is a book about copy, most of what follows are copy-ads. Sorry about that.

THIS IS AN ADVERTISEMENT FOR CHIVAS REGAL.
IF YOU NEED TO SEE THE BOTTLE,
YOU OBVIOUSLY DON'T MOVE IN THE RIGHT SOCIAL CIRCLES.
IF YOU NEED TO TASTE IT,
YOU JUST DON'T HAVE THE EXPERIENCE TO APPRECIATE IT.
IF YOU NEED TO KNOW WHAT IT COSTS,
TURN THE PAGE, YOUNG MAN.

An ad for Chivas Regal that broke every booze-ad rule. But the Chinese drinker is arrogance personified, so the ads matched the consumer.

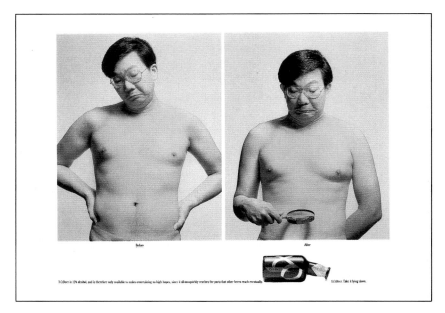

Above: The Chivas campaign ran to twelve ads, and was an enormous success. To such an extent that this, the final ad, didn't even have to mention the brand-name.

Above: Here are two ads for XO Beer. It didn't actually exist as a product when we ran the campaign; the intent was to convince advertisers that you could sell beer in newspapers. But there was such a demand that a local brewer started making the stuff. We tested two approaches: One with a picture and a pack shot; one with a headline and a pack shot; six of each. Recall was about the same, except that people could actually parrot the entire headlines back to us. So in my book, they win. This particular picture ad was, in fact, banned, which is an excellent way of making sure a product and a campaign become famous. The strategy, by the way, was basically, "Gets you drunker quicker".

Right: A picture-only ad. (Well alright, there's a caption/headline/tag-line underneath, if you must be picky). Actually, the regulations wrote this one: The product is a hair-tonic, but we weren't allowed to say hair-tonic, and we couldn't show the pack, 'cos that said 'Hair-tonic'. And no pictures of bald men. And no pictures of hairy men, implying that they used to be bald men. So, hairy eggs, hairy billiard balls, and a hairy Chihuahua. (Don't ask!).

THERE IS A SPELLING MISTAKE IN THIS ADVERTISEMENT. THE FIRST PERSON TO SPOT IT WILL RECIEVE $500.

No, it's not i ı this line.

Or, you'll have guessed, in this line, either.

You're going to have to read this entire page, with the eyes of a school examiner, to spot it.

Which, when you think, makes it rather a good advertisement, doesn't it? Since ads, like the editorial they sidle up to, are written to be read.

How many of the other ads in this week's 'Media' are going to get this amount of attention?

One, maybe? Two?

It's more than likely that you haven't read *any* of them. Be honest, now:

You've given them the same treatment you give those suspiciously friendly encyclopaedia salesmen, who knock on your door and ask for five minutes of your time.

No, thank you: Slam the door. (Or in this case, turn the page.)

No sale. And we don't blame you. You saw the sell coming. Why waste your time?

The majority of ads are like that, too. Predictable, dull, and not very well presented.

They resolutely ignore the fact that the average consumer sees one thousand, six hundred advertising messages every day, and would be perfectly content not to see any at all.

You see, with the possible exception of seven year old brats with a passion for Teenage Mutant Ninja Turtles, PEOPLE DON'T LIKE ADS. There, we've said it. In a publication dedicated to the creed that advertising is a profession comparable only in its saintliness and altruism with being one of Mother Teresa's little helpers, we've spilt the beans:

We are not universally popular: If spacemen came down and took every person connected with advertising away for dissection, it would be a long time before we were missed. And even then, it would be because people discovered that their newspapers had become more interesting, and their TV programmes more enjoyable, for our absence.

(See? Heresy spoken out loud. And still we write. No thunderbolts from on high. God doesn't like ads, either.)

And yet...

And yet, in the face of reams of irrefutable evidence to the contrary, the majority of advertising agencies (and let's spread the blame a bit, their clients, too), persist in the belief that this just ain't so.

They sincerely believe that buying a space also guarantees readership of whatever they fill it with.

Sadder still, the higher the cost of the space, the more tense and creatively constipated they become, and the more safe and generic is their message: It's a new rule; the bigger the budget, the blander the ads.

Even the relatively enlightened feel that if they find, and mention, some semblance of a benefit in that space, they've *really* done a good job.

That by some miracle, the consumer is going to home in on their ad, shrieking "Just what I've always wanted!"

Sure. If your benefit is "Free Beer".

OK; *definitely*, if your benefit is "Free Beer". But if it's not, you're in big trouble.

You're going to be thrown in there with washing powders that get clothes whiter, toothpastes that taste nicer, tires that grip better ...

In other words, you're going to be ignored.

Don't misunderstand us, please. If your product has a substantial benefit over its competitors, you'd be mad not to tell everyone. The point is, it'd be mad to think that's *all* you had to do.

The public, as we've said, has become immune to everyday advertising.

For an ad to succeed these days, it has to work on many levels. It has to be relevant to the reader: It has to speak to him in language he can relate to: If there *is* a benefit to crow about, it has to be a benefit that's important to the *consumer*, not just to the manufacturer: To revert to the door-to-door salesman analogy, it has to look good ...the sort of person you'd invite into your home; the sort of advertisement you'd welcome into your mind...

But most of all, it has to be 'different'.

It has to jump from the page, or leap off the screen, screaming "Read me! Watch me!"

And it has to do so with a degree of seduction in its voice, rather than the foot-in-the-door brazen insistence, that leads only to the zap, the flip, and the broken toe.

Now. Doubtless there are sceptics out there who may say that this particular advertisement meets none of the criteria that it has been at such pains to expound.

That it is visually dull, dull, dull.

That it's criminally overwritten: That it's also a stupid concept, and that the one and only reason that they're reading it is to find the spelling mistake and qualify for $500 in the currency of their choice.

They may, of course, be right. (Found it yet, by the way? Keep going; concentrate.)

But at the Ball Partnership we'll do anything to get people to read ads.

Ours. Or yours.

This advertisement has cost us $22,336 to run. As you can imagine we're more than happy to give away $500 to make sure that everybody reads it. If you've found the spelling mistake (and if you haven't by now, you've missed it), call The Ball Partnership in Hong Kong, Malaysia, Singapore, Taiwan or Thailand and ask to speak to the Managing Partner. Of course, you're almost certainly too late to get the five hundred bucks, but call anyway. We like to chat about ads.

IS THIS THE BEST AD EVER WRITTEN?

MEN WANTED for Hazardous Journey. Small wages, bitter cold, long months of complete darkness, constant danger, safe return doubtful. Honour and recognition in case of success — Ernest Shackleton.

When this little advertisement ran, in 1900, Ernest Shackleton was snowed under with replies.

Why? Surely, by all the accepted rules, he shouldn't have been. For a start, the 'promise' is entirely negative. And there's no picture.

So let's rewrite the ad, according to the rules.

"Men wanted for exciting journey. Good money, excellent conditions, certainty of massive royalties from publishing and movie rights. Reply now!"

Brilliant. Run it.

And if they had, you know instinctively that, even though they might have had a bagful of replies, it's very doubtful that they'd have got anywhere near the South Pole.

And certainly, no-one would have returned, to cash in on the deal.

And we wouldn't now be talking about the ad either. Would we?

Isn't the strength of that advertisement, then, in its simplicity? Isn't its sheer power in its honesty?

And is not its most brilliant quality the way it appeals precisely, and absolutely exclusively, to the very specialised section of the market it addresses?

'Wimps need not apply' would be superfluous. It's written large enough between the lines.

No doubt Shackleton wrote the ad straight off the cuff, pausing only to count the words, and the cost. It works because it has passion, and belief, and you can feel the leadership, if not fanaticism, in every phrase.

But *this* advertisement is written for an agency. An advertising agency. We produce ads, every day, for a living.

And frankly, rarely for as romantic a cause, or as inspiring a journey, as Ernest's.

But we do like to think that, at times, our work is as focussed, and as simple, as his: We know for certain that it can be as effective.

To help us, we've evolved systems that *force* us to take a fresh look at every problem; to wring the very last drop of information out of the product and the market; and to avoid at all costs, the trite, the formula-led, and especially the downright boring.

We've even produced an example, to show how, in all likelihood, our system would have led us to the same conclusion to which Shackleton's inspiration led him. (To his ad, that is. Not to the South Pole.)

If you'd be interested in finding out how we work, give us a call. We're in Hong Kong, Malaysia, Thailand, Taiwan, and Singapore.

We're The Ball Partnership.

Here are three of the dozen or so ads I wrote for The Ball Partnership. The first was a recruitment ad. The next two were part of the continuing statement of principles of the agency. (Interestingly, though we had stacks of attempts to win the money, only my secretary actually spotted the spelling mistake).

There are plenty of excellent reasons for leaving the country.

Frankly, 'The chance to do better ads' isn't usually regarded as one of them.

For most advertising people, England, and London in particular, has become a sort of benign prison. And not always that benign.

"If I'm not here," you hear them say, "I won't be able to do great ads." As if the air itself, polluted and carcinogenic as it is, in some way contributes to the creative process.

But in all seriousness, how many great ads have you seen lately?

More importantly, how many have you done, yourself? Honestly, now.

(Of course, it may be that you're basically inept, in which case, you're probably no longer reading this, and good riddance).

Some of those still with us may, however, have a nagging suspicion that we have a point. Or may eventually get round to making one.

So. Why do people flock, Whittington-like, to London, when, these days, the entire world is their mollusc? Fear is the key.

Not just the fear of 'not being at the heart of things'. It's the greater fear... of the unknown. That, once you leave, you can never return.

Nonsense, of course. If you're good, you can go anywhere. For instance, Paul Leeves worked in Singapore for a while, and it didn't slow him down.

But in any case, is it so crucially important that you should return? Why would you want to? Is London really that special?

Today, take a look around you.

Is it the weather that keeps you here? (This is, quite clearly, a joke. There are few major cities in the world with as unattractive a climate as ours. Minsk, perhaps. Or possibly Melbourne).

Is it the absence of crime? If it is, you must live in Gwent. Or Downing Street.

The freedom of the individual? The justice and sanity of having your car clamped for hours in the very position in which it was, presumably, causing an obstruction in the first place?

Perhaps you're just proud of being British? Haven't been abroad lately, have you? Not where they play football, anyway.

You believe, possibly, that despite it all, this is still a great place to bring up a family. That must be it. There are no drink problems, no drugs and no violence: The education system and sickness service are in splendid shape: And for the young, these days, buying a home is so easy. Right?

Seriously, now. What are you doing here?

The Option.

You could live somewhere else.

Give yourself a moment to get over the shock of the concept, and then get the world map out of your Filofax. First time you've ever needed it, yes?

Over on the right is the Pacific. It's the large blue bit. All the land in and around it is called the Pacific Rim. And for the next few decades, that is where the action's going to be.

Japan, of course, and Australia. And some day, China. But right now, Hong Kong, Thailand, Taiwan, Malaysia, Indonesia, South Korea. And Singapore.

All the major agency groups are already in position there. They have to be. But only one was actually 'born' there, and predictably, it is quickly becoming the most successful. The name can wait for now, because first let's talk about just one of those countries.

Singapore is a small island, with ambitions to become the Switzerland of Asia. Its population of 2.5 million is swollen by a constant invasion of visitors. Singapore has more First-Class Hotels per square mile than anywhere else on earth. And they include the tallest, and one of the oldest, in the world.

It is practically free of street-crime. Burglary is rare. Corporal punishment is mandatory for rape and violence. Drug-pushers are hanged.

It has the most modern subway-system in the world. Parking is easy. Traffic-jams are cause for remark.

The city is clean, green, bursting with life. It is, admittedly, hot and humid. But air-con makes a welcome change from central heating. It rains in stair-rods occasionally. No hurricanes, though, or earthquakes.

The people are Chinese, Malay, Indian and Caucasian. Most speak English. Their commercial history is one of trading and entrepreneurship. Consequently, they tend to be marvellous, brave, clients. (Not all, of course. But a lot).

Finally, the cost of living well is rather lower than in the UK. And tax is a lot lower.

What about this 'better ads' bit? Singapore produces some of the best ads in the world.

Bullshit? Not at all. Every year, some of the world's top admen fly to Singapore to judge their awards (it's known as the Gong Show), and every year they're amazed at the standard.

Ask Steve Grounds, Jeff Stark, Peter Harold, Suzie Henry, or Tony Brignull. Call Helmut Krone, Ed McCabe, Andrew Rutherford, or Ron Mather.

At the moment, one agency in Singapore is very hot indeed. It's called The Ball Partnership. Creatively, we're No.1. (As we are in Malaysia).

But the fact that we won the lion's share of Singapore's Awards may not mean much to you. Even the fact that we walked off with more Asian Awards than any other agency may not impress. A wallfull of Clio finalists? No?

OK, then. How many ads did you get in the D&ADA Annual this year? We got seven.

We're understandably cocky. But we want to do better. We're looking for a Creative Director. Ideally, an art-director who can write. Definitely a thinker. Without doubt, a leader. Possibly not from London at all, but a denizen of the rather more ballsy 'provinces'. (I'm a Brummie, myself).

If you're interested, write to Neil French, at The Ball Partnership, 172 Drury Lane, London WC2, with your C.V. and examples of some of your best work, (stats will do). Don't bother to call in or phone, though; I'll be somewhere in Asia. In the sun.

Top: By now it may have dawned on you that, layoutwise, I'm severely limited! Here is layout No. 2a. But I like the copy, and the argument, and for this book, it's appropriate.

Bottom right: A bit of fun, this; an ad for an aquarium where you walk through a glass tube, and the fish swim around you. The old role-reversal idea.

Bottom left: An oddity. Is this all headline or all copy? Continental were intent on publishing their (check) ownership and this translated into a 'no nonsense' approach, so the ads had to match.

YOU HAVE EXACTLY THIRTY SECONDS TO READ THIS AD.

Starting now.

Of course, you know at a glance that it can't be done, which is probably why you're reading this far, to find out what's going on.

Is this an advertisement for an entirely new method of speed-reading? What a marvellous thing that would be: To be able to knock off the entire contents of the South China Morning Post in about half an hour.

Well, no. It's not.

And to save you a lot of time, if you're not in the advertising business, or at least don't have an advertising budget to spend, now would be a good time to stop, and turn over.

DOES YOUR ADVERTISING SELF-DESTRUCT AFTER THIRTY SECONDS?

This is what it's all about.

The old chestnut about whether you should advertise in the newspapers or on the television.

The first argument is an obvious one.

A newspaper is entirely in the power of the reader. If he wants to read your ad, he can: If he wants to read it again, no problem: If he wants to tear it out and keep it, fine.

But a sneeze, or a phone call, or indeed any distraction during your TV ad, and, sorry, but your time's up. No refunds.

And, of course, here we're only talking about involuntary distractions.

Which brings us to another fascinating question.

WHAT DO *YOU* DO DURING THE COMMERCIALS?

Well, *you're* at least marginally connected with advertising, so you're more likely to sit and watch them, than, say, an office worker or a housewife.

But honestly now, don't you, too, go and put the kettle on, or go and get rid of the effects of the previous kettle, or see how the kids are getting on with their homework, or glance at the TV programme guide to see what's on the other channel?

And where do they print the programme guide? In the newspaper. Exactly our point.

The standard response to this is that the reader can turn the page, and miss *your* ad, too. But this neatly ignores the main argument; the viewer can (and does) zap your commercial, either by fast forwarding if it's on video, or by channel switching.

The big difference is that, when someone picks up a newspaper, it's an 'active' decision. He or she, is going to read. And assuming your ad is visually interesting, and relevant to him or her, it'll get read. There are no compulsory ads, interrupting the editorial. No-one blows a whistle, and tells the reader to stop reading what he's reading, and look, at the ads.

But on TV, that's exactly what happens. Isn't it? You *know* it is.

BUT WHAT ABOUT THE RESEARCH?

The figures can tell you, fairly accurately, when the TV is switched on. They can even tell you what sort of people have the TV on; what socio-economic group they belong to; what age or sex they are.

But they can't tell you how much attention is being paid to your ads. Just because no-one has bothered to switch the TV *off*, doesn't mean anyone is watching it.

Now, research into TV viewership, coupled with attitude research into the details, is expensive. It is therefore usually carried out by TV companies. It's hardly surprising that you don't hear much bad news, is it?

But ask yourself this. If current methods proved conclusively that TV ads were more effective than press, would it not be the most effective weapon in the TV arsenal? Why is it *not* then?

And, finally, let's get rid of that old story about TV being a "housewives' medium: In the evening, when the family's home, who does most of the tea-making, the kid-coddling, the meal-fixing... The ad-missing?

"BUY SOME TODAY!"

Seriously, don't you find it infuriating when you hear an hysterical voice-over instructing you to "Buy now!"?

It's nine o'clock in the evening; it's dark outside; possibly raining; you're settled in for the night... do they *seriously* expect you to dash out and buy soap-powder?

Of course they don't. They hope you'll remember all that high-pitched enthusiasm tomorrow. Or when you finally decide to go shopping.

Meanwhile, you'll watch more programmes and more ads; close up the home, sleep for eight hours or so; get up, shower, have coffee...

And read the newspaper.

If you're going to buy anything today, that newspaper just might be where you'll read about it.

IT'S TRADITIONAL. AND I'M A SHEEP.

The last bastion of marketing conservatism.

"Sorry, some products are always advertised on TV. That's the way it is." "Our competition is on TV, so we have to be." "You can't demonstrate a product in press."

Oh dear. Oh dear.

How very sad. Follow-my-leader, me-too-marketing. No wonder so many new products fail.

Imagine a soap-powder being launched in newspapers. It would stand out. People would remember it... and they'd see it *just* before they went shopping, not the *night* before.

The same applies to a bug-killer, or a breakfast cereal (especially a breakfast cereal, come to think of it). Or a bakery...

The first rule of advertising: Get noticed. Easy in newspapers.

Second rule of advertising: Dominate your medium. For these products, impossible on TV. Easy in newspapers.

And "you can't demonstrate in the press"?

If you believe that, you're using the wrong advertising agency.

But that's another story.

NO PICTURES OF SMILING STEWARDESSES.

NO PICTURES OF SMILING PASSENGERS.

NO PICTURES OF GLASSES OF CHAMPAGNE, OR TRAYS GROANING WITH HAUTE CUISINE.

JUST ONE SMALL LINE OF INFORMATION.

WE THINK YOU'LL GET THE PICTURE.

▼

Continental. The folks who fly the planes own the airline.

ESSAY COMPETITION WINNER

"WHAT I DID AT THE WEEKEND."
by A. Shark.

"It was wet outside, so that was a good start to the day.

On the other hand, it's always wet outside. It'd be a tough world for a fish if it was dry outside, come to think of it.

I decided to go and take a look at the new place, called Underwater World.

(Though, again, why they call it that I've no idea, since as far as I can see, the entire world's under water anyway. Still what do I know? I only work here.)

The great thing is that, if you're a fish, entry's free!

Apparently, the non-fishy exhibits shell out $9 to be gawped at, which just goes to show that a human being has all the intelligence of a giant sea-cucumber.

And take it from me, they're *thick*.

In fact, in the contest for the most remarkably stupid sea-creature, your giant sea-cucumber would romp home by a short head, (which is exactly what he's short of), from the common jelly-fish, if only either of them could work out the entry-forms.

Where was I?

Right. Yes. At Underwater World. Well, you know what we sharks are like. If there's something happening, we're *there*. It's like a fifth sense. Always first to the action, that's us.

Anyway, me and my pals turned up in the morning, and spent the whole day being jostled by other fish.

The entire marine population, so it seemed, had decided that an hour or two laughing their fins off at a bunch of dumb two-legged mammals gliding through a transparent tube was just what they all needed. Good for stress, I expect.

The plaice was *packed!* Eels, rays, big guys, small ones, the little fat chaps in weird suits, starfish. Jellyfish, even! All peering at the humans on display.

Actually, to be honest, I don't find humans very interesting.

For a start, they all look the same to me. Very boring lot. No fun.

They don't even seem to eat each other very often.

They just drift past, mouths gaping like a school of terminally dim gold-fish, pointing at us with their fins.

After a couple of hours, I was fed-up to the gills with it. For some reason, it's forbidden to eat the exhibits, and since nobody can jostle a shark and get away with it, I ate a couple of the visitors and went home. The end."

UNDERWATER WORLD IS NOW OPEN, FREE OF CHARGE, TO ALL FISH. HUMANS PAY $9 AT THE DOOR; THEY WILL THEN ENTER A HUGE TRANSPARENT TUBE AND GLIDE ALONG MOVING WALKWAYS THROUGH ENORMOUS TANKS, SO THAT THE FISH CAN GET A GOOD LOOK AT THEM.

FISH ARE EXPRESSLY FORBIDDEN TO EAT THE EXHIBITS, WHICH, WE ADMIT, IS EXTREMELY UNFAIR, SINCE FOR YEARS THE EXHIBITS HAVE EATEN *THEM*. SUCH IS LIFE.

A FEW ENCOURAGING WORDS FOR THE TOTALLY INCOMPETENT.

It's perfectly alright to be incompetent for hours on end.

I am. And so is everyone I know.

Of course, being of this persuasion, I shall never be able to afford a bottle of Beck's Beer. Which is why the people who sell Beck's Beer got me to write this ad.

They see it as a sort of public service announcement; as a way of consoling those who moan at the unfairness of it all. A way of making the 'have-nots' feel glad that they 'haven't'.

So here, for the first time, are the great names: The people who were so bad in their chosen sphere of endeavour that they achieved greatness.

People who believed that success is overrated.

And who believed, as G. K. Chesterton once said, that 'If a thing's worth doing, it's worth doing badly."

THE WORST BOXING DEBUT

Ralph Walton was knocked out in 10½ seconds of his first bout, on 29th September, 1946, in Lewison, Maine, USA.

It happened when Al Couture struck him as he was adjusting his gum-shield in his corner. The 10½ seconds includes 10 seconds while he was counted out.

He never fought again.

THE LEAST-SUCCESSFUL WEATHER REPORT

After severe flooding in Jeddah, in January 1979, the Arab News gave the following bulletin: "We regret that we are unable to give you the weather. We rely on weather reports from the airport, which is closed, on account of the weather. Whether or not we are able to bring you the weather tomorrow depends on the weather."

THE WORST SPEECH-WRITER

William Gamaliel Harding wrote his own speeches while President of the USA, in the 1920's.

When Harding died, e. e. cummings said, "the only man, woman or child who wrote a simple, declarative sentence with seven grammatical errors, is dead".

Here is a rewarding sample of the man's style. "I would like the government to do all it can to mitigate, then, in understanding, in mutuality of interest, in concern for the common good, our tasks will be solved."

THE MOST UNSUCCESSFUL ATTEMPT AT DYING FOR LOVE

When his fiancee broke off their engagement, Senor Abel Ruiz, of Madrid, decided to kill himself for love.

Reviewing the possibilities available on such occasions, he decided to park himself in front of the Gerona to Madrid express. However, jumping in its path, he landed between the rails and watched, gloomily, as the train passed over him.

He suffered only minor injuries, and promptly received First Aid at Gerona Hospital.

Later that day, he tried again. This time he jumped in front of a passing lorry, again only acquiring some more bruises. His rapid return to the hospital led doctors to call a priest, who made Sr. Ruiz see the folly of his ways. Eventually, he decided to carry on living, and to seek a new girlfriend.

Glad to be alive, he left the hospital and was immediately knocked down by a runaway horse; he was taken back to Gerona Hospital, this time quite seriously injured, for the third time that day.

THE WORST JUROR

There was a rape case at a Crown Court in Northern England in the late 1970's at which a juror fell fast asleep, during which time the victim was asked to repeat what her attacker had said prior to the incident.

To save her embarrassment, the girl was allowed to write it on paper, instead. This was then folded, and passed along the jury. Each member read the words which, in effect, said "Nothing, in the history of sexual congress, equals the comprehensive going-over which I am about to visit upon your good self."

Sitting next to the dozing juror was an attractive blonde. After reading the note, she refolded it, and nudged her neighbour, who awoke with a start.

He read the note, and looked at the blonde in astonishment. To the delight of the entire court, he then read the note again, slowly. Then he winked at the blonde, and put the note in his pocket.

When the judge asked him for the piece of paper, the recently dormant juror refused, saying that 'it was a personal matter'.

THE LEAST-SUCCESSFUL WEAPON

The prize for the most useless weapon of all time goes to the Russians, who invented the dog-mine. The rather ingenious plan was to train the dogs to associate food with the underside of tanks, in the hope that they would run hungrily beneath the advancing Panzer divisions. Bombs would be strapped to their backs, which endangered the dogs to a point where no insurance company would look at them.

Unfortunately, they associated food solely with *Russian* tanks, and totally destroyed half a Soviet division on their first outing.

The plan was quickly abandoned.

THE WORST BUS SERVICE

Can any bus-service rival the fine Hanley to Bagnall route, in Staffordshire, England? In 1976 it was reported that the buses no longer stopped to pick up passengers.

This came to light when one of them, Mr Bill Hancock, complained that buses on the outward journey regularly sailed past queues of elderly people; up to thirty of them sometimes waiting in line.

Councillor Arthur Cholerton then made transport history by stating that if the buses stopped to pick up passengers, it would disrupt the timetable.

THE LAST WORD

"They couldn't hit an elephant at this dist..." The last words of General John Sedgwick, spoken while looking over the parapet at enemy lines during the Battle of Spotsylvania, in 1864.

This is what the label on a bottle of Beck's Beer looks like. Since its the closest you'll probably ever get to one, we've given you a dotted line, so you can cut it out, and put it on your wall as a kind of ikon. When you've finished cutting it out, plasters can be bought from any pharmacy.

OH, ALRIGHT, THEN; HERE ARE SOME MORE

Typography has never been our strong point, so here are a few more determined losers, to fill out the column: The Welsh choir who were the sole entrants in a competition, and came second; the Swiss pornographer who was heavily fined because his wares were insufficiently pornographic; the writer of this ad, who, unable to master the art of précis, copied the entire thing, word for word, from Stephen Pile's 'Book of Heroic Failures', thereby incurring almost certain legal action.

There, feel better now, don't you? After all, the price of a bottle of Beck's Beer may well be so high as to be audible only to highly-trained bats, but at least you're not the only one who'll never be able to afford it.

(Oh, no. Three more lines. How about a jingle? Beck's diddly-dee-de-dah, Beck's, tiddly-pom. The end).

On the other hand, there's Becks. The strategy was "expensive lager", and since we couldn't bring ourselves to rip off the lovely UK work for Stella Artois, we went for an interminable read. There are three in the series, and they're my all-time favourite ads. I did them with Ben Hunt. I like the headline treatment on this one.

Steve Hayden, George Orwell's favourite copywriter, sports many fearsome titles, including President, Worldwide Brand Services, Ogilvy & Mather.

But he is quite simply one of the pre-eminent creative talents in advertising today and has been responsible for many of the most influential and highly acclaimed campaigns ever to run. These include fourteen years of work for Apple Computer, the most famous being the commercial "1984". As well as the mid-eighties print campaign that gave Porsche its highest ever sales in North America, Steve has worked on a wide-ranging list of consumer accounts which include Pizza Hut, Nike and Home Savings of America.

In 1986, Steve was recruited by BBDO to head the special Los Angeles office set up to handle Apple. Subsequently, Steve took over the creative leadership of all BBDO accounts in Los Angeles and San Francisco. In 1992, the Los Angeles and San Francisco offices won over 60 creative awards including two of the industries most coveted: the Belding Sweepstakes and the Grand Effie.

In late 1994, he moved to Ogilvy & Mather Worldwide to head up the recently consolidated IBM account to atone for his past life.

Over a twenty year career which began in business and industrial advertising, Steve has won all of the most prestigious laurels advertising hands out, some of them many times over. On that list is the Belding Best of Show, Canne Gold Lion, the Clio, the New York Art Directors Club, the One Show, and British D&AD awards.

A graduate of USC, Steve is also an alumnus of several agencies from MacManus, John & Adams in Detroit to Foote, Cone and Belding in Los Angeles.

If you want to be a well-paid copywriter, please your client. If you want to be an award-winning copywriter, please yourself. If you want to be a great copywriter, please your reader.

Copywriting is perhaps the only non-criminal human activity that allows you to make a comfortable living off your character defects. These will usually include, but are not limited to, pride, anger, gluttony, greed, lust, envy, sloth and fear.

All of them are useful, depending on the circumstances, so make sure you're familiar with each in all its facets.

This may be why some of the more successful copywriters are so familiar with the original creative black book, the Bible.

It not only explains everything you need to know about human frailty, but also serves as a very useful style guide (where do you think all those "Ands" in copy come from?). It's also the most powerful selling document ever written. In a world full of parity scriptures, it's persuaded billions to buy the totally intangible, often at the ultimate price a human can pay, for nearly twenty centuries. Forty, if you just count the scary parts.

It also embodies the principle of Anonymous Power. No one knows who wrote it. We barely know who translated it. But they were very, very good.

How many of us, even after winning a D&AD pencil, have our work referred to as The Word of God?

Thus, it's not a bad idea to emulate them rather than the flashier types you come across in awards books. In other words, make your work The Word of Proctor, or The Word of IBM, or The Word of Callard and Bowser.

Which brings us to hearing voices, and developing your own. A few great copywriters like Hal Riney and Howard Gossage can get away their whole lives with one voice.

Most of us, though, have to adapt our style to our clients, our audiences, our countries, and our mortgage payments.

That's why it helps to meet the president or managing director of whatever it is you're writing about. If they were great speakers and brilliant thinkers, and if you were able to sweep aside the stupidity and cupidity that drives most businesses, what would they sound like? Yours job is to create your clients' Best Self. So look for the angel in them, and bring it out.

Now then there's the matter of getting people to read your copy. Large promise, as Johnson pointed out, is the soul of the advertisement.

Search for some way to relate the tiny, constricted world clients live in to the larger, sunnier world people actually care about. Deodorants aren't about keeping dry, they're about being loved. Computers aren't about getting more work done, they're about power. Cars aren't about transportation. Food isn't about hunger. Drink isn't about thirst. And so on.

It's always useful to get yourself genuinely excited about a product or service that seems incredibly dull to everyone else. Package delivery, for example. Find how to relate it to the larger world, and you'll make yourself famous, at least in the copywriter's anonymous fashion.

The opening line of your copy is probably more important than the headline. A creative director at FCB once told me that four per cent of the readership will slog through seventy per cent of body copy no matter how bad it is. Your job is to beat these odds.

The Bible, save for Genesis, is a great source of book titles, but only occasionally of opening lines. For these, study Country and Western lyrics, the very font (if not wellhead) of common emotion, everyday irony and freighted pith.

My favourite Country and Western lyric: "If your phone don't ring, it's me."

A brilliant example of morphemic loading for everyone who toils in the dank trenches of commercial prose.

Most people's lives are brutish, dull and long. If you can bring a momentary diversion, a promise that there is something interesting out there that might make a difference, they will love you.

If you are lying, of course, they will tear you to pieces. So make the truth as interesting as it can be, and never look down on your audience. They're wiser than you, and will live longer.

Now, one last piece of advice.

Avoid drugs if you possibly can, alcohol as much as you can, and cigarettes at all hazard.

You will spend most of your life creating artificial pearls for genuine, well, clients. If you win awards, they will hate you for it. If you don't win awards, they'll dump you for someone who does.

Ultimately, this will drive you to addiction and death, unless you're able to achieve a healthy perspective on your existence as a copywriter. After all, it's the only career in the world that allows you the life of an artist and the income of a foreign currency manipulator.

So make sure you give at least ten percent of your earnings to worthy causes. Give of your own time in love and service to others. Learn compassion and beware of the ego sickness that devastates so many in our trade.

Of course, that does bring us back to the Bible, preferably the version scripted by the anonymous scribes of King James' court. It's better written.

We began setting Apple's brand persona back in 1980 with ads like this – true stories of how Apple computers fit in people's lives – without the bits and bytes, speeds and feeds featured in most computer ads.

Baked Apple.

Last Thanksgiving, a designer from Lynn/Ohio Corporation took one of the company's Apple Personal Computers home for the holidays.

While he was out eating turkey, it got baked.

His cat, perhaps miffed at being left alone, knocked over a lamp which started a fire which, among other unpleasantries, melted his TV set all over his computer. He thought his goose was cooked.

But when he took the Apple to Cincinnati Computer Store, *mirabile dictu*, it still worked.

A new case and keyboard made it as good as new.

Nearly 1,000 Apple dealers have complete service centers that can quickly fix just about anything that might go wrong, no matter how bizarre.

So if you're looking for a personal computer that solves problems instead of creating them, look to your authorized Apple dealer.

You'll find everything well-done.

The personal computer.

Welcome, IBM. Seriously.

Welcome to the most exciting and important marketplace since the computer revolution began 35 years ago.

And congratulations on your first personal computer.

Putting real computer power in the hands of the individual is already improving the way people work, think, learn, communicate and spend their leisure hours.

Computer literacy is fast becoming as fundamental a skill as reading or writing.

When we invented the first personal computer system, we estimated that over 140,000,000 people worldwide could justify the purchase of one, if only they understood its benefits.

Next year alone, we project that well over 1,000,000 will come to that understanding. Over the next decade, the growth of the personal computer will continue in logarithmic leaps.

We look forward to responsible competition in the massive effort to distribute this American technology to the world. And we appreciate the magnitude of your commitment.

Because what we are doing is increasing social capital by enhancing individual productivity.

Welcome to the task apple

I don't believe the cleverest ads always have clever headlines. We ran this ad in 1981, welcoming IBM to the personal computer market. Somewhat like Belgium welcoming Hitler to the border. Oh well. The clever bit was that, even though Apple was tiny at the time, this ad made a two horse race out of a twenty horse race, and Apple–IBM have forever after been hyphenated.

For the second year of the campaign, after people had purchased about a billion dollars' worth of PowerBooks, we realised how very personal these little notebooks can become, and developed the "Contrasts" campaign. The copy is nothing more than what these very different individuals have on their PowerBooks, but the readership scores were amazing. Art direction by Susan Westre and photography by Michael O'Brien.

What's on your PowerBook?

Father Don Doll
Priest

Wedding homilies
Student addresses
Fax/modem
Faxes to Jesuit missionaries in Nairobi, Bangkok and Rome
Entire photo layout of book I'm writing on the Sioux Indians
Grant proposal for my book
Reflections on scripture
Letter template, with my letterhead and signature
Envelope template
QuarkXPress
Microsoft Word
FileMaker Pro
Scans of photos I took in Ireland
A Campus Planning memo
A calculator
A spellchecker
A calendar
Design for wedding programs
Design for my Christmas card
Syllabi and assignments for my classes
My mechanic's phone number

Todd Rundgren
Interactive artist

The dates of my concert tour
Songs I've written
Computer programs I've written
Scanned photos I retouched for my new album cover
Fax/modem
Sequencer that lets the PowerBook control my synthesizers onstage
A letter to the editor
A bunch of type fonts
Flowfazer, the screensaver I codeveloped
CompuServe
Microsoft Word
Adobe Photoshop
Think C Code
ToasterLink
A lecture I delivered on interactive music
A lecture I delivered to the New York State Bar
Animation clips
An alarm clock
My last video
Storyboards and graphics for my next video

BEFORE
*This is me before I started listening to
KFAC. Overweight, poor, unhappy and alone.*

AFTER
*This is I after 16 short years as a
KFAC listener. Rich, trim and sexy.*

How classical music changed my life.

The other day at Ma Maison, as I was waiting for the attendant to retrieve my chocolate brown 450 SLC, the Saudi prince I'd been noshing with said, "Say, Bill, how did an unassuming guy like yourself come to be so rich, so trim, so…sexy?"

My eyes grew misty. "It wasn't always this way, Ahmed, old buddy…"

My mind raced back to the Bad Time, before the investment tips, the real estate empire, before Dino bought my screenplay and I bought my Columbia 50…

Once I was a lot like you.
Working at a nowhere job, hitting the singles bars, watching situation comedies in my free time. I tipped the scales at a hefty 232, but my bank balance couldn't have tipped the bus boy at the Midnight Mission.

Finally, I hit bottom…picked up by the Castaic police for barreling my old heap the wrong way over some parking lot spikes.

My last friend in this lonely world, Hardy Gustavsen, set me straight while he was driving me back to L.A.

"Bill, get hold of yourself! Start listening to KFAC!"

"Gosh, Hardy, don't they play classical music? I'm not sure I cotton to that high brow stuff!"

Aside from a couple of summers at Tanglewood and Aspen, and one semester in Casals' Master Class…
I knew absolutely nothing about classical music.

"Bill, who would be wrong if you got better?"

Looking into his steely blue eyes, I

realized Hardy was right. I resolved to give KFAC a shot.

At first, it was quite painful. Listening to all those 100-piece groups was confusing—I was used to having the drums on the right and the bass on the left and the singer in the middle. All those semidemihemiquavers made my head spin.

But I started to feel the beneficial effects of classical music listening in just one short week.

In no time, I was using napkins with every meal, I switched from Bourbon to an unpretentious Montrachet and I became able to hear sirens even with my car windows rolled up.

Soon I was spending every night with KFAC and a good book, like Aquinas' *Summa Theologica*.

I realized that some of the wealthiest, most famous people in this world listened to classical music—Napoleon, Bismark, George Washington, Beethoven…and many others who are yet alive today.

Then I met Marlene. The first girl who knew there was more to *Also Sprach Zarathustra* than the theme from *2001*. And I fell in love.

Today, I'm on top of the world with a wonderful wife, close friends in high places and a promising career in foreign currency manipulation.

Can classical music do for you what it did for me?

A few years back, scientific studies showed that when dairy cows are played classical music the quantity and quality of their milk dramatically

improves.

Now if it can do that for plain old moo cows, imagine what it can do for you!

You might use it to control disgusting personal habits and make fun new friends. The possibilities are endless!

Can you afford KFAC?

Is lox kosher?

Even though marketing surveys show that KFAC's audience is the most affluent assemblage of nice people in Southern California, yes, you *can* afford KFAC! Thanks to their Special Introductory Offer, you can listen FREE OF CHARGE for *as many hours as you like* without obligation!

Begin the KFAC habit today.

Remember, the longest journey begins by getting dressed. Don't let this opportunity slip through your fingers. Tune to KFAC right NOW, while you're thinking about it.

And get ready for a spectacular improvement in your life.

Warn your family and friends that you may start dressing for dinner.

You may lose your taste for beer nuts.

And the next time you're on the freeway thinking about playing with your nose, you'll find yourself asking:

"Really. Would a KFAC listener do this?"

KFAC
1330 AM 92.3 FM

Selling a classical music radio in LA is only slightly less challenging than selling bikinis in Rejavik, but I thought this tried and true advertising form would at least get us readership. It also got me a job at Chiat/Day.

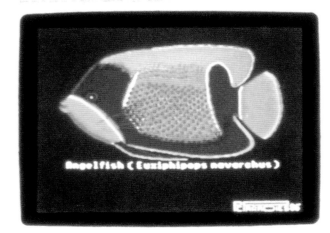

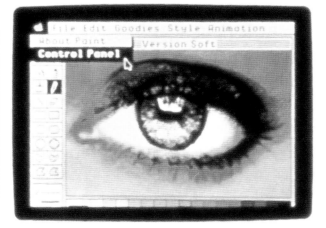

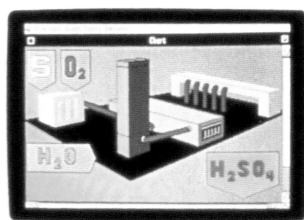
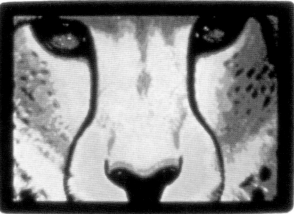

You won't believe your ears, either.

The recent PowerBook campaign is some of the best print we've ever done for Apple. This is one of my favourites, featuring Steve Wozniack, Apple founder, and his son, Jess. I wrote the copy with Chris Wall and came up with "The next thing" theme for the campaign, which Apple never particularly liked, but Dan Weiden rather enjoyed.

Born in Hong Kong, 1955. During a hurricane.

Formal First in English Literature, Oxford University. 1978. Copywriter GGT, 81 — 85. Worked on: London Docklands, London Weekend Television, Holsten Pils, Time Out. 85 — 87, Group Director at WCRS. Worked on: Carling Black Label, Midland Bank, Prudential, Tennents Extra.

Set up Howell Henry Chaldecott Lury in 1987. Favourite clients include: Molson lager, Marie Claire magazine, Thames Television, First Direct bank, Maxell Tapes, Fuji Film, Mercury Communications, Healthcrafts, Danepak

Bacon, MTV, BhS, Britvic Soft Drinks (including Tango), Golden Wonder Pot Noodles, Red Mountain Coffee, Lego, Avon Cosmetics, the Automobile Association, and Mazda Cars.

HHCL and Partners was voted Campaign Agency of the Year 1989 and in 1994. Fuji was voted Advertiser of the Year 1990. Tango was voted Campaign of the Year 1992. No other company has won all three awards within its first five years.

Steve is 38, married with two daughters, and lives in Wandsworth in South London.

Life's too short to read body copy. Let's face it – life's too short to read this book.

Skim it. Look at the pictures. Nobody reads body copy.

Sometimes, I have this fantasy that a piece of copy goes out. And it hasn't been read by anybody – not even the proof-reader. And, hidden down in paragraph 13, is a typo that reveals the secret of the universe. But nobody gets to see it. (Because nobody reads body copy.)

However. Sometimes art directors need body copy to balance the design of an ad. Or a client insists on saying lots of things. Or else you just have a moment of blind optimism, and imagine that people do actually read body copy. (I've made that mistake myself.)

Whatever. Sometimes you find yourself opening up a new file on your Apple, and stabbing away with two fingers.

And let me confess something right now. Although I fully understand the futility of writing body copy, I love doing it.

So, if you're still obstinately insisting that you can learn anything valuable from this handsome work of reference, I'll inflict four tips on you. Then talk you through the examples I've been half-nelsoned into including.

Tip One is work closely with the art director, designer, typographer, Mac operator, etc.

Tip Two is do anything to make the body copy readable. If all else fails, keep your sentences so short that someone with the IQ of an orang-utan can keep up. Right? Got that? Terrific.

Tip Three is one which a lot of top copywriters ignore. Every piece of body copy you write should be different. It should have your personal input but it shouldn't have your recognisable signature on it. Your clients are all different, and they deserve something unique.

Tip Four is do it differently. Don't try and emulate anybody else's style. The most important thing about any ad is to do it differently. Write it upside down, in Jamaican patois, or with every fifth letter missing.

(Tip Five is read the other contributions in this book. There are much better copywriters than me in this volume.)

Having said all this, I went to dig out some examples of body copy from the plans chest and immediately realised that I hadn't been quite as revolutionary as I wanted to be.

My first, panicky thought was to send in ads with as few words on them as possible — like the old Time Out poster with a candle burning at both ends, or the First Direct poster with a deliberately bland shot of rather stubby grass stretching across 96 sheets of prime London poster-site.

Then I thought, grow up, mate. This book is about words, and you don't despise words that much, do you?

So I dug out some ads with words on 'em. And I hit another problem. As a creative director, you don't always get to write the ads you most want to.

So some of these ads aren't my body copy at all.

So what.

MTV. This was an MTV trade ad in which we introduced the idea of "optional body copy". The copy was put on a rub-down inserted into the magazine. You could add as much of it (or as little) as you wanted to by rubbing on the sheet like a transfer. This came from a team called Justin Hooper (copywriter) and Christian Cotterill (art director). A BMW April Fool's ad from

WCRS. I like this because I had to write to a style set by Robin Wight, but I was able to inject some of my own sense of humour into it. At least, it raised a smile or two for me when I re-read it. Plus, it's even more topical now than when it was done eight years ago.

Fuji. Forget the body copy as such — I just like the captions. The fun was in making short captions describe the missing pictures in your head.

Vitachieve for Healthcrafts. Looking through all the print work we've done here, I felt this had a real urgency to it. I love it. Axel Chaldecott and I creative-directed it but it was *top copy-writer in her own right* Liz Whiston who wrote the words.

Idris Soft Drinks. A chance to indulge — which I feel I only half-took. Undoubtedly this is the sort of ad which David Abbott would have written much better.

Thames TV. I love the way the copy is spread out around the page, so you avoid that normal block-wodge look of body copy. The ad was a lot of fun to write. And it was written several years before Ben Langdon met Chris Still.

First Direct. In this campaign, small cut-out heads enjoyed short dialogues in small-space press ads. They had the feel of cartoons (i.e. they looked approachable), but I felt they were very fresh and different.

This idea originated from Axel Chaldecott. Which goes to show you that the copywriter's best friend isn't a dictionary, a Thesaurus or an HB2 pencil. It's his or her art director.

Most of the ads in the campaign were written by other people (Naresh Ramchandani, Dave Buonaguidi and Steve Girdlestone). I can't remember who wrote this one.

Call me perverse, if you want to but I like body copy that doesn't look like body copy. Which isn't that surprising when you consider that I first learnt about advertising from a man who took a very individual approach to copywriting.

Fresh from studying English Literature at Oxford University, I was told by Dave Trott that the best bit of body copy he'd seen was on a Land Rover ad from TBWA. There were actually no words at all. Just symbols.

He was right.

Now the question you've got to ask yourself is this. What's the next bit of genuinely revolutionary body copy going to look like? Not like anything in this book, that's for sure. Because these ideas have all been done before.

MTV Trade ad.

WHEN YOU CROSS THE CHANNEL, OUR STEERING WHEEL CROSSES OVER WITH YOU.

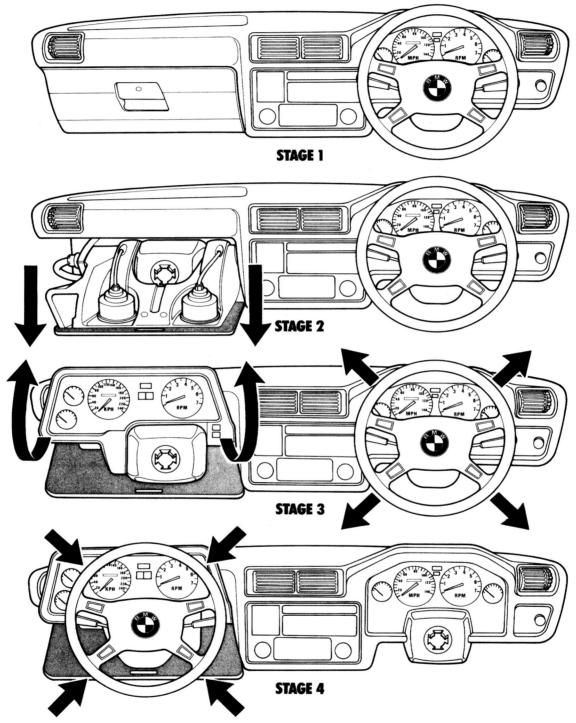

STAGE 1

STAGE 2

STAGE 3

STAGE 4

Since the 'Droit de Seigneur' act, passed in 1867, the French have always driven on the right-hand side of the road.

This is not merely a matter of inconvenience for British drivers; it is also a potential safety hazard. And yet car manufacturers have been ignoring the problem completely.

With one notable exception. Because BMW engineer Aap Rilfühl discovered, just three years ago, that the problem could be tackled; and, with ingenious modifications, a test vehicle was designed that incorporated a unique BMW feature – the multi-dashboard facility.

By incorporating a second-unit steering wheel socket and instrument panel into a conventional glove compartment, Dr Rilfühl was able to provide the basis for a secondary driving position.

The fascia, naturally enough, conforms to 'Continental' standards – with a kph speedometer, and the 'Lawson' fuel gauge reading in litres.

Then, by the insertion of a lynch-pin into the steering wheel column, fellow engineer Hans Grabbem was able to devise the first quick-release steering wheel. (Incorporated, too, into the column is a secondary 'Continental' horn – the 'Vorin-Drivers' 80 decibel air-horn.)

The final problem, of the foot-pedals, was easily resolved; Herr Grabbem made them transferable, too, with a dual position facility.

At present, this option is only available on the BMW 3 Series, but it is expected to be available on all models in time for the proposed opening of the Channel tunnel.

And then, for the first time, British drivers will be able to drive abroad without getting on the wrong side of the natives.

To: Uve Adjuri-Egpuhld, BMW (GB) Ltd, Ellesfield Avenue, Bracknell, Berks, RG12 4TA.
Please send me more details of the BMW multi-dashboard facility.
I intend to drive abroad: ☐ for business. ☐ for pleasure. ☐ for ever.
Name
Address
Postcode

THE ULTIMATE DRIVING MACHINE

BMW April Fool's ad.

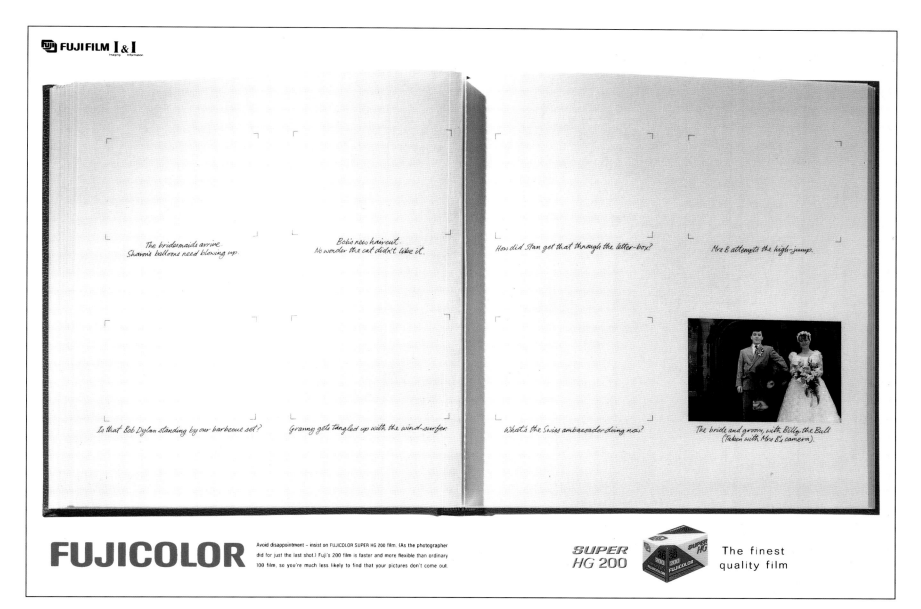

Fuji Film.

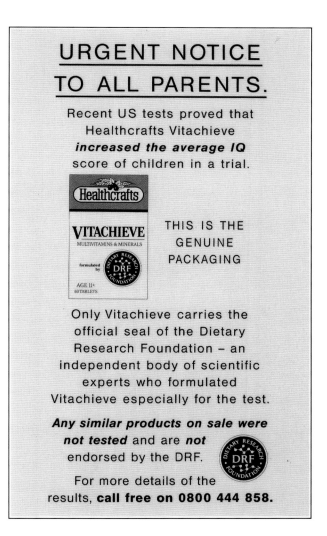

Vitacheive.

REMEMBER...

THAT TIME AFTER SCHOOL, in the summer, when you could go outside and play till ten o'clock at night? ¶ THAT LONG DRIVE to the seaside, when you

first saw the blue of the sea through a gap in the hills? ¶ PUTTING UP A TENT in the garden, and drinking Lemonade made cloudy by the real lemons in it, as the sun shone through the canvas? ¶ GETTING OFF THE BUS a stop early, so you could spend the fare money you saved on sweets? ¶ PLAYING 'TAG' in the garden all afternoon, as the shadows lengthened across the lawn? ¶ GOING FOR A LONG WALK, just with

your best friend, and giving yourself a reward in the sweet shop a mile away from home? ¶ MAKING AN ICE CREAM float, with vanilla ice cream and Cream Soda, and taking it carefully outside

with your two favourite comics? ¶ PICKING WILD BLACKBERRIES, and thinking you could run away and survive for ever on the delicious, free fruit? ¶ ROLLING DOWN A long bank, and standing up and feeling all dizzy as you ran up the bank to do it again? ¶ THE TASTE OF Dandelion and Burdock (if you ever drank it, how could you ever forget it)? ¶ PLAYING CATCH AGAINST a wall, and giving yourself a target of 10 in a row, to help England win the match?

¶ COMING HOME ONE DAY, to find that your family was the proud owner of a dog, and you had to think of a name for it?

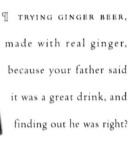

¶ TRYING GINGER BEER, made with real ginger, because your father said it was a great drink, and finding out he was right?

IDRIS
TRADITIONALS

Idris Soft Drinks.

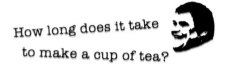

How long does it take to make a cup of tea?

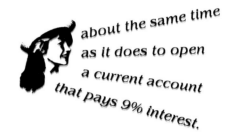

about the same time as it does to open a current account that pays 9% interest.

put the kettle on then.

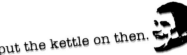

first direct is a division of midland bank plc. Interest is paid monthly on any amount in credit increasing to 9.25% for £500+ rate quoted is net p.a. and may vary

first direct
0800 22 2000

First Direct.

THE WORST THINGS AN ADVERTISING AGENCY CAN SAY TO ITS CLIENTS.

1. "Great news. We've merged."

13. "Sorry. Looks like we can't afford London on the schedule."

2. "Meeting...what meeting?"

3. "You know what's causing the problem here. Your logo's too big."

12. "I know we've made a hash of your advertising for the last 10 years. But we'll really try hard from now on."

4. "Can I give you a lift to the station? My Ferrari's just outside."

11. "Blimey. Did we do that?"

5. "Here, this'll make you laugh. We've gone a bit over budget."

10. "You'll notice we've left your sales conference off the timing plan."

6. "Sorry about the punch-up in reception."

9. "Here's the finished film. I guarantee that people will be able to make sense of it in research."

7. "Hello. I recognise you from somewhere don't I?"

8. "Yea, yea. But clients don't know much about advertising, do they?"

YOU CAN'T AFFORD NOT TO ADVERTISE IN LONDON. YOU CAN AFFORD TO ADVERTISE ON THAMES.

THAMES TELEVISION XXI

(CAMPAIGNS FROM £73,000. SPOTS FROM £500. EVEN LESS FOR LOCAL ADVERTISERS).

Thames TV Trade ad.

Susie Henry has been copywriting since 1972. She worked at Cogent Elliot, French Gold Abbott and Doyle Dane Bernbach, before leaving to become a founding partner in Waldron, Allen, Henry and Thompson, where she was also a creative director.

In 1992 she was reunited with her original art director, Gary Denham, when she joined CME.KHBB. "We're just the same people," says Susie. "Only now we've got eight children between us." Susie owns five D&AD Pencils for her work on Commercial Union, Bob Martins and the Government's Drink Drive campaign.

My first day in advertising I was given a very simple piece of advice.

"Remember kid, today's press ad is tomorrow's chip paper."

At the time it seemed a rather odd thing for my boss to say. Did he mean the advertising word was of so little value it wasn't worth the craft? That ultimately its only use was to stop vinegar dripping on your trousers. I was 22, nervous and not a little confused. But I soon twigged what he'd been on about.

The life of a press ad is brief. So let it be brilliant. You have one chance to entice and interest your reader. Tell them something they didn't know or hadn't thought of. Be provocative, beware the cliché, be believable. That in essence is what he meant. It's a good discipline, and one I've tried to live by.

How do I write copy? At the last minute, almost always. With fevered brow and even after all these years, with a good deal of angst.

People who know me will tell you there's nothing I like more than a jolly good natter. Give me a garden fence and I'll be leaning over it. When I first started writing, the 'chattiness' of my copy prompted one creative director to comment that I wrote "like a Butlins Redcoat". I remember being rather indignant. But on re-reading one of my early ads for Commercial Union ('Floods' circa 1978) I can see his point. It's not so much a press ad, more a Daily Mirror-style scoop. (Both my mother and aunt were journalists, so maybe that's where I get my tabloid turn-of-phrase.)

On the subject of journalists, I've lost count of the number of times they've borrowed the Commercial Union line and tweaked it to suit their editorial. I'm very flattered. Certainly, it gives the line an added currency.

I've grown up, quite literally, with Commercial Union. After seventeen years and four agencies, I'm still writing for them. What I've enjoyed most of all is the opportunity to tell a ripping yarn. Not having to pepper the copy with selling points. It's good to have that freedom. The hard bit has been to keep giving the campaign an edge, without losing its personality. We know that case histories work, the trick is how you tell 'em.

The last batch of ads, 'Toupee', 'Cow' and 'Jam', are less reportage and are written more like short stories. They're some of my favourites. Another reason why they're the only examples I'm including is because I had a savage clear out about twelve years ago. I've never hung on to anything since. It's meant a lot more drawer space, but it's a bit embarrassing when you're asked by D&AD to provide evidence of a lifetime's work.

I've given up trying to write copy at the office. Too much going on. If my art director sharpened his chinagraph my concentration would be in shreds. I remember there was this little old lady who used to come in and polish the phones. I could never do any writing when she was about, I'd be too busy watching her buffing up the receivers and working her way round the dials with her impregnated tissue. She used to wear white gloves, like a magician. She had me spellbound.

Writing at home with my grubby telephone unplugged seems much the best way. I make myself a coffee in my special mug — the one with the floppy-eared goat on, bought at the Hawkshead Show in aid of the Nubian Goat Society. It has become an essential prop to the 'creative process': no other mug will do. I don't write on to a screen. I write on to paper. With my Pelican poised? Sadly, no. It's usually a two-inch pencil stub (more suited to a greengrocer's ear), which is all the children leave me after raiding my desk.

I almost forgot. I've been asked to comment on the craft of copywriting. Now, that's a tough one. Whatever the skill is, I cannot define it. For me, it's more a feeling for words than a formula for putting them down. One thing I learnt early on was if someone says of your copy "I don't understand it," don't try and explain it. Just re-write it, so it's not only clear to you, but it's clear to him too.

To convey genuine enthusiasm, I think that's important. If your reader senses you're excited by the product, there's a pretty good chance he'll feel the same way.

Me, I'm still excited by this business. I hope it shows.

Commercial Union, 1978.

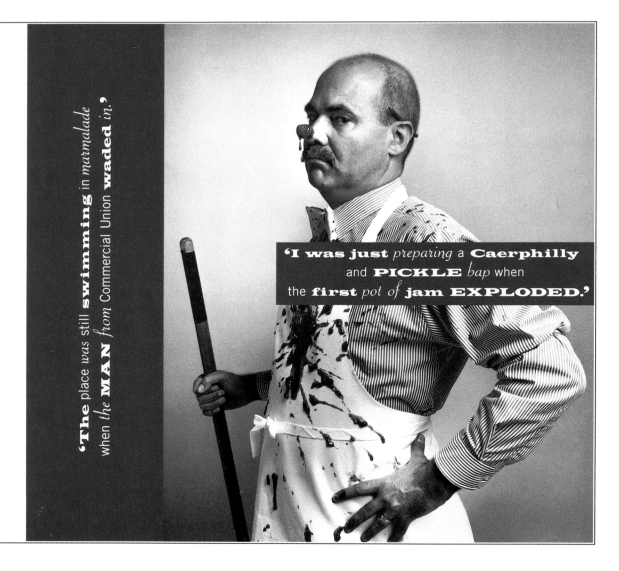

The Colonel strode out of the club house, his jaw set, his face etched with grim determination.

He was not in the best of humour.

Only moments earlier he'd been happily cocooned in the members' bar. Old Higgins had just ferried across a large 'pinky' and a bowl of cheese straws.

All seemed right with the world.

Then the phone rang. It was the dreadful Marjorie from the office.

Higgins listened impassively, holding the receiver at arm's length so the Colonel could follow the flow without moving from the comfort of his wing chair.

Some problem on the course. Intruders running amok. Must be dealt with immediately.

For a man who hadn't seen action since Suez the Colonel was still remarkably sprightly. Armed with a 3 Iron, a bucket and shovel, and several yards of rope, he moved ever closer to the shadowy figures lurking in the spinney.

The minefield of cow-pats around the 14th hole gave an important clue to their identity.

With one bound he was amongst them. A surprise attack.

The stampede that followed had not been part of the game plan. Golfers looked on aghast as the Friesians tore down the fairway, and tore up the turf.

By the time the farmer arrived, his herd had moved to pastures new, and were lunching in the herbaceous border around the club house.

The Colonel stood in the driveway brandishing a large bunch of headless marguerites.

His language was colourful, his message abundantly clear. The farmer's mumbled apology simply would not do.

The golf club demanded compensation.

That night the farmer checked his insurance policy. Thankfully it was just as he thought. Commercial Union had tailor-made his cover to include Third Party Liability.

Which meant that when the bill from the landscape gardeners came in, the golf club didn't pay, the farmer didn't pay.

We did.

'Commercial Union **were QUICK** to understand this was **not** simply a case of replacing a **few** divots.'

'**No sooner** had I **SHOOED** one of them **off** the fairway, than **four more** appeared from a **BUNKER**.'

COMMERCIAL UNION

We won't make a drama out of a crisis.

Commercial Union, 1994.

The mistletoe dangled invitingly over the door of the delicatessen.

Inside, the shelves were laden with seasonal goodies.

Mrs Bumkin's home-baked Dorset nobs, ribboned boxes of marrons glacés, pickled quails' eggs, Drambuie truffles.

And in the very centre of the store, a splendid pyramid of Christmas puddings.

Mr Johnson, his head framed between two well-hung garlic sausages, stood behind the cheese counter and smiled.

This was his shop, his empire.

A bustling business of which he could be proud.

Gently closing the lid of the wholemeal bap he'd been preparing, he thought of those few precious days at home over Christmas.

Then it happened.

A hideous noise. Like the clatter of a hundred saucepans being dropped from a great height.

It came from the room at the back of the store.

Mr Johnson darted through the shop like a gazelle.

It was as he had feared. The shelving in the stock room had collapsed under the weight of five thousand jars of jam, delivered that morning.

He opened the door to an explosion of colour.

Green and red dribbles of gooseberry and damson preserve laced the walls. Whole black cherries dripped from the ceiling.

A river of Greek honey swirled around the floor. Broken glass twinkled menacingly in dollops of whisky marmalade.

So it was that Mr Johnson's Christmas stock came to a sticky end.

With a shop full of customers, and a store room splattered with fruits of the forest, he did the sensible thing and called Commercial Union.

A good move.

Our man was on the doorstep that very afternoon.

And in true festive spirit agreed to Mr Johnson's claim on the spot.

After all, he could see the jam he was in.

'**The** place was still **swimming** in marmalade when the **MAN** from Commercial Union **waded in**.'

'**I was just** preparing a **Caerphilly** and **PICKLE** bap when the **first** pot of jam **EXPLODED**.'

COMMERCIAL UNION

We won't make a drama out of a crisis.

he recipe said "Sauté lightly with a knob of butter."

Godfrey tossed the confetti-thin King Edwards into a pan and reached for his pepper grinder.

There could be no denying, the apron suited him.

Patting the pocket for the friendly rattle of Swan Vestas, he moved towards the hob.

His head momentarily lost in steam as he peered into the rumbling pot of stewed rhubarb on the back burner.

The aroma mingled menacingly with the pilchard mornay, gently toasting under the grill.

But here was a man who liked his flavours well-defined. In an atmosphere that would have sent others reeling, he sniffed the air with obvious pleasure.

He turned on the gas and struck a match.

What followed was nothing short of hair-raising.

For beneath Godfrey's luxuriant curls lurked a pate as smooth as a billiard ball.

Normally well-anchored by an ingenious combination of glue and clips, the mop had mischievously worked itself loose in the steam.

Without warning, and with deadly accuracy, it plopped into the flames.

His mercy dash to the soda syphon was, alas, too late to save the charred tufts.

It was a tragic case of toupee flambé.

The chef was understandably distraught. To replace the golden locks would cost hundreds. Money he didn't have.

At two minutes past nine the following morning, a man in a dark brown Homburg walked purposefully into his local branch of Commercial Union.

It was Godfrey.

The frizzled evidence of his culinary catastrophe in a carrier bag by his side.

One peep, and the girl at the claims desk understood the problem.

Cheered by the promise of a speedy settlement Godfrey went on his way.

Sure enough, a cheque in full compensation arrived within days.

Telephoning his thanks to our young lady, he summed up his appreciation quite simply.

He took his hat off to her.

COMMERCIAL UNION

We won't make a drama out of a crisis.

'without Commercial Union *I'd have* been stuck **in a HAT** *for weeks.'*

'**As** *I* **BENT down** to **light** the **gas** *stove* my *toupee* **MUST** have **slipped.'**

Just as "Heineken refreshes the parts other beers cannot reach" has entered the language, so has Commercial Union's "We won't make a drama out of a crisis" message. Interestingly, both campaigns were in the 1970's. Both require a genuine dialogue between reader and advertiser. Both have been regularly hijacked by the media. Both have been misquoted, but rarely misunderstood.

Adrian Holmes got his first copy writing job in 1976, having studied Film and Photographic Arts in London.

He worked at a frankly alarming number of agencies before finally settling down as joint creative director of Lowe Howard-Spink in 1989.

He is now Chairman of that agency, but still manages to squeeze in the odd ad between meetings.

This is my favoured approach to writing a piece of copy.

After carefully studying the copy brief, I put one of Beethoven's late String Quartets on the gramophone and sit down at my desk overlooking Hyde Park.

I extract one sheet of handmade 150 gm/m² Swiss vellum from my drawer, and place this in front of me.

I unscrew the cap from my 1936 Waterman tortoiseshell pen and fill it from a bottle of Prussian blue engraver's ink which I have specially blended for me by a man in Cairo.

Approximately two hours later, I am ready to review the results. These typically constitute the following:

(i) A series of increasingly frenzied zig-zag indentations in the paper where I've tried to get the goddamn 1936 Waterman pen to write anything at all.

(ii) My preliminary design proposals for a sixteen-wheeled combined spaceship/all-terrain vehicle.

(iii) A lot of half-hearted opening sentences and jottings, all of them crossed out, and then the crossings-out carefully inked in so as to achieve an eye-catching chequerboard design.

(iv) Not a lot else.

The truth of the matter is I've never found writing copy a particularly easy business. A good 90 per cent of what I commit to paper ends up being scrubbed out, abandoned halfway, completely rewritten or thrown into the bin in disgust.

There are of course writers — the Mozarts of our business — who seem to be able to *extrude* wonderfully crafted copy straight onto the page like so much toothpaste.

With me, it's more a case of hacking and hewing away at an unyielding rockface, with just the occasional nugget to show for my labours.

After nearly twenty years of writing, it would be nice to think that things have got a bit easier. But they haven't.

My hacking and hewing techniques might have improved a little. And each piece of copy seems to produce a slightly less mountainous slag heap than it used to.

But I still find the going tough. And the bits of writing I'm most pleased with always turn out to be the toughest to do.

However, for what they're worth, here are my Ten Tips for Copywriters — techniques I've either developed myself or picked up along the way.

They've certainly helped me down at the bottom of the mineshaft. I hope they do the same for you.

1. Make the most of your deadline.

Call me irresponsible, but I always wait until the traffic man appears at the door, purple-faced and screaming for my copy. *Then* I write it. I find there is a direct correlation between rising panic and burgeoning inspiration. Incidentally, I've fully exploited this technique for writing the piece you're reading now. My apologies to all at D&AD.

2. Before starting your copy, work out where it'll end.

To me, the process of writing a clear, logically-argued piece of copy is a bit like erecting a telephone line from A to B. The first thing you do is to establish the route your poles are going to take, and then put them up in a nice orderly line. Only then do you actually string the wire between them. In other words, get your basic structure right before you're tempted to start writing. If I don't observe this discipline, I usually end up in a hopeless tangle of wire.

3. Keep the reader rewarded.

Any copywriter has to strike a deal with the reader. And as far as the reader is concerned, the deal is this. *I'll keep reading for as long as you keep me interested.* So always ask yourself: have I expressed this in as original a way as possible? Have I been ruthlessly concise? Have I kept my side of the bargain?

4. Don't over-egg the mix.

Beware loading your prose with too many jokes and verbal conceits. As a rule, the plainer you keep things, the greater effect of the occasional flourish.

5. Read poetry.

And why not? Indeed, I think the best copywriting is a form of poetry. We fuss and fret about the way things sound just as much as poets do. So study their techniques, see how they use language, rhythm and imagery to achieve their effects. Anyway, it's good for you. What do they know of copywriting that only copywriting know?

6. Read your copy out loud to yourself.

This may well earn you some funny looks. If it helps, pick up a phone and pretend you're presenting the copy to someone on the other end. There again, this may earn you funny looks from switchboard. Either way, make sure you do it. I know of no better way of revealing awkwardnesses of expression. For instance, try reading that last sentence out loud. See? Straight in the bin.

7. Don't get too precious about your words.

Normally I'm no fan of research — except when it comes to my own copy. I get my art director to read it, I get other writers down the corridor to read it, in fact I pester anyone who'll spare me the time. I ask them: are there any bits which you had to go back and read again? Any jokes that didn't quite work? If there are, I re-write them. No questions asked.

8. Treat your copy as a visual object.

For some reason, copy that looks good on the page has a knack of reading well, too. One trick I have is to stand back from the finished typescript until I can't actually decipher the words.

Does it have balance? Do any of the paragraphs seem excessively long or heavy-looking? Does it, in short, look inviting to the eye? I work closely with my art director and the typographer to achieve this. If they want extra words here, or to lose a paragraph there, I usually try and oblige.

9. Observe the sonata structure

There is a convention in classical music whereby a piece is said to be divided into three distinct phases: the Exposition, the Development and the Recapitulation. In writing terms, this is just a posh way of saying that the end of your copy should somehow refer back to the headline thought. It's nice if you can pull it off — but if you can't, you can at least tell everyone down the pub that you have decided to break free of the tyranny of the sonata structure in your writing.

10. The good is the enemy of the great.

You've completed your 15th draft. You finally sit back and say to yourself: yup, that's good.

Congratulations. Now tear it up and do it again.

Only better.

I told you this writing business was tough.

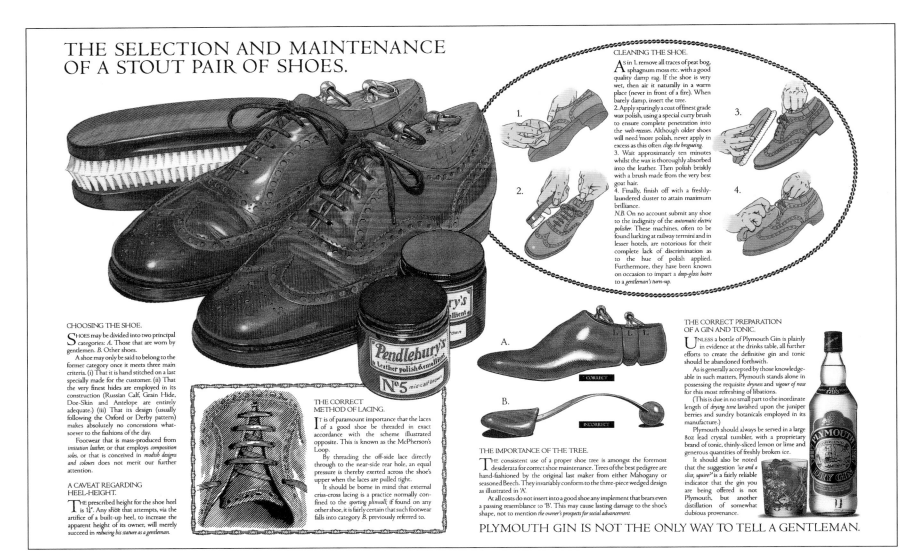

A rare instance of long copy that was a real joy to write. Once I had fixed the snooty, Jeevesian tone of voice in my head, the words came relatively easily. Alan Waldie, the art director, did a wonderful job, even getting the type set in hot metal. Agency: Lowe Howard–Spink.

This was written at the height of the 1980s financial boom, when the Army was losing its graduate recruits to the fat cats in the City. The brief was to make the life of a broker sound as dull as possible, even if you were on a couple of hundred grand a year. The opening is perhaps a bit heavy–handed, but the copy bows out neatly enough. Art Director: John Foster. Agency: Collett Dickenson & Pearce.

Are you making plans for your wife's death?

Come on now, own up. The thought hasn't so much as crossed your mind, has it?

All along, you've blithely assumed that you'll be the first to go.

That your wife will be the one who will need the financial looking-after.

That yours is the life that should be insured, not hers.

Noble and worthy sentiments indeed. But, if we may say so, short sighted ones, too.

There's no guaranteeing that your wife will outlive you. (According to statistics, little more than a 60% chance in fact).

So have you ever thought what would happen to you if the unthinkable happened to her?

Not in the dim distant future.

But tomorrow, Friday, 24th June 1983? Could you cope?

On the purely practical front, think of the cooking, the washing, the hours of housework

After hours of office work, could you face hours of housework?

Could you be an executive by day and a chambermaid by night?

that you'd have to put in. More importantly, there's the children to consider. Could you ever devote the sort of time to them

they need and deserve?

The nightly bedtime stories? Helping them out with their maths homework? Teaching them what's what in the big wide world?

Heaven knows, you'd need help. Lots of it. And like everything else nowadays, that sort of help doesn't come cheap.

According to a recent survey, the average mother of three ploughs through eighty hours of housework a week.

Eighty hours, mind.

At £2.50 an hour, that comes to a staggering £10,400 a year. Where on earth are you going to get hold of that sort of money?

Well, you could start at the bottom right hand corner of this page.

For as little as £15.00 a month, Albany Life can provide cover worth over £50,000 tax free.

If you prefer, we can even draw up a combined 'Husband and Wife' policy that pays out in the event of either of you dying.

If you'd like to discuss things further with us, post off the coupon straight away.

Planning for a wife's death may be no pleasant matter for a husband.

But for a father, it's a very necessary duty.

Could you afford £2,000 a year for a family cook?

Who'll play nursemaid if the kids fall ill?

To learn more about our plans, send this coupon to Peter Kelly, Albany Life Assurance, FREEPOST, Potters Bar EN6 1BR.

Name
Address
Tel:
Name of your Life Assurance Broker, if any:

Albany Life
A member of the American General Corporation group.

*Figure quoted is nett of premium relief at 15% and applies to a woman aged 25 next birthday.

Tony Brignull and Alfredo Marcantonio had already shown the kind of writing that was possible on this account — it does help when you've got a standard to aim for. Looking at the ad afresh, I think we should have done something about that rather awkward type run-round at the bottom of the left hand column. Art Director: Andy Lawson. Agency: Lowe Howard-Spink.

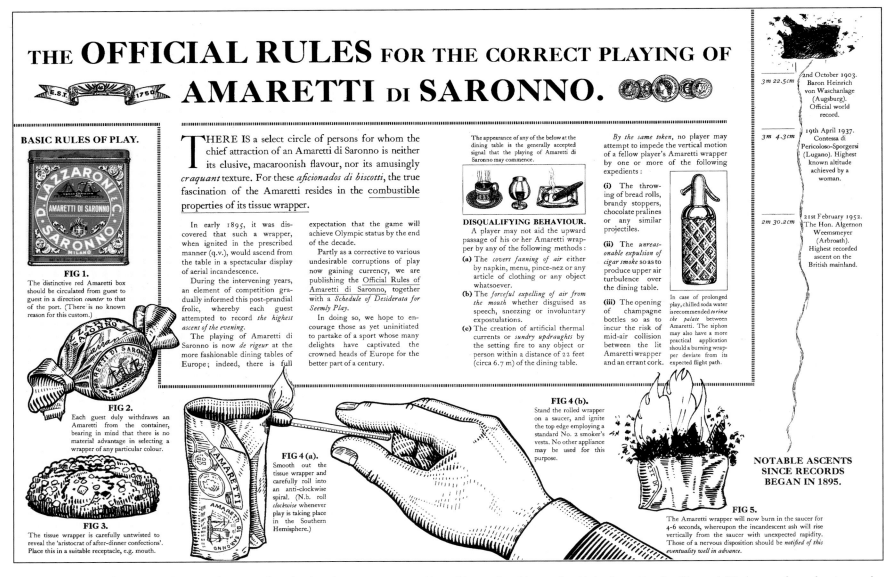

THE OFFICIAL RULES FOR THE CORRECT PLAYING OF AMARETTI DI SARONNO.

BASIC RULES OF PLAY.

FIG 1.
The distinctive red Amaretti box should be circulated from guest to guest in a direction *counter* to that of the port. (There is no known reason for this custom.)

FIG 2.
Each guest duly withdraws an Amaretti from the container, bearing in mind that there is no material advantage in selecting a wrapper of any particular colour.

FIG 3.
The tissue wrapper is carefully untwisted to reveal the 'aristocrat of after-dinner confections'. Place this in a suitable receptacle, e.g. mouth.

THERE IS a select circle of persons for whom the chief attraction of an Amaretti di Saronno is neither its elusive, macaroonish flavour, nor its amusingly *craquant* texture. For these *aficionados di biscotti*, the true fascination of the Amaretti resides in the <u>combustible</u> properties of its tissue wrapper.

In early 1895, it was discovered that such a wrapper, when ignited in the prescribed manner (q.v.), would ascend from the table in a spectacular display of aerial incandescence.

During the intervening years, an element of competition gradually informed this post-prandial frolic, whereby each guest attempted to record *the highest ascent of the evening.*

The playing of Amaretti di Saronno is now *de rigeur* at the more fashionable dining tables of Europe; indeed, there is full expectation that the game will achieve Olympic status by the end of the decade.

Partly as a corrective to various undesirable corruptions of play now gaining currency, we are publishing the <u>Official Rules of Amaretti di Saronno</u>, together with a *Schedule of Desiderata for Seemly Play.*

In doing so, we hope to encourage those as yet uninitiated to partake of a sport whose many delights have captivated the crowned heads of Europe for the better part of a century.

The appearance of any of the below at the dining table is the generally accepted signal that the playing of Amaretti di Saronno may commence.

DISQUALIFYING BEHAVIOUR.

A player may not aid the upward passage of his or her Amaretti wrapper by any of the following methods :

(a) The *covert fanning of air* either by napkin, menu, pince-nez or any article of clothing or any object whatsoever.

(b) The *forceful expelling of air from the mouth* whether disguised as speech, sneezing or involuntary expostulations.

(c) The creation of artificial thermal currents or *sundry updraughts* by the setting fire to any object or person within a distance of 22 feet (circa 6.7 m) of the dining table.

By the same token, no player may attempt to impede the vertical motion of a fellow player's Amaretti wrapper by one or more of the following expedients :

(i) The throwing of bread rolls, brandy stoppers, chocolate pralines or any similar projectiles.

(ii) The *unreasonable expulsion of cigar smoke* so as to produce upper air turbulence over the dining table.

(iii) The opening of champagne bottles so as to incur the risk of mid-air collision between the lit Amaretti wrapper and an errant cork.

In case of prolonged play, chilled soda water is recommended *to rinse the palate* between Amaretti. The siphon may also have a more practical application should a burning wrapper deviate from its expected flight path.

FIG 4 (a).
Smooth out the tissue wrapper and carefully roll into an anti-clockwise spiral. (N.b. roll *clockwise* whenever play is taking place in the Southern Hemisphere.)

FIG 4 (b).
Stand the rolled wrapper on a saucer, and ignite the top edge employing a standard No. 2 smoker's vesta. No other appliance may be used for this purpose.

NOTABLE ASCENTS SINCE RECORDS BEGAN IN 1895.

FIG 5.
The Amaretti wrapper will now burn in the saucer for 4-6 seconds, whereupon the incandescent ash will rise vertically from the saucer with unexpected rapidity. Those of a nervous disposition should be *notified of this eventuality well in advance.*

3m 22.5cm — 2nd October 1903. Baron Heinrich von Waschanlage (Augsburg). Official world record.

3m 4.3cm — 19th April 1937. Contessa di Pericoloso-Sporgersi (Lugano). Highest known altitude achieved by a woman.

2m 30.2cm — 21st February 1952. The Hon. Algernon Weemsmeyer (Arbroath). Highest recorded ascent on the British mainland.

An unforgivable instance of a writer plagiarizing the style of another campaign, even if it was his own. I could argue that this is a better idea than Plymouth Gin because the product is central to the joke, and not just an adjunct. This ad never actually ran because someone at the client end decided it was a fire risk. These things happen. Art Director: Paul Arden. Agency: Saatchi & Saatchi.

My mother happens to be a sufferer of what she calls 'bells in the head' and it was the surreal image conjured up by that simple turn of phrase that led us to the idea you see here. (The verse is hers, by the way). Re-reading the copy now, I flinch at one or two bits of clumsy phrasing. This feels like draft number 15 and not 16. Art Director: Paul Arden. Agency: Saatchi & Saatchi.

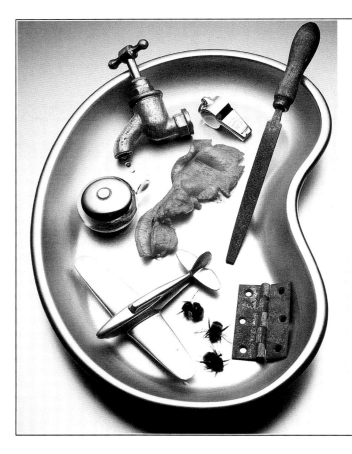

Some of the things we've removed from people's heads.

We know a lady who's had a slice of bacon frying inside her head for the last thirty years.

We know a man whose only idea of silence is the incessant roaring of a jet aircraft.

And we know a little girl who wishes somebody would answer the telephone she hears ringing all night.

These people we know aren't mad (although a few may end up in psychiatric wards).

They aren't in the grips of some fatal disease (although every year an average of five or six commit suicide).

They are sufferers of a little known condition called *tinnitus*: from the Latin meaning 'the ringing of bells.'

Put simply, tinnitus is a malfunction of the inner ear that causes the brain to 'hear' sounds that aren't really there.

A lady from Hythe in Kent recently described her sounds in a poem she sent us:

Bells are malign that ring for me.
No pause or blessed lull.
Only this wild cacophony,
This howling in the skull.

Today the British Tinnitus Association needs funds more urgently than at any time in its history.

Particularly as the search for a cure is proving to be a long and expensive one.

If you'd like to help us, please send anything you can to the BTA, 105 Gower Street, London WC1E 6AH.

Or, if you have a credit card, dial 01-387 8033 (extension 208) and make your donation directly over the phone.

Just this once, the incessant ringing of bells is what tinnitus sufferers are desperate to hear.

BRITISH TINNITUS ASSOCIATION

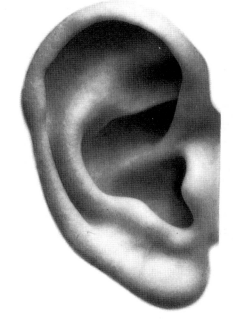 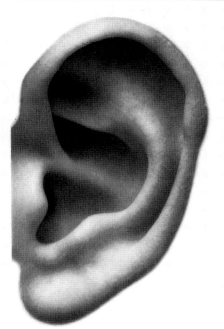

They're odd shaped, quirky looking things.

But they do give you great stereo sound.

They're odd shaped, quirky looking things.

But they do give you great stereo sound.

Supposing a pair of ears came up for review in a hi-fi magazine. Just what would the reviewer say?

No doubt there'd be references to their 'startlingly accurate frequency response'.

Praise would be heaped on the 'uncannily natural sound reproduction'.

And there'd certainly be a mention of 'the superb stereo effect wherever the listener is sitting'.

Well, *there's* a coincidence.

Because that's exactly the kind of thing that hi-fi reviewers have been saying about Canon's new S-50 loudspeakers.

The reason they've been saying it is a breakthrough called Wide Imaging Stereo technology.

No, that's not a marketing man's feeble attempt to deafen you with science.

It's a radically different method of creating stereo sound images.

And, as you'll observe, it's resulted in a radically different looking stereo speaker.

For a start, the enclosure is not the familiar box-shape, but domed.

And instead of pointing outwards, it's directed downwards onto a precisely angled 'acoustic mirror.'

This reflects sound out into the room, and in doing so achieves something quite remarkable.

A stereo 'hot spot' at least six times the size produced by conventional speakers.

Most impressive. But what does that mean in plain English?

It means simply that you can enjoy balanced stereo sound over a much larger area of your living room.

In other words, whether you're sitting on the left end of the sofa, or the right end, it'll still sound as though you're sitting exactly in the middle.

If you'd like to witness this remarkable phenomenon with your own ears, may we suggest you call in at your local Canon Audio outlet listed opposite.

On the other hand, to understand more about the technical story behind the S-50, we'd recommend a pair of scissors.

They're odd-shaped, quirky looking things. But they're great for cutting out coupons.

For a free brochure on the S-50 loudspeaker, send this coupon to: Canon Audio Ltd, Unit 6, Genesis Business Park, Albert Drive, Woking, Surrey GU21 5RW. Or Tel: 0483 740005.

Mr/Mrs/Ms _____ First Name _____

Surname _____

Address _____

_____

_____ Postcode _____

Canon
WIDE
IMAGING
STEREO.

Getting copy started can be one of the trickiest parts of writing an ad. In this case I remember feeling mightily relieved when I had the notion of a hi-fi magazine reviewing a pair of ears. The ending strikes a distinctly jazz note. Art Director: Rod Waskett. Agency: Lowe Howard–Spink.

Lionel Hunt had the perfect start to a career in advertising when he left school in England in 1960 and joined The St. Pancras Borough Council as an audit clerk. Some may have viewed this as a strange move as mathematics was his weakest subject in school. But it wasn't that weak, as the clerk's job paid £8 per week when most other school leavers were only getting £5. After six months this brief exposure to the high life convinced him that his real future lay in advertising and he joined Pritchard Wood in Knightsbridge as a despatch boy. His greatest achievement there was to get despatch boys' wages paid on Thursday, like everybody else, not Friday. The view had been that if you paid despatch boys on Thursday they wouldn't come in on Friday. So began a lifetime's fight against discrimination.

Wrapping so many packages for exotic destinations in outer London and the southern counties gave him the urge to travel and in 1961 he emigrated to Australia to be a cowboy (another vital component of the advertising executive's make-up). After this there was a brief stint on a sewer-pipe laying gang and, his training complete, he joined an agency in Tasmania as a copywriter. Eleven years later in 1972 — after jobs as account executive, advertising manager, copywriter and creative director — he co-founded The Campaign Palace with art director Gordon Trembath where he is still employed as chairman and national creative director. The Campaign Palace which now has offices in Melbourne, Sydney and Auckland, is generally regarded as the most creative agency in the country.

Lionel Hunt has won many awards for his work including gold and silver awards at Cannes, The New York One Show and Australian AWARD. He has three times been voted creative director of the year in Australia, was chosen Advertising Man of the Year in 1984 and is a member of both the AWARD and Australian Awards Halls of Fame.

He now lives on a small farm outside Sydney where his previous cowboy and sewer-pipe experiences are continuing to prove useful.

Can you imagine the time and trouble that has gone into all the portraits of the eminent copywriters who grace these pages?

Egos? What egos?

I know in my own case it took all morning to strike up exactly the right balance between casual aloofness, debonair nonchalance and sporting prowess.

I can almost guarantee you that most of us spent a lot more time on our pictures than we did on our written pieces.

Which is an important lesson to learn.

Copywriting for print ads isn't about writing copy. It's about creating a picture that powerfully communicates the proposition. Most of the world's best ads are a combination of pictures and words. Some are just a picture. Even all-type ads create a picture of their own.

The best example I can give you of this is the ad Rob Tomnay and I did for Bluegrass jeans. I'm cheating here because it was actually a poster but imagine it as a double page spread print ad. It doesn't even contain one complete word but it speaks volumes about the jeans.

All of which has led me to the conclusion that the most important part of being a good copywriter is working with a great art director.

In my case I was very lucky to have started our agency with Gordon Trembath who was the best art director in Australia in 1972 and still would be one of the best if he hadn't retired at the grand old age of 40. (They're also smarter than writers).

What this meant for me was that it didn't matter what rubbish I wrote as Gordon would always make it look fabulous. So on those rare occasions when what I wrote wasn't half bad, the ad was virtually guaranteed great results and loads of awards.

There are, I know, some great copywriters who sit alone at their typewriters and come up with their ads in isolation but for me this would be a miserable experience, like going to prison.

So lesson one is to beg, borrow or steal the best art director you can find. It'll make your ads much better, your life a bit more fun, and your lunches so much more enjoyable. And if you're really lucky they'll think up most of your ideas and headlines for you which is like having your cake and eating it too.

Gordon worked on the Woman's Day "How to kill a baby" ad with me. I remember distinctly that we only had half a day to do it and that, before lunch, the line was "How to kill a baby seal slowly". At lunch, somewhere into the second bottle of Chardonnay I said "I know! How to kill a baby!"

Gordon looked at me as if I'd gone insane then had another glass himself, took a deep breath and said "let's go and sell it."

There are two important lessons buried in here. The first is that you should go to lunch every day with your art director no matter how busy you are. In fact, the busier you are the more important for you to go because it's the only place you can get any work done. The only interruptions come from people who want to put nice things in your mouth which is a pleasant change from the office.

The second is to have courage. All good ads are hard to sell and you need a steely resolve to get the good stuff through. I suppose it's better for your health if this courage is natural, rather than Dutch courage, but no-one's perfect.

You might notice in my photograph, I hope you do, seeing how much time was spent on it, that I am not carrying a table tennis bat. This is misleading. I have found that when you are up against an impossible deadline (like now) then it's vital to use up lots of that precious time and play several games of table tennis. Excuse me while I go off for a quick hit.

That's better. All the stress has gone, the adrenalin is pumping, I am flushed with success and now feel I can do anything.

Which is exactly how Campaign Palace Sydney creative director, Ron Mather and I came up with the Ansett Airlines Hostess ad.

We had a morning to come up with the launch ad for the 'new' airline and then go off and present it to Rupert Murdoch, one of the owners. This was a reasonably terrifying prospect and I remember worrying about the presentation of an ad that didn't exist. The more we thought about the presentation, the less we could think of anything for the ad.

Three games later and we had it but it was touch and go. So don't present your own work. It won't give you enough time to do the ad, play your games, and have your lunch.

But this absolutely requires that you surround yourself with the most brilliantly effective account directors in the business. As I have said to somewhat lesser suits on occasion "If the creative team takes the brief, develops the strategy, does the ad, sells it, and produces it, where does that leave you exactly?"

The hostess ad caused a huge controversy with talk-back radio running hot with disgruntled ex-hostesses ('old-boilers', Sir Reginald Ansett publicly called them) and church groups so it was a huge success. So much so that we were able to spoof it two days later for a TV station client who was running an airline sit-com. Killing two old birds with one stone, as it were.

The medical insurance ad for Underwriting and Insurance Ltd won a silver in Australia for the most outstanding copy in a consumer advertisement. As far as I remember, I copied most of it out of the client's own brochure. Another important lesson. If the headline (and picture) isn't riveting it doesn't matter what the body copy says. I'll bet my bottom dollar that most of the judges didn't read more than the first few lines of the body copy they so richly awarded but assumed from the headline, picture and layout that it was probably pretty good. Consumers some-times do the same.

The headline coincidentally is dead straight, isn't it? It always pays to remember that if there is a compelling proposition you shouldn't bury it in so called creativity. In this case the straight headline works with the picture to confront the over 50's worst fears about getting insurance.

The only other thing I've got to say is make sure you spend most of the day laughing. This is meant to be a fun business, not some kind of grim science, like embalming for example. In fact, our motto at The Palace is the same today as it's always been. Do great ads, and have a laugh.

So there you have it. Always work with a great art director. Always take him out to lunch. Be brave. Take up table tennis. Don't sell your own work. Surround yourself with brilliant account directors. Concentrate on your headlines before your body copy. Don't bury the proposition. And have a laugh. Yes, I think that about covers it.

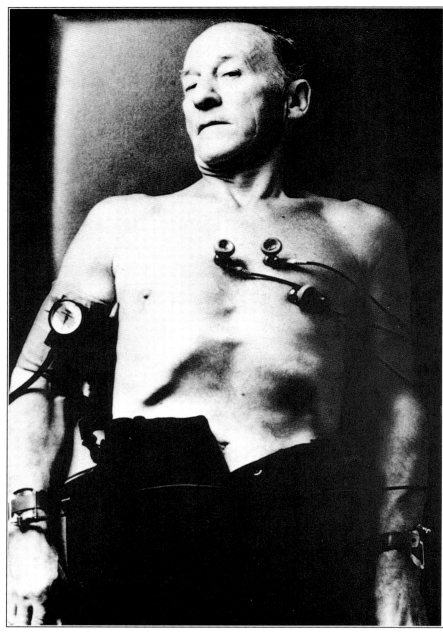

How to insure your life without a medical if you're over 50.

Trying to buy life insurance is a bit like trying to get a bank loan. The more you need it, the harder it is to get. In your fifties and sixties when you feel you most want life insurance, you find that nobody seems to want to give it to you.

You find yourself up against a probing medical examination, or at the very least, a barrage of questions on the state of your health.

As a result many older people are so certain they can't qualify that, not surprisingly, they don't even bother to apply.

Which often results in bitter hardship for those they care about most. You may think this is all very unfair. We do. So we've done something about it.

THE GOLDEN YEARS PLAN

The Golden Years Plan provides lifetime cover for people now aged 50 to 70 without medical examination and regardless of their state of health.

It offers the protection of life assurance to people who might otherwise be denied it.

HERE'S HOW IT WORKS

The Golden Years Plan is offered in units. The amount of cover it provides is based upon your age at the time the policy is issued. The table below shows the cover provided at each age.

TABLE OF BENEFITS & PREMIUMS

Age when you buy Policy	No. units bought — monthly cost			
	1 unit	2 units	3 units	4 units
	$9.50	$19.00	$28.50	$38.00
	Sum assured (excl. bonus) bought			
	$	$	$	$
50-52	1487	3104	4721	6337
53-55	1318	2750	4182	5615
56-58	1169	2440	3711	4982
59-61	1040	2171	3302	4432
62-64	930	1941	2952	3963
65-67	836	1745	2654	3563
68-70	755	1575	2395	3216

To ensure that everyone now between 50 and 70 can get this policy, Underwriting & Insurance Limited have developed special benefits for the first two years.

Should death occur from natural causes during the first two years your beneficiary will receive every cent of premium you have paid plus interest at 6% per annum compound.

Should death be the result of an accident at any time during the first two years the full amount of the sum assured plus any bonus allotted will be paid.

After the first two years the full benefit of the sum assured plus all bonuses allotted is paid in the event of the death of the Life Assured from any cause whatsoever.

NO MEDICAL EXAMINATION IS REQUIRED.

To apply for the Golden Years Plan you do not require a medical examination nor do we ask you any questions about your state of health.

Simply fill in the application form and send it to Underwriting & Insurance Limited.

THERE ARE NO SALESMEN.

Remember, this advertisement is our only approach to you. No salesman will contact you, but should you require any advice, simply ring our office on 51 1471 and our staff will be very happy to assist you.

THE GOLDEN YEARS PLAN LETS YOU INSURE HUSBAND OR WIFE.

You are able to insure your marriage partner by a simple cross proposal. Simply fill in clearly the name of the person to be insured and sign the form as indicated.

YOUR POLICY IS GUARANTEED RENEWABLE.

As long as your premiums are fully paid within the normal 30 days grace period, your policy cannot be cancelled by us, nor can we refuse to renew it. The sum assured does not decrease. In fact it increases as we add bonuses each year.

A 30 DAYS INSPECTION PERIOD WITH EVERY POLICY.

The Golden Years Plan is offered by Underwriting & Insurance Limited, a wholly owned subsidiary of C.E. Heath & Co., who are one of the largest non-marine syndicate managers at Lloyd's of London.

You are further protected by a money back guarantee as follows:

The Golden Years Plan gives you a 30 day Inspection Period. When you receive your Policy Document, please read it carefully. If, for any reason, you are not completely satisfied with the policy, you may return it to us within 30 days of receipt and your money will be refunded. This offer is guaranteed by Underwriting & Insurance Limited, 578 St. Kilda Road, Melbourne, 3004.

HOW TO JOIN THE GOLDEN YEARS PLAN

1. Complete the Application Form in full, date and sign.
2. Cut along the dotted line.
3. Place in envelope together with your cheque, money order or postal note for the first month's premium only, made payable to Underwriting & Insurance Limited.

CLOSING DATE THURS. APRIL 12.

APPLICATION FOR GOLDEN YEARS PLAN LIFE ASSURANCE

Underwriting & Insurance Limited Head Office, 578 St Kilda Rd. Melbourne 3004

Full name of person to be insured _____

Residential address _____

State _____ Postcode _____
Sex _____ Date of birth _____
Place of birth _____
Name of Policy Owner or Proposer _____

I hereby propose for the Golden Years Plan. I would like to pay future premiums   I require

☐ Monthly   ☐ 1 unit
☐ Quarterly   ☐ 2 units
☐ Half Yearly   ☐ 3 units
☐ Annually   ☐ 4 units

I enclose premium payment for $ _____ being the first month's premium.

I understand that if for any reason I am not satisfied with the policy I may return it within 30 days of receipt and a full refund will be made to me.

Signature of Proposer _____
Dated _____

Won a copy award but did the judges read it?

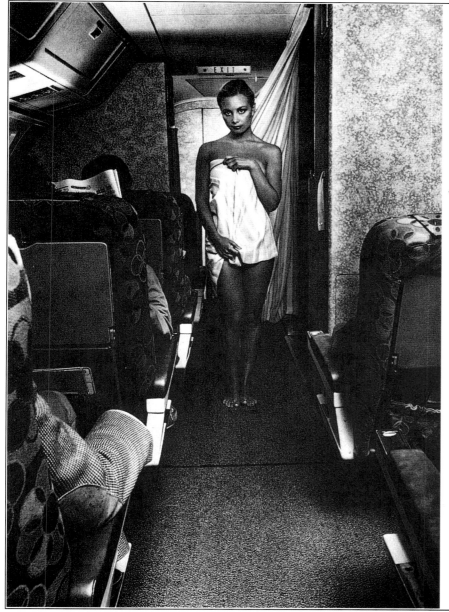

If the hostess was out of uniform would you know which airline you were flying with?

Until recently probably not.

But from next June you won't be in any doubt at all.

Ansett will be offering you a real choice of the planes you fly in, the times you depart, and the services you get both in the air and on the ground.

In June we start taking delivery of our new fleet of 12 Boeing 737's and new generation 727's and start pensioning off our DC9's.

This means we'll soon be offering you Boeing comfort and reliability on all our jet routes.

Just as important, more planes will mean far greater frequency. And no more identical schedules.

You'll be far more likely to find a departure time that suits you, rather than one that just suits the airline.

And you'll check-in faster, get on and off quicker, and get your baggage sooner.

We'll also be offering major service benefits that we can't reveal now for reasons that will be obvious to readers who are also in a highly competitive situation. But don't wait until next June to try the new Ansett. Our competitive philosophy is showing up right now in lots of little ways that already make flying with us just that much better.

But you ain't seen nothing yet. **ANSETT**

Lots of complaints but Rupert was happy.

Hardly a word, but volumes spoken.

Pilots walk out over sexist airline ad.

But they'll be back in time for tonight's exciting episode of 'Skyways'. 9.30 tonight on Seven. Rated 'A'. ⑦

Spoofing our own ad and the complaints it caused.

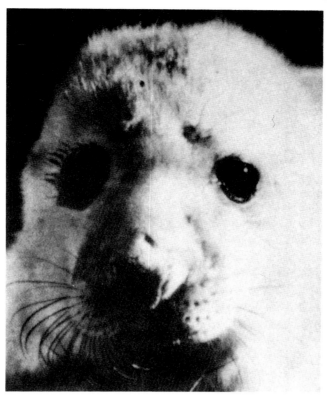

How to kill a baby.

It's easy. All you do is walk up to it. It won't run away.

Then, as it looks up at you trustingly, mistaking you for its mother, you smash in its skull with a baseball bat.

That's what happens to baby seals in Canada every year in a bloody ritual that lasts six weeks.

In Japan they do it a different way. They herd dolphins into the shallows, wait for the tide to leave them stranded, then go through the same grisly process.

Then there's the whales. You know what happens to them.

Doing it is dead easy if your mind is warped enough. Stopping it is a whole lot harder, but there is something you can do.

In this week's Woman's Day we're running a thought provoking article on what's happening to these beautiful creatures.

We're also running a simple competition that you and your children can enter. All you have to do is tell us in less than twenty words what the seals, the dolphins or the whales would say to us if they could speak.

There are cash prizes, but far more importantly, for every entry in the competition Woman's Day will donate 10 cents to Greenpeace to help their work in bringing this ghastly business to a halt.

Look for this week's Woman's Day. It's the one with the baby seal on the cover, seconds before it dies.

Woman's Day.

Circulation up 10% and Gold in New York One Show.

Mike has been a writer and cre-ative director at three prominent agencies: Fallon McElligott, Hill Holiday and Leagas Delaney. Currently on his second

stint with Fallon, his work for dozens of clients has been honoured by the One Show, D&AD, CA Annuals and the Cannes Advertising Film Festival.

I start the writing process long before I start writing. That's because I've found that a lot of what you end up writing in an ad depends on decisions that get made in the early, planning stages of the project. Working with an art director, an account person and the client, I try to help create a brief that leaves room for great executions.

Once all have agreed on the information we want to convey, the art director and I tend to spend the first few hours working separately. This way, when we convene to review initial concepts, we have two distinct perspectives on the same brief, as opposed to just having ideas generated from one, communal line of thought. We then start consolidating our thinking, usually ending up with a few ideas that we want to explore further. Oftentimes, I find the exercise of creating headlines useful, whether the ad ends up using a headline or not. It focuses my thinking.

If the ad calls for body copy, I think the tone, style and length of that copy should be determined by the product I'm writing about. People probably want to do some reading about a bottle of bourbon that will cost them $60, for example. So for the Booker's Bourbon ads, I took my time making an argument for why this bourbon was worth a premium price. With an almost reverential tone, the copy pays homage to the virtues of distill-ing. It is written to reflect the personality of the distiller, Booker Noe, whose family had been making Bourbon for 200 years. It was the right approach, and it worked.

Not everything works, however, and I'd have to say that for me, the real key to producing good work has been editing out the bad. Co-workers can help. Partners can help. And whether you want them to or not, clients will help. What works best for me is the overnight test. It's amazing how dumb a great line can get between six o'clock in the evening and nine o'clock the next morning.

I don't follow a lot of rules, and I would encourage young people to ignore them as much as possible. I say this not because every ad has to become a kind of revolution, but because I believe we think differently when we are following strict guide-lines. We become mechanical in our thinking, expecting ideas to come after a given number of carefully thought out steps. Any of the talented people writing in this book will tell you that coming up with ideas is not so much a step by step process as it is a silent, lonely vigil interrupted infrequently by great thoughts, whose origins are almost always a mystery.

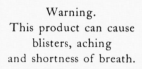

Warning.
This product can cause
blisters, aching
and shortness of breath.

The damp morning air wheezes in and out of your healthy lungs as if each breath might be your last. The hill you've been climbing seems to get steeper with every step. Was that a twig snapping? Or was it your knee creaking?

Congratulations.

You are enjoying the countryside with the help of an Ordnance Survey map.

Enjoying? Don't we really mean to say enduring? The truth is, with our maps you'll be able to do more than your share of each.

You see, at Ordnance Survey we believe when it comes to travelling through the wilds of Great Britain, the best route to take isn't always the easiest one.

That's why maps like our Landranger Series will not only show you quiet country roads, but also very quiet country pathways.

They'll help you to discover many little known public rights of way, which often lead to some even lesser known picnic spots.

And they'll point out the hill that's over

the hill, and has a better view of the lake.

All of which might induce you to expend a little more energy. But is sure to be well worth the effort.

Fair Quiet have I found thee here, and Innocence, thy sister dear,

Mistaken long, I sought you then, in busy companies of men.

Your sacred plants, if here below, only among the plants will grow.

Society is all but rude, to this delicious solitude. - Andrew Marvell

Each weekend, thousands of people escape the crowded, noisy cities of Britain only in order to meet up with each other a few hours away at crowded, noisy tourist spots. [So much for finding delicious solitude].

The problem, of course, is that everybody seems to go to the same few places.

Well, in addition to all the things an Ordnance Survey map can help you find, there are also some things it can help you avoid. Like other people.

With more details on your map, you'll have more places to choose from for a day away. Including many that aren't overrun with your fellow travellers.

Moreover, wherever you decide to go, you can always trust those details will be the most accurate available.

After all, at Ordnance Survey we've had exactly 200 years practice making maps.

The first Ordnance Survey maps were

commissioned in the late 18th century for one reason. To map the South Coast in case of attack from Napoleon.

Naturally, the job had to be done to an exacting standard. And we still create maps today as if someone's life might depend on them.

Although nowadays people use our maps to plan peaceful weekends, instead of battles.

You finally reach the crest of the hill and look up from your aching feet. Suddenly, you find yourself staring out in utter awe across thirty miles of folding hills and valleys.

If you need an incentive to keep yourself striding boldly up a challenging hillside, nothing can beat the views you are bound to encounter when you go out rambling with an Ordnance Survey map. You can gaze down upon ancient stone monuments. Spy way off in the distance what might be the site of King Arthur's first court. Or perch high up above famous medieval battlefields, [seeing them from a safe distance, just as the generals did].

But even if the vista has no known historical significance, you will still be able to enjoy something the road-bound traveller rarely experiences. Nature.

Or what William Wordsworth called 'The anchor of my purest thoughts, the nurse, the guide, the guardian of my heart, and the soul of all my moral being'.

In Wordsworth's Lake District alone, Ordnance Survey maps can guide you to well over a hundred waterfalls, dozens of ancient earthworks and countless historic houses.

One of these houses, in fact, was lived in by a Mrs Heelis, a prosperous lady sheep farmer whose hobby was writing and illustrating stories under her maiden name, *Beatrix Potter.*

It seems Beatrix Potter Heelis enjoyed a quiet walk in the country as much, if not more, than sitting in her Lake District home and writing some of the world's most famous tales for children.

'I loved to wander the Troutbeck Fell,' said the much admired author in a 1942 interview. 'Sometimes I had with me an old sheepdog, more often, I went alone. But I was never lonely. There was company of gentle sheep, and wild flowers, and singing waters.'

Meanwhile, Beatrix had written in a letter to her publisher, 'These d____d little books... I am utterly tired of doing them, and my eyes are wearing out'.

Still, she did do them, and you can see the study she toiled in even today, as long as you know where to look.

You look down one last time at the green and yellow quilt of fields below, and stand to start your descent. This time, you're glad for the extra weight around your middle. Gravity will be doing most of the work.

There are three kinds of walking maps made by Ordnance Survey, and you can get one to cover every field, every wood, every lake and every stream in Britain.

In the more popular touring regions of the countryside, one of our Outdoor Leisure maps will help you know your way around as well as the locals, maybe even better.

If you're planning to travel to other areas, we suggest the Landranger Series or the larger scale Pathfinder Series maps.

Each has dozens of helpful symbols in its key that point out important features you won't find on other maps.

For instance, you'll find three different symbols used just for marking churches, with tower, with spire, without tower or spire.

Are we going overboard? Does anyone really need this much detail in a map?

Well, considering that most of our customers are on foot, yes, we think they do.

Ramblers don't have motorway signs to go by, and need landmarks to find their way.

Landmarks that are mapped accurately, since getting lost on the moors is somewhat more unsettling than getting lost on the M6.

So if you're going to venture out to those places where there might not be anyone to ask for directions, we strongly suggest that

you take along a map from Ordnance Survey.

Because we wouldn't want you to suffer from any more blisters, aching and shortness of breath than you absolutely have to.

Ordnance Survey.
The most detailed maps in the land.

"I may be the only guy in the country who's happy about what he made this year."

~ Booker Noe

BOOKER NOE *pauses along a* GRAVEL ROAD *in the grounds of the* JIM BEAM DISTILLERY *at* CLERMONT, KENTUCKY, *rests his* BIGGER THAN LIFE HAND *on a cane,* and gazes up at a warehouse that holds hundreds of barrels of aging bourbon.

"Nothing could possibly make a man feel richer," he says, "than knowing he's got the best whiskey there is."

Booker Noe is the grandson of Jim Beam. He has lived here his entire life. And as you might imagine, there's a lot of bourbon know-how passed on down to kin in this part of Kentucky.

Witness the two essential things Booker learned from his legendary grandfather about whiskey making. The When. And the Where.

Knowing "when" to harvest fine bourbon from the barrel is a talent. Some might even call it a gift.

You see, unlike Scotch whisky, bourbon doesn't necessarily get better when you simply age it longer.

> "*T*HE BOURBON *I believe is the best there is comes straight from the center barrels here at the Jim Beam warehouses. The charred white oak of these barrels gives this natural proof bourbon a nutty, fruity taste that you don't get in any other whiskey. Now I'm making a small amount available to the public. It's hand-labeled, hand-sealed & hand-wrapped. Plus it's in a nice wood gift box. But once you try it, chances are you won't be giving any away.*"

Leave bourbon in the barrel too long and it could end up with a heavy, overbearing constitution. Bottle it too early, and the whiskey's character won't yet be fully developed.

Since the rate of aging depends on the temperament of the seasons, the only way to know for certain when the time is right for a bourbon is to taste it.

As a master distiller, that's where Booker Noe comes in. Booker makes frequent checks on the bourbon as it ages. And somehow he knows the exact moment at which a barrel of bourbon couldn't possibly get any better.

He also knows the place you'll find conditions the very best for aging whiskey. Which brings us to the Where.

On this crisp autumn day, Booker makes his way down the gravel road to the warehouse and heads on up to the middle floor, where rick after rick of barrels reaches from floor to ceiling.

LOOK for the ORIGINAL WOODEN BOX *that holds* BOOKER'S *BOTTLE.*

This area is what he refers to as the "center cut." It is the place where temperature, humidity and sunlight are likeliest to combine in perfect proportion. The place where the marriage between whiskey and charred white oak will most often produce the most beautiful offspring.

Here, in the center of the building's middle floor, Booker knocks the bung out of a barrel.

Now this bourbon is uncut and unfiltered. It's at its natural proof, which, since every barrel ages differently, can measure anywhere from 121 to 127.

You don't drink it quickly.

What you do is what Booker does, and what his granddad did before him. You pour an ounce or two into a brandy snifter and pause to admire the deep amber hue. You lift the glass to your nose and take a moment to savor the rich aromatic nature of natural proof bourbon whiskey.

Then, finally, you take a sip. Just a small one. And you let the subtle shades of the oaky flavor dance a two-step across your tongue and bring nature's own warmth to the back of your throat.

THE "center cut":

ONE OF THE FAMOUS AGING WAREHOUSES AT JIM BEAM. BOOKER'S BOURBON COMES FROM THE AREA INDICATED.

Of course, savoring a bourbon at this stage of the distilling process, and with all of its integrity intact, is an experience most anyone would appreciate.

So a few years ago, Booker began bottling some of this very rare bourbon to be presented as gifts to special friends.

The response has been something more than simple gratitude. Collectively, these friends, many of whom might be considered connoisseurs of fine spirits, have reported that this is simply the best whiskey they've ever tasted.

Did this surprise Booker in the least? "Course not." And now that his belief in this bourbon has been confirmed, he's decided to make a limited supply available to the public.

As you might guess, all barrels destined to become Booker's Bourbon are tasted by Booker personally, so that you can be assured every bottling has what he calls "that certain something."

Each bottle of Booker's is marked with a tag indicating its batch number, its proof and its age. (Booker believes aging from six to eight years provides the ideal flavor.)

Booker's is not inexpensive bourbon. Where you can find it, the hand-sealed bottle sells for around $40. Although, apparently in response to the law of supply and demand, some retailers are charging a good deal more.

If you want to look on the bright side, consider that all your searching for Booker's will no doubt make you enjoy it even more when you do find some.

And isn't it reassuring to know that even though money may be a little rare this year, there's still something out there that's a whole lot rarer?

Booker's™ Kentucky Straight Bourbon Whiskey, 60.5%–63.5% Alc./Vol. Bottled by James B. Beam Distilling Co., Clermont, KY. ©1991 James B. Beam Distilling Co.

"I know bourbon gets better with age, because the older I get, the more I like it."

~ Booker Noe

BOOKER NOE *will never forget* THE FIRST TIME HE sampled *the legendary* bourbon from his grandfather Jim Beam's distillery.

Even as he tells the story today, his face twists into a grimace, his head shakes slowly back and forth and his big hand swats at the air in front of him.

"I didn't like it at all," he says, without apologies.

Now, if that confession sounds a bit strange coming from a man who's devoted his life to making fine whiskey, there is a perfectly reasonable explanation.

Booker Noe, perhaps better than anyone else, understands that an appreciation for bourbon isn't something people are born with.

You see, in his time as Master Distiller at the Clermont, Kentucky home of Jim Beam Bourbon, Booker has come to cherish the subtle flavors found in the world's finest whiskey.

And he's discovered he's especially fond of bourbon in its

> **"***L****IKE MOST PEOPLE,** learning to love fine bourbon took me a certain amount of time. But as the years have gone by, I've decided there is just nothing better than the taste of whiskey aged in charred white oak to the peak of its flavor. It's uncut, unfiltered and straight from the barrel. This is the bourbon I've chosen to put my name on."*

purest form, taken straight from the barrel, at its natural proof.

It is this bourbon, Booker Noe believes, with all of its rich, oaky body intact, that is the very best of the best.

Until recently, uncut, unfiltered bourbon like this was the domain of the Master Distiller alone. And while he's no doubt appreciated having the privilege, Booker has always wished that other people, people who truly love fine spirits, could taste this whiskey for themselves.

Which is why Booker Noe recently began bottling his unique bourbon and making it available to the few connoisseurs who can appreciate it.

Considering the special pride he takes in his favorite whiskey, it's not surprising that Booker has put his own name on the label. Nor should it come as any shock that he personally approves

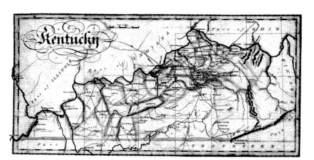

BOOKER NOE grew to love BOURBON in his home state of Kentucky.

every batch of Booker's Bourbon before he allows it to be sent along to you. Fact is, only someone of Booker's experience can determine whether a straight-from-the-barrel bourbon is at the very peak of its flavor.

Depending on the temperament of the seasons in the Bluegrass State, Booker's Bourbon reaches that peak anywhere from six to eight years into the aging process. And since every barrel of whiskey ages differently, each batch of Booker's has a different proof, which can measure anywhere between 121 and 127.

Once selected, the bourbon is painstakingly handsealed in a hand-labeled bottle and marked with a tag showing its unique proof and age.

With any luck, you'll find Booker's Bourbon at your local liquor retailer. But since, by its nature, this is not a mass produced bourbon, you may have to look further.

If you should find Booker's impossible to locate,

BOOKER'S BOURBON comes straight from the barrel, UNCUT and UNFILTERED.

we suggest you call the toll-free number listed at the bottom of the page, and see about obtaining your Booker's Bourbon that way.

Regardless how you obtain it, Booker Noe believes you'll find his bourbon well worth the time and effort you spend searching.

Especially if, like Booker himself, the years have done for your taste what they do for a bourbon's.

TIMBERLAND GIVES YOU BACK THE COAT FOUR MILLION YEARS OF EVOLUTION TOOK AWAY.

There was a time when Man could venture into the wilderness clad in nothing but the coat God gave him.

But that was quite a while ago.

Sometime during the Lower Paleolithic Era, Homo Erectus became a creature of the great indoors. The thick hair that once covered his entire body was gone, and in its place came a man-made imitation.

Hampered by a brain the size of a walnut, man's earliest attempts at outdoor clothing were, needless to say, somewhat primitive.

Fortunately, however, our species has continued to evolve, and today can produce coats that protect us when the need for food, recreation and a disposable income forces us outside our central heated caves.

At a company called Timberland, in Hampton, New Hampshire, we design outerwear whose natural practicality rivals the coats our animal relatives were born with. Coats that provide shelter from howling wind, pelting rain and mornings as cold as an ice age.

Witness our Timberland leather coats.

They're made from the best hides we can find, and believe us, we spend a lot of time looking.

We insist upon cowhides from the open range, to avoid ugly nicks from barbed wire fences. Which means we often have to travel as far as other continents in order to find a supply that meets our standards.

We use two styles of leather on our outerwear at Timberland, Split Suede, and in the coat you see here, Weatherguard Newbuck.

Each is given a thorough dunking in waterproofing agents before getting a special finish to protect its suppleness and colour.

But we make more than leather coats that will help to keep you dry in the rain.

In other Timberland outerwear, we use a material that keeps you free of perspiration.

To let these coats 'breathe' (just like the ones Mother Nature used to make) we include a layer of Gore-Tex. This man-made fabric, with over nine billion pores per square inch, allows moisture to escape from your body, but remains waterproof.

Of course, we wouldn't take all this trouble finding perfect materials only to turn around and make a coat that doesn't last.

To make doubly certain a Timberland Trenchcoat holds together, we double stitch the seams that will be exposed to the heaviest

wear, a practice that's all but extinct today.

On other Timberland coats, we overstitch many seams to prevent wind and rain from penetrating the tiny holes left behind by our sewing needles.

The result is outerwear that leaves Man as well adapted to the outdoors as he's been in millions of years.

Our sturdy coats are just one example of the Timberland Clothing range, albeit a good one, since   everything we

make is built to last you for aeons.

Using workhorses like canvas, cotton, wool and denim, Timberland puts together sweaters, shirts and trousers, even the duffle bags to carry them in. And since practical clothing doesn't ever seem to go out of fashion, you'll be able to wear them season after season.

Naturally, if you own a pair of Timberland boots or shoes, you're already familiar with the way we do things.

You may know, for example, that we impregnate the leather of all Timberland footwear with silicone to give it a longer life and to keep your feet dry no matter what.

That we pre-stretch our leathers on a special geometric last to keep them from cracking with time.

And that seams on many Timberland boots are sealed twice with latex, because that's the only method sure to keep the water out.

The truth is, here at Timberland, we wouldn't really know how to go about things any other way.

We've even gone as far as to find a machine that can test our waterproof leathers better than we ever could by hand. It's called a Maser Flex, and it helps us make sure that our leathers will withstand 15,000 flexes. Which, by the way, is equal to the highest standard demanded by the U.S. Military.

But while we admit that our practices may seem a little obsessive, there is method to our madness.

We use solid brass eyelets in our boots, not because they look better, but because they don't rust when they get wet.

We use self oiling raw-hide laces for the simple reason that they don't get soaked with water and rot.

And we certainly don't construct our footwear using double knot pearl stitching because we think it's fun. (Even in Hampton, New Hampshire, there are more entertaining things to do).

We do it so that the seams won't unravel, even if they're accidentally cut open on the sharp rocks and thick brush that Timberland wearers often find themselves in.

As you might suspect, all of these time consuming steps in constructing them don't serve to make Timberland boots or clothing any cheaper.

In fact, the chances are very good you'll pay more for a Timberland coat than you would most others.

But like everything Timberland makes, you'll be wearing it long after you've forgotten the price you paid.

Which even someone with a shelf-like forehead and one continuous eyebrow can tell you is a very good thing.

In fact, even mankind's most distant ancestors would certainly have preferred a Timberland coat to their own hairy variety.

Ours, after all, have pockets.

Timberland (UK) Limited, Unit Four, St. Anthony's Way, Feltham, Middlesex. TW14 0NH. Telephone enquiries, please ring 081 890 6116.

Timberland

IN ONE AMERICAN STATE, THE PENALTY FOR EXPOSING YOURSELF IS DEATH.

In the winter of 1968, Mount Washington in New Hampshire was the unlucky recipient of 566 inches of snowfall. Or to put it another way, that's just a little over forty-seven feet.

Snowstorms with winds in excess of a hundred miles an hour are not uncommon. Which makes the wind-chill factor too cold to measure with existing instruments.

The weatherman simply warns that at times like these, exposed flesh freezes instantly.

Some of the old folks in the state can recall the time in '34, when the Mountain was the site of the strongest wind gust ever recorded on earth: 231 mph.

They can recite articles from the local paper, The Littleton Courier, about hikers freezing to death up there in the middle of summer.

And they'll tell you, in no uncertain terms, that it's less important to dress according to the latest fashion than it is to dress according to the latest weather report.

It is this almost inbred respect for nature's wrath that compels the people at Timberland in Hampton, New Hampshire to design their outdoor clothing the way they do.

This clothing is ideal for people who venture outdoors regardless of the forecast and who pride themselves on being ready for the worst.

Take, for example, our Timberland leather coats. The leather is the best you can find, because it's the best we can find.

To get hides that meet our standards, we travel the world looking for sources of supply. A search made more difficult by our insistence on hides from animals raised on the open range. While that may sound pernickety, you'll never see scarring from barbed wire on a Timberland coat.

But we're not just concerned about how our hides are treated while they're raised. We also give them special treatment once we get them back to our workshops.

All the leathers used by Timberland get a dunking in chemical agents for water repellency. Then, to keep them looking new in any kind of weather, we give them special finishes that will never wear off.

When we use Split Suede, for instance, we give it a light-resistant finish to avoid fading. So it's not only rainproof, but sunproof, as well.

As for our Weatherguard Newbuck leather, it's given a unique chrome-tan finish so it stays supple throughout its life.

Partial as Timberland is to leathers like Newbuck and Split Suede, we realise that man cannot live by leather alone.

Which is why in some Timberland outerwear we use Gore-Tex, a man-made fabric with over nine billion pores per square inch. These microscopic openings are too small to let water in, yet large enough for perspiration molecules to get out.

Once we have the right materials in place, we start sewing coats that will last year after year after year.

On the coat you see here, we double stitch the seams that will be exposed to the heaviest wear. We run a pull cord through the waist of the coat to keep cold air from creeping up underneath. And we fit zippers of solid brass, so they'll never rust.

Since people who wear Timberland coats often venture off the beaten path, we've also taken special care that the pockets won't get torn in heavy brush. Each one is closed up with a thick leather cover and secured by buttons made from brass and bone.

And to make sure you never end up looking for those buttons in the woods (worse than looking for a needle in a haystack), we use heavy cord thread and reinforce each one on the backside with quarter-inch guards.

The finished product is a coat that will protect you from cold, wet and, on one of its more hospitable days, perhaps even the Mountain itself.

But it's not just outerwear that Timberland makes to last. Our clothing range also includes the kind of things you might wear when the temperature soars to above freezing.

Starting with stalwarts like wool, denim, canvas and cotton, Timberland makes a range that's always at home in the wild. Sweaters, trousers, jackets and shirts, even the duffle bags to carry them in.

Each item designed to withstand the twin tests of weather and time.

Of course, if you own a pair of our boots or shoes, you're already familiar with the unique way Timberlands hold together.

What you may not know is why they do.

We tape seal the seams of some of our boots with latex to make sure water can't get through to your feet.

We impregnate our shoe and boot leather with silicone, to give it a longer life. We sew in doubleknot pearl stitching that won't come undone even if it's accidentally cut. We use self oiling laces that won't rot, and solid brass eyelets that won't rust.

The list, like the winters up on Mount Washington, goes on and on.

Suffice to say that at Timberland, making outdoor clothing and boots is not just a way of life. It's a way of living.

Timberland (UK) Limited, Unit Four, St. Anthony's Way, Feltham, Middlesex. TW14 0NH. Telephone 081 890 6116.

Timberland ⬤

Bob Levenson is an internationally known and admired advertising copywriter and creative director. He has been called "the writer's writer," and "the best print copywriter ever."

Levenson's relationship with Bill Bernbach began in 1959, when Bernbach hired him at the Doyle Dane Bernbach agency. In the 26 years that followed, Levenson won every major award that the advertising business could offer, many of them several times. In 1972 he was elected to the prestigious Copywriter's Hall of Fame. He rose through the ranks to become chairman of Doyle Dane

Bernbach International and the agency's world-wide creative director.

The business relationship between the two men grew into a firm friendship that lasted until Bernbach's death in 1982. In his first book, titled Bill Bernbach's Book, Bob Levenson notes: "This is a book by one man about what another man's book might have been if either of them had ever written a book before."

Bob is married to Kathe Tanous, a well known American painter. They live in East Hampton, New York and Useppa Island, Florida, where they grow roses, paint pictures and avoid trade publications.

ANSWERS NOBODY WANTED
TO QUESTIONS NOBODY ASKED

"I know every trick in the book" does not apply to advertising copy.

There are no tricks and there can be no book. Including this one. Too bad.

There are, however, three ingredients for a decent piece of advertising prose:

1. You must know what you're talking about.

In order to be informative — never mind persuasive — you need to know how the car is put together, how the chicken is taken apart, what the surfactant does, what to expect in the foreign country, in what way is the oil refinery 'refined', etc, etc.

In the absence of such knowledge, you will be doomed to rely more and more on adjectives; always a mistake.

2. You must remember who is doing the talking.

We use words like image, character, tone, texture, even personality, almost interchangeably. But whatever we choose to call it, it must be recognisable, distinctive and consistent. This is even more important than friendly, approachable or accessible.

The writer who attempts to put the agency's mark on the client's copy or — God forbid — his own mark should pay with his job. And his severance should be that of his writing hand.

3. You must know who you're talking to. (Or, better still, to whom you're talking.)

This can be knotty in the extreme. 'Males, 18 to 34' or 'Households above £30,000 pa' are categories worse than useless; they are destructive. You may actually have to enter the Hades of the focused group. (Purchase a round-trip ticket, with no advance reservations required).

The very best tactic is to create your own customer or prospect. Keep your creation a secret and real life need never touch you.

Keep in mind, at the same time, that your prospect (even of your own creation) is likely to be smarter than you are and much warier. He is, after all, not in advertising; you are.

One final thing: being a copywriter is hard enough, hiring one is worse. "We need more (fewer) (better) (cheaper) (livelier) talent" has been heard in agency hallways since before agencies had hallways.

Talent might just have something to do with writing ability. But I'm not sure. Many people have a way with words; often that's all they have.

Now that it doesn't matter any more, I'd look for a teacher-turned-salesman (or a salesman-turned-teacher) and take my chances.

DO THIS OR DIE.

Is this ad some kind of trick?

No. But it could have been.

And at exactly that point rests a do or die decision for American business.

We in advertising, together with our clients, have all the power and skill to trick people. Or so we think.

But we're wrong. We can't fool *any* of the people *any* of the time.

There is indeed a twelve-year-old mentality in this country; every six-year-old has one.

We are a nation of smart people.

And most smart people ignore most advertising because most advertising ignores smart people.

Instead we talk to each other.

We debate endlessly about the medium and the message. Nonsense. In advertising, the message *itself* is the message.

A blank page and a blank television screen are one and the same.

And above all, the messages we put on those pages and on those television screens must be the truth. For if we play tricks with the truth, we die.

Now. The other side of the coin.

Telling the truth about a product demands a product that's worth telling the truth *about*.

Sadly, so many products aren't.

So many products don't do anything better. Or anything different. So many don't work quite right. Or don't last. Or simply don't matter.

If we also play this trick, we also die. Because advertising only helps a bad product fail faster.

No donkey chases the carrot forever. He catches on. And quits.

That's the lesson to remember.

Unless we do, we die.

Unless we change, the tidal wave of consumer indifference will wallop into the mountain of advertising and manufacturing drivel.

That day we die.

We'll die in *our* marketplace. On *our* shelves. In *our* gleaming packages of empty promises.

Not with a bang. Not with a whimper.

But by our own skilled hands.

DOYLE DANE BERNBACH INC.

A new American plant.

After 27 years (and nearly 6 million VWs) in the U.S.A., we feel enough at home here to make a home here.

So we've opened a factory in Westmoreland, Pennsylvania, to make VW Rabbits as fast and as well as we know how.

Over the past years, you've found that we make good products. Over the coming years, you'll find that we make good corporate citizens, too.

Long ago, someone said, "I don't want an imported car. I want a Volkswagen."

How wunderbar that it turned out to be true.

$1.02 a pound.

*SUGGESTED RETAIL PRICE, EAST COAST P.O.E. LOCAL TAXES AND OTHER CHARGES, IF ANY, ADDITIONAL.

©1963 VOLKSWAGEN OF AMERICA, INC.

A new Volkswagen costs $1,595.*

But that isn't as cheap as it sounds. Pound for pound, a VW costs more than practically any car you can name.

Actually, that isn't too surprising when you look into it.

Not many cars get as much put into them as a Volkswagen.

The hand work alone is striking.

VW engines are put together by hand. One by one.

And every engine is tested twice: once when it's still an engine and again when it's part of the finished car.

A Volkswagen gets painted 4 times and sanded by hand between each coat.

Even the roof lining is hand-fitted.

You won't find a nick or a dimple or a blob of glue anywhere because VW isn't above rejecting a piece of car for a whole car if it has to.

So you can see why a Volkswagen is so expensive when you figure it by the pound. It's something to think about.

Particularly if you haven't bought a Volkswagen because you thought they didn't cost enough.

AUTHORIZED DEALER

This we change.

Now you can see for yourself where we make most of our changes. Way down deep.

Every part you can see (and every part you can't see) has been changed again and again and again.

But we never change the Volkswagen without a reason. And the only reason is to make it even better.

When we do make a change, we try to make the new part fit older models, too.

So you'll find that many VW parts are interchangeable from one year to the next.

Which is why it's actually easier to get parts for a VW than for many domestic cars.

This we don't.

And why VW service is as good as it is.

The same principle holds good for the beetle shape. We made the rear window bigger one year so you could see other people better. We made the tail lights bigger last year so other people could see you better. But nothing drastic. Any Volkswagen hood still fits any

VW ever made. So does any fender.

And, in case you hadn't noticed, every VW still looks like every other VW.

Which may turn out to be the nicest thing of all about the car.

It doesn't go in one year and out the other.

We don't take off until everything is Kosher.

Kosher is sort of slang for "A.O.K." Literally, it means "fitting and proper" in Hebrew.

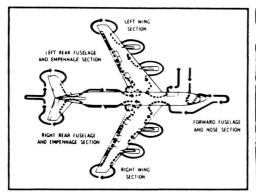

We spend more time walking than flying.

And we take it very literally indeed.

Before we let one of our Boeing 707's off the ground, our crews do some fancy footwork to make sure that everything is just so.

To begin with, the ground crew takes a nice long walk all around the plane. Every inch of the wings, the fuselage and the engines gets scrutinized.

The things that are supposed to be open are opened.

The things that are supposed to be closed are closed.

Every item on a very long checklist must be initialed one by one, and the man who checks the checker must sign the completed form.

When the walk is over, the work has only begun.

One member of the ground crew goes into the cockpit to test all the controls. Another man stays outside to see what happens.

They speak to each other in a language all their own. When the man inside turns the control wheel to the right, the man outside says, "Left tabs up, left inboard ailerons down, left spoilers down, right tabs down, right inboard ailerons up, right spoilers up."

There are even tests to test the tests. Horns

blow and lights light to show that things are working properly.

And if something isn't Kosher, everything

We check 597 controls...

stops until everything is.

If you took care of your car this carefully once a month, it would probably last forever.

Every EL AL jet gets the full treatment twice a day.

Meanwhile, there's the little matter of whipping up 3 square meals for 152 guests of this flying hotel.

What a job that is! Especially when you can't run out to the store if you're missing something at the last minute.

So we make sure that there's a little extra of everything; it hurts us to think of anyone going away hungry or thirsty.

We stock more than a dozen kinds of liquor on board; plus cigars, cigarettes, playing cards, olives, onions and cherries.

There's almost no end to the variety of things: from diapers to 2 sizes of doilies to 3 sizes of paper cups.

We even have 2 kinds of toothpicks: 1 kind for picking hors d'oeuvres and the other kind for picking teeth.

All of which brings us to the basic definition of Kosher that has to do with food.

Since we're the Israeli airline, we cook in the great Jewish tradition.

And the great Jewish tradition includes

some tasty morsels (like matzo ball soup, kreplach, and gefilte fish) that are usually served only on festive occasions.

...one at a time

But we figure that an EL AL trip is a festive occasion all by itself, so we go all out and bend the rule a little by serving them every day.

Actually, the dietary laws can get pretty involved, but what it boils (or broils or roasts) down to is that we don't mix meat and dairy products during the same meal.

So there won't be any butter for your bread with the sumptuous roast beef, and there won't be cream with your coffee afterward.

On the other hand, when breakfast comes, you'll find gobs of butter to go with your lox, bagels and cream cheese, enough milk to bathe in, and all the cream you want for your coffee.

Above all, you get to fly with a bunch of enthusiastic people who don't have to work at being hospitable because that's the way they were brought up.

And you can be doubly sure that everything's Kosher. Inside the plane and inside you.

Hold it! Something isn't Kosher.

The Airline of Israel EL AL

For more information contact your travel agent or EL AL Israel Airlines, 8 South Michigan Ave., Chicago, Ill. 60603   (312) 236-3745.
For information on travel in Israel contact the Israel Government Tourist Office at 5 South Wabash, Chicago, Ill.

Till death us do part.

It may be beautiful to die for love in a poem.

But it's ugly and stupid to die for love in a car.

Yet how many times have you seen (or been) a couple more interested in passion than in passing? Too involved with living to worry about dying?

As a nation, we are allowing our young to be buried in tons of steel. And not only the reckless lovers—the just plain nice kids as well.

Everyone is alarmed about it. No one really knows what to do. And automobile accidents, believe it or not, continue to be the leading cause of death among young people between 15 and 24 years of age.

Parents are alarmed and hand over the keys to the car anyway.

Insurance companies are alarmed and charge enormous rates which deter no one.

Even statisticians (who don't alarm easily) are alarmed enough to tell us that by 1970, 14,450 young adults will die in cars each year.

(Just to put those 14,450 young lives in perspective, that is about 4 times the number of young lives we have lost so far in Viet Nam.)

Is it for this that we spent our dimes and dollars to all but wipe out polio? Is it for this that medical science conquered diphtheria and smallpox?

What kind of society is it that keeps its youngsters alive only long enough to sacrifice them on the highway?

Yet that is exactly what's happening. And it's incredible.

Young people should be the best drivers, not the worst.

They have the sharper eyes, the steadier nerves, the quicker reflexes. They probably even have the better understanding of how a car works.

So why?

Are they too dense to learn? Too smart to obey the obvious rules? Too sure of themselves? Too un-sure? Or simply too young and immature?

How can we get them to be old enough to be wise enough before it's too late?

One way is by insisting on better driver training programs in school. Or *after* school. Or after work. Or during summers.

By having stricter licensing requirements. By rewarding the good drivers instead of merely punishing the bad ones. By having uniform national driving laws (which don't exist today). By having radio and TV and the press deal more with the problem. By getting *you* to be less complacent.

Above all, by setting a decent example ourselves.

Nobody can stop young people from driving. And nobody should. Quite the contrary. The more exposed they become to sound driving techniques, the better they're going to be. (Doctors and lawyers "practice;" why not drivers?)

We at Mobil are not preachers or teachers. We sell gasoline and oil for a living and we want everyone to be a potential customer.

If not today, tomorrow. And we want everyone, young and old, to have his fair share of tomorrows.

Mobil

We want you to live.

Fresh-killed chicken.

Bravo.

Let's hear it for the winner.

That's him lying there the dead one.

Or is he the loser?

You can't tell. Not that it matters very much. Because in the idiot game of "chicken," winners and losers both die.

In the idiot game of "chicken," two cars speed straight for each other. Head on.

With luck, one car steers clear in the nick of time. Without luck, neither car steers clear. And the winner and the loser are equally dead.

Some "game."

It took God Almighty to stop Abraham from making a blood sacrifice of his son.

What do you suppose it will take to make us stop sacrificing our children?

We who bear them in sterilized hospitals, stuff them with vitamins, educate them expensively, and then hand over the keys to the car and wait with our hearts in our mouths.

Too bad we educate them only to make a living and not to stay alive.

Because right now - this year - car accidents kill more young people than anything else. Including

war. Including cancer. Including *anything.*

Yet we allow it.

Incredibly enough, fewer than half the young people who get drivers' licenses every year have passed a driver training course.

Which leaves well over 2 million (!) youngsters who get licenses every year *without* passing such a course.

And this is the price we pay: 13,200 young people between 15 and 24 died in automobile accidents in 1965. (The exact number for 1966 isn't in yet; it will probably be higher.)

It's a gruesome answer to the population explosion.

And if we all sit still about it, we ourselves are guilty of "chickening out."

Yet we mustn't frighten our youngsters; they're frightened enough.

We must teach them.

Does your school system have a driver training course?

Are there books in your school library or public library on driving? (Did you know such books exist? Do *they* know?)

Are the requirements for getting a driver's

license in your state tough enough?

Are your radio and TV stations paying any attention to the problem? Your newspapers?

Does anyone in your community give awards for good driving? The PTA? Or the Boy Scouts? The Chamber of Commerce? The churches or synagogues?

What kind of driver are you yourself? Do you set a good example or a poor one?

Would your company insist on a driver training course before they'd hire someone?

Would your schools insist on a training course before they'd turn a youngster loose?

Would it help?

Yes, it would. Education works. Drivers in large truck fleets are trained to drive safely. And some of them have dropped accident rates to only about half that of the general public.

It would cost little or nothing to get these things going. And we haven't a minute to spare. It's blood that we have on our hands, not time.

We at Mobil sell gasoline and oil for our living *to* the living. Naturally, we'd like young people to grow up into customers. But for now we'd be happy if they'd simply grow up.

Mobil

We want you to live.

My son, the pilot.

by Tillie Katz

Believe me.

I'm not saying this just because he's my only son.

But who ever thought a boy from Jacksonville, Florida would grow up to be the Chief Pilot for a whole airline?

It's funny, but Bill wasn't even interested in flying when he was young. Which was all right with me. Frankly, it made me a little nervous even when he played football.

Then something got into him. Just when we all thought he was going into some nice business, he enlisted in the Air Corps.

Pretty soon, he was a group commander with the 8th Air Force in Europe. By the time he came home, it was *Captain* Katz.

With a Distinguished Flying Cross, if you please.

Afterwards, it was flying, flying, flying.

I don't know if you could call him a pioneer or anything, but he was right there when EL AL was only a tiny little airline.

And now? Now you can call him Chief Pilot.

And does he keep an eye on that airline!

Sometimes I think he worries about it too much.

Do you know how many miles he's flown? Over 2 million! Do you know how long he's spent in the air? Over 12 thousand hours!

But if that's what it takes to make the airline so good, that's what he does.

The other pilots even tell a joke on him. They say he only comes down to collect his pay.

But *I* know better. I have two beautiful grandchildren who live in Israel with Bill and my daughter-in-law.

They come to see me now and then, but I wish I could spoil them more often. It's a good thing they have Bill for a father. He spoils everybody. Except himself.

So if you fly on EL AL and see him, tell him I said to dress warm.

After reading History at Oxford, and learning to dig sheep in Australia, James Lowther decided to put the combined skills thus acquired to work in advertising. He worked at Hobson Bates and Wasey Campbell Ewald, until in 1977 he joined Saatchi and Saatchi, where he eventually became Joint Creative Director and Deputy Chairman.

As a copywriter he has been responsible for award winning campaigns for Castlemaine XXXX, British Rail, Schweppes, The Health Education Council, the COI and Cunard. He has an ad in the book of The Hundred Best Advertisements.

In 1995, he resigned from Saatchi and Saatchi to become a founder member and Creative Director for the New Saatchi Agency.

Here's some ideas of how to be a copywriter who writes but doesn't copy.

1. RULE NO 1. NO RULES.

Everything I am about to say are things that have helped me write good ads. But at the end of the day, you could ignore every one of them and do a great ad.

More great ads are done by breaking rules than by following them.

2. LEAVE THE OFFICE

Before you even open your pad, open five other things. Your ears, your eyes and your mind.

You'll never be a good writer of anything if you just sit in your office and stare at the desk. Your raw material isn't in the office or in Groucho's for that matter. It's out on the streets. Look at pictures. Listen to music. Go to films. See plays. And more importantly look at people. They're those funny things with two legs we're meant to be writing about remember.

It sounds obvious but it's amazing how many people in our incestuous little business just spend their spare time with other people in this incestuous little business.

Get outside. And observe.

For instance, the Castlemaine XXXX campaign would never have happened if my parents hadn't sent me to Australia to make a man of me. This it conspicuously failed to do. But it did teach me how to get bitten by a wild cockatoo, how to cheat at poker, and fifteen years later how to write a XXXX ad.

3. CHUCK OUT THE BRIEF.

Don't always accept the planner's brief. It's sometimes just a form of words which manages to get into one sentence all the contradictory things that the client and the account team wanted to say. As a result it can be about as informative as the communique after a dodgy EEC summit. In my experience the best planners are often creative people.

4. RELAX

I know this sounds odd in the pressurised world of fast lead times. We are all under pressure. We just shouldn't behave as if we are.

Sit back and sniff around the problem.

Have fun. Tell stories or jokes around the subject. That way you might come at the problem from an unexpected angle. (The script with which we launched XXXX was based on a revolting joke about a man who got a snake bite on his willy). If you get stuck, walk away from it for a while. It's amazing how much clearer it is when you revisit it.

5. FISH FOR BIRDS

In the last century, the American writer Washington Irving visited the magnificent Alhambra Palace in Grenada where the local birds had become so accustomed to being shot at by the locals, that they had become very adept at avoiding this particular Valhalla.

One enterprising urchin had a wonderful idea. He got fishing nets and cast them off the battlements. The birds circling the battlements were caught hopping by this unfamiliar angle of attack and were trapped for the pot in their hundreds.

So next time you're tempted to go down the old familiar path, why not try fishing for birds and you'll probably get lions. Big gold ones.

6. DO THE OPPOSITE

Here's a way of fishing for birds that may be worth a try.

Think of what everybody does in the category of product you're advertising and do the opposite.

Why do all our car ads look the same? Why do all our washing powder ads look the same?

Why not do a car ad like a washing powder ad? Or vice versa.

It may not work but it just might.

7. DON'T WRITE.

Just because you're called a copywriter, don't start thinking about writing.

The best copywriters are often highly visual. After all, a newspaper ad is just a blank sheet of paper in which you can do absolutely anything you want. As long as it makes a point.

The press ad I'm proudest of – the "headlights" ad happened when I was looking at a photograph of a car in mist and I put my fingers over the headlights. After that, it didn't need a John Milton to come up with the headline.

John Hegarty once said to me that communication through the written word was being replaced with communication through images.

He said the Celtic civilisation never wrote down stories because they could make them more memorable by passing them down orally or visually. It's a great argument until I asked John where the Celtic civilisation was today. Still I take his point.

8. CRAFT IT.

When I first thought about this piece, I was going to write the word 'care' a thousand times and leave it at that.

Because that is what distinguishes good copywriters from average ones.

The best copywriters are not always the ones with the highest ability but the ones with the highest standards.

Who knows that 90% good ad is not enough. And who will keep going until its 100% right.

When I did the BR press ads, Alex Taylor's brilliant layout was done is such a way that meant not only that every ad had just nine lines of copy but also every line had to have between 20-24 letters. I did point out that Shakespeare did not labour under such typographical tyranny, but I gave it a go.

It was incredibly hard work and took twice as long as a long piece of copy. But it was worth it.

9. FIGHT FOR IT.

People don't like great ideas. They're original. Which means they're unfamiliar and therefore frightening.

This explains why mediocre advertisements sail though without touching the sides, whereas people always find a million and one reasons why a great idea should never run.

The best teams just never give up. One art director I had, now a respected creative director in London used to jam recalcitrant account executives between our door and the wall.

The less drastic, though probably more successful method is to take the account team and client along with you. Explain why you're doing what you've done.

Why you've rejected other approaches. Charm them. Have drinks with them. Remind them over and over again of your thinking.

And if that fails, them you hit them.

10. THE ONE I DON'T KNOW

I'm sure there's something else that would make me better. I'm still looking for it.

"Guinness has bought the wrong companies...... far too many for its management to be able to effectively man...."

"The principal acquisitions made during the two years ended 30 September 1985 are ...Arthur Bell & Sons, Gleneagles Hotels, Canning Town Glass, Lewis Meeson, Martin the Newsagent, Neighbourhood Stores, Champneys, Richter Brothers, R.S. McColl, Natures Best Health Products, Hediard."

Perhaps the head of Guinness should listen to the head of Guinness

Argyll. We can revive Distillers' spirits.

OH AND THE MOST IMPORTANT RULE:

If you want to be good, never think that anything you have done is quite good enough. As you can see, I don't.

Born in England but of Italian parentage, Alfredo Marcantonio began his advertising career as Head of Advertising for Volkswagen in Great Britain.

He left to become a copywriter and joined French Gold Abbott in 1974. In 1976 he moved on to Collett Dickenson Pearce, which was then widely regarded as one of the most creative agencies in the world.

Four years later Marc helped Frank Lowe and Geoff Howard-Spink to found Lowe Howard-Spink. He remained

there throughout its formative years but quit his post as Creative Director and Deputy Chairman in 1987 to join Wight Collins Rutherford Scott which added his long name to its already lengthy title. He left in 1990, following the agency's takeover by French group Eurocom.

Marc ran BBDO's London office for a short time before its merger with Abbott Mead Vickers reunited him with David Abbott and gave him the opportunity to return to his first love, writing ads.

I write copy the way my grandmother made minestrone soup. I throw in every interesting ingredient that I can find and slowly reduce them down. When you start off you have this rather thin, unpalatable solution but with constant stirring you should end up with something quite substantial.

Where do you get the ingredients?

Well, if you're anything like me, you'll have a clutch of headlines you couldn't sell your art director when you first did the ad. Then there are the notes you took on the factory visit. (You don't take notes? Well, body copy is good reason to start.)

Next, search the client's previous advertising for anything interesting or persuasive. And the competition's campaigns. (The most awful ads can often harbour the most interesting facts.)

After that, read through any brochures, technical sheets, independent test results and press cuttings you can find. Even the company's annual report can contain a few gems.

Most of these sources will provide you with rational reasons for purchase. You have to look to the customer rather than the client to find emotional ones.

What is the target audience like? What's important to them? How do they feel about the product, the manufacturer, the marketplace? What role does it play in their lives?

Write to people's hearts as well as their heads. That's where most decisions are taken.

When you're all written out on the subject, review your findings, rejecting the weak points and re-writing the strong.

Always remember that self-praise is no commendation. (If I say I am the best copywriter in Britain, you wouldn't listen, if Tom McEllicot said so, you might be fooled into believing it.)

Also, raw statistics are far more convincing than polished opinions. (Do you want a car that does 68 miles per gallon or one that's 'outstandingly economical'?)

Beware of adjectives. They don't always do what you think they do. (We're all concerned about kitchen cleanliness but how many of us would frequent a snack bar called 'The Hygienic Cafe'?)

Don't be ashamed of mimicking the style of your hero copywriters at first. In my early days my best efforts all read a bit like Bob Levenson on a very bad day. (Tim Delaney thinks they still do.)

Obviously, you need to put the facts into some logical order. An advertisement is like a door-to-door salesman. It is an intrusion in people's lives. The headline may have got you onto the threshold but it's up to your sales patter to keep you there.

Put the most surprising, most persuasive or most intriguing fact first. (My opening line about soup is about as interesting as this article is going to get.)

As with any form of creative writing, you will need to develop a tone of voice. A way of talking that's chosen not to reflect the agency, or the category but the product or service being advertised.

Should you sound like some *eminence gris* talking from a distant podium? Or the bloke in the next seat on the railway train? I've heard tell that Bill Bernbach once suggested to a young writer that he make his copy more conversational by writing it as though it was a letter to an Uncle he had met, but rarely saw.

For me, copywriting is closer to speechwriting. It's not simply about informing, entertaining or amusing the audience. It is about winning them over to a product or a point of view.

In his book, *Our Masters Voices*, Max Atkinson analyses the devices that orators have used since ancient times. The seasoned copywriter will recognise almost all of them.

Perhaps the most useful is the 'list of three'. From God the Father, the Son and the Holy Ghost, through Hip, Hip Hooray to the archetypal Englishman, Scotsman and Irishman, there is some magical power that a list of three words, three phrases or three sentences exerts over the human psyche.

Explain it, I cannot. Disprove it, I cannot. Time and time again, I have found that two facts or phrases are inadequate but four are unwieldy.

It's a Marcantonio family tradition that stretches way back to 44 AD; "Friends, Romans, Countrymen, lend me your ears."

1900 years later Abe Lincoln announced "Government of the people, by the people, for the people."

And rather more recently Winston Churchill declared; "Never in the field of human conflict has so much been owed, to so many, by so few."

You can't stump up a list of three? Fear not. Neither could many of the great orators. Turn to their other great weapon, the contrasting pair.

This groups two items that are as different as chalk and cheese. (That's one to start with.) "Famous names at unheard of prices", "The big network for small phones". There can't be a writer on the planet that hasn't used this device in a headline or body copy.

Why does it work? I think it's the way that it disarms the reader; the first word or phrase sets him off in one direction but the second takes him back in a completely opposite one.

William Shakespeare wrote perhaps the most famous contrasting pair on Earth; "To be, or not to be."

While Neil Armstrong delivered the most famous on the Moon; "That's one small step for man, one giant leap for mankind."

Dr Martin Luther King also made moving use of the genre; 'I have a dream that one day my four children will not be judged by the colour of their skin, but by the content of their character."

In the very best examples the number of words and even syllables, in each of the two phrases balances each other perfectly, a symmetry that adds to the impact and memorability.

Alliteration is another powerful weapon in the writer's arsenal. Look at Dr King's use of alliteration with the words 'colour' and 'content'. I find alliteration enormously rewarding, both to write and read. And it can be combined with the two previous devices to great effect.

Add it to the list of three and you have Julius Caesar's "Veni, Vedi, Vici."

Add it to the contrasting pair and you have the phrase one British politician used to describe her party's concern for the poor rather than the rich; "We are more about Bermondsey than Burgundy".

So there you are. You have written and re-written the facts until only the strong survive. You have woven them into a persuasive argument that will win over the hearts and minds of all fair minded folk. You have developed a tone of voice that exactly matches the personality of the product.

It's end-line time.

There are a number of ways to sign off. One is the final telling fact that completes the sale. Another is the call to action. Most popular of all there's the light, witty line that relates back to the headline in some way.

(Hint: you know those rejected headlines I mentioned at the beginning of this article? One of them might be just the job.)

Dun writin'? Right, now sit back and read the whole thing aloud. Yes, aloud. Preferably in the tone of voice you've written it in. Failing that, do what I do and impersonate the voice over from the 'Jones and Krempler' Volkswagen commercial.

Am I mad? Quite possibly, but I've heard David Abbott doing it too.

Will you be as fortunate finding a second career?

Heaven knows, you are going to need a second career more than this gentleman.

Compulsory retirement at 55 is on its way.

No matter how long your service, no matter how high your position, you could be out of a job, come your 55th birthday.

The company car will disappear.

The expense account will disappear.

The private health insurance will disappear.

Sadly, your mortgage won't. You may well find yourself repaying that until you are 60 or 65.

Civil servants should be alright. They have indexed-linked pensions, courtesy of the poor old taxpayer.

Members of trade unions should make out too. They often have an army of negotiators to battle on their behalf.

No, it's the private sector business-man who will be in trouble.

His retirement age is going down, but his life expectancy is on the up and up. Today's 40 year olds can expect to reach 80. You could easily be faced with 25 years in retirement.

How will you manage?

That fixed company pension that looked oh-so-generous ten years ago, won't be worth much in another ten year's time, never mind twenty or thirty.

State pensions aren't famous for keeping up with inflation either.

Of course, with the two added together, you may just have enough to survive.

But is that all you want to do? Survive?

Wouldn't you prefer to do some-thing positive with the second half of your adult life?

Albany Life and the Inland Revenue can help you.

Start salting away a regular sum each month. £15, £50, whatever you can spare.

We will bump up your contributions by claiming back from the taxman every last penny of tax relief we can.

We will then invest the total amount on your behalf.

We receive what is arguably the best investment advice there is. We retain Warburg Investment Management Ltd., a subsidiary of S.G. Warburg & Co Ltd., the merchant bank.

Start saving in your thirties or forties and you will amass a considerable sum, well before your 55th birthday.

When you are pensioned off, you will have a wad of tax-free money to cushion the blow.

Enough to set up shop in some sleepy Devon village.

Enough to pursue some half-forgotten craft, like working with cane or stained glass.

Enough to buy you a stake in some successful small business near your home.

Whatever you decide to do, you'll be better off mentally as well as financially. People vegetate if they have nothing but the garden to occupy their minds.

There is no reason why you shouldn't be active and working at 73, like Mr. Reagan here.

Though hopefully you won't have to carry the worries of the world on your shoulders.

To learn more about our plans send this coupon to Peter Kelly, Albany Life Assurance, FREEPOST, Potters Bar EN6 1BR.

Name

Address

Tel:

Name of your Life Assurance Broker, if any

Albany Life

Albany Life

WHAT A PART GOES INTO
BEFORE IT GOES INTO A BMW.

The very liquids that keep a car going can cause many a car part to break down.

Petroleum has the power to soften some plastics.

Hydraulic fluid has an unhealthy appetite for certain forms of rubber compound.

While anti-freeze solutions can interfere with electrical contacts.

So, no sooner do BMW's engineers perfect a part, than BMW's lab technicians try to destroy it.

Components are immersed in any suspect substance they're likely to come into contact with. As well as a few they're unlikely to meet.

Critical items like the ABS braking sensor face even sterner tests.

Generously coated with petroleum, diesel oil, hydraulic fluid, detergent and brake fluid, it is placed in an oven for 24 hours, at 115°C.

If the sensor is still in working order, the ordeal is repeated for 16 hours at 150°C.

All being well, it is then given a vigorous impact and collision test. Not once, not twice, but 72 times.

Such testing not only helps BMW design parts and components, it helps them develop the materials they are made from.

The alloy wheels now fitted to many BMW cars are a case in point.

They are constructed from a metal that is created to BMW's own formula.

A formula they continuously monitor and test. Ten wheels from each delivery are hammered with an iron pendulum.

It simulates the effect of hitting a kerb at 20mph. And if the wheels aren't up to it, the whole consignment is consigned to the scrap heap.

If they do survive, each wheel is given an X-ray

before being passed fit for the production line.

There is a principle behind all these procedures.

Creating parts that perform outstandingly well creates a car that performs outstandingly well.

And for BMW, that is the true acid test.

THE ULTIMATE DRIVING MACHINE

BMW

Will the muse visit you during your stay at the Gritti Palace in Venice? You will certainly enjoy the same sources of inspiration as Mr Hemingway.

The Grand Canal still laps the hotel entrance as it has for five hundred years.

Titian's 16th century portrait of Doge Andrea Gritti continues to grace the hotel's walls.

ERNEST HEMINGWAY WROTE A NOVEL HERE. PERHAPS YOU MAY BE MOVED TO WRITE A MEMO OR TWO?

And the view from your window, across to the church of La Salute, is the same one that greeted the American author on his arrival in October 1949.

The Gritti Palace became not only the place where he wrote, but also the place that he wrote about, in "Across the river and into the trees".

In truth, other Ciga Hotels have proved equally inspiring. And neither satellite communications nor air conditioning have robbed them of their historic charm.

In Asolo, amid the hills of the Veneto, you will find the Villa Cipriani. Once the home of Robert and Elisabeth Browning.

But perhaps the most literary of our hotels is the Meurice, which borders the Tuileries in Paris.

For more than thirty years, its renowned restaurant served as headquarters to France's most noted literary circle.

An era immortalised in Fargue's "Les Piétons de Paris". And commemorated by the portrait of its Patron, Florence Gould, which presides over diners to this day.

If you are a person more attracted by the beauty of a traditional building than the sterility of a tower block, consider a Ciga Hotel next time you travel.

There are currently 36 to choose from, with room rates much the same as ordinary five star hotels.

To obtain a brochure describing them all, simply fax your letterhead or business card to Milan (02) 76009131. Alternatively, telephone Milan (02) 626622.

CIGA HOTELS

CIGA

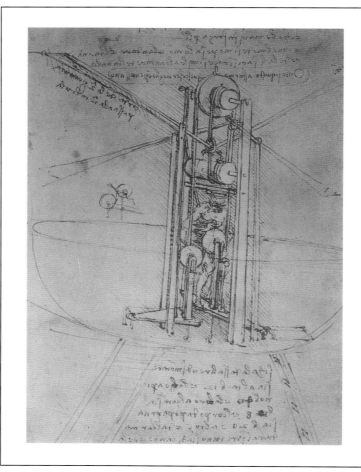

Florence, birthplace of air travel. It's taken 500 years to organise a direct flight.

No sooner did man walk upon the Earth than he began to dream of flying above it.

A fantasy that was given form by Leonardo Da Vinci, almost five centuries ago.

The Glider. The Helicopter. The Parachute. All were born on the drawing board of this Florentine Maestro. But, aeronautical visionary though he was, Leonardo could never have predicted the trials of reaching his native city by air. Ask any of the major international airlines to take you to Florence and they will promptly take you to Pisa. A pleasant enough city, but a good hour or two's drive from the joys of the Uffizi. Thanks to Meridiana you'll soon be able to take a less roundabout route. Starting September 1st, Meridiana will fly you direct from London's Gatwick to Florence's Amerigo Vespucci Airport. And fly you there in style. Tourist passengers travel in Business Class comfort, while those in Electa Club enjoy facilities that put many a First Class in the shade. The spacious cabin has unique seats with winged headrests and the international menus are created by some of Italy's finest chefs. To learn more about Meridiana and its new scheduled service direct to Florence, call your travel agent. It's the ideal airline for those who don't have a leaning towards Pisa.

Direct daily flights leaving London at 10am and Florence at 8.05am.

Meridiana
Your Private Airline

Meridiana

Little wonder they don't build cars like they used to.
Building a pen is difficult enough.

Oh, the elegant lines of the 1925 Hispano Suiza. Oh, the elegant lines of the 1927 Parker Duofold.

The car may no longer be available but happily the pen is making a welcome return.

We have long yearned to recreate this favourite Parker design. And our approaching centenary has provided a suitable excuse.

Like today's top cars the Parker Duofold Centennial boasts working parts that are 'state-of-the-art.'

But unlike them, it boasts workmanship that is somewhat old fashioned.

Rather than mould the cap and barrel 'en masse,' we machine them as we did in the old days, from a solid block.

Rather than cut the nib from some modern metal, we stay true to gold.

Rather than slit the nib on some new fangled contraption, we still do the job by hand, using a blade no thicker than a human hair.

And just as Hispano Suiza road tested its cars thoroughly after manufacture, we put our pens through their paces.

Upon completion, each Duofold Centennial is examined by a white gloved inspector. If deemed perfect, it is filled, written with and cleaned before being released for sale.

It is an exhausting way to produce a pen. But, as with the Hispano Suiza, the looks and handling provide ample reward.

ɸ PARKER

Parker

THE GUARDIAN Thursday October 9 1980   5

By kind permission of the Daily Mail.

By kind permission of The Guardian.

They obviously felt like shooting each other.

Who can blame them?

They've got their hands on an Olympus XA. Automatic exposure control and a coupled range-finder ensure a perfect seaside snap.

A great help, whether you are an accomplished photographer, like the gentleman on the right. Or a less experienced one, like the gentleman on the far left.

It's nice they're seeing eye to eye over something.

THE OLYMPUS XA.

Olympus XA shown actual size. For further details write to: Olympus Optical Company (UK) Limited, 2-8 Honduras Street, London EC1Y 0TX. Tel: 01-253 2772.

Olympus

Born in Chicago in 1938, Ed McCabe started working at the age of eight as a paper boy and then as a Good Humor man. He began his career in advertising by chance at the age of fifteen, in the mailroom of McCann-Erickson.

In 1959, he moved to New York City and landed a job as copywriter at Benton & Bowles, then at Young & Rubicam. In 1964, he joined Carl Ally, a small agency focused on doing great creative work. During the three years McCabe was at Ally, the agency's billings increased tenfold.

In 1967, McCabe co-founded Scali, McCabe, Sloves. During the next nineteen years, he created enduring and effective campaigns including many of Volvo's most memorable advertisements.

In 1974, he was elected to the Copywriter's Hall of Fame, the youngest person ever so honoured. McCabe is as renowned for his ability to teach creative people as he is for creating advertising himself. He has been trainer and inspiration to at least a dozen people who have gone on to found agencies of their own.

He resigned from Scali, McCabe, Sloves as President and Worldwide Creative Director in 1986, to seek fresh challenges. In early 1991, he founded McCabe & Company, an advertising and communications company.

Pencils, I work with pencils. Sometimes pens and paper or computers. Lacking one of those, I'll write with someone's lipstick or eyebrow pencil. In extremis, give me a twig and some dirt, a stone and a sidewalk, a fingernail and anything it can be scratched into.

I scrawl things on pieces torn from the shopping bags of unsuspecting old ladies I accost on the subway. I scribble on sodden cocktail napkins. Even on lavatory walls, then send someone back with a Polaroid.

For years, I had a table in a restaurant in New York. I wrote some of my best ads and the body copy for them on tablecloths. Every morning, the cloth from the night before would arrive at the agency, oily with dinner drippings and blackened with notes. We'd copy the tablecloth, then send it back so they could launder it fresh and white, only to be assaulted by me yet again.

When I have an idea, wherever I have an idea, I write it down. This compulsion knows no bounds. I've written ads on the soles of my shoes. I've written on the skins of friends and lovers, on my own hands or feet, on the clothing of total strangers, cajoled them into following me to a source of paper, and then paid for the damage done.

But that behaviour only occurs in the later stages.

In the early stages – that is, while I'm doing my studying and my research and memorising, before I know what I'm doing inside out, and outside in – when I'm in that empty state of ignorant acquisition, you couldn't get me to pick up a pencil for love nor money.

I make it a practice to never do anything until I know everything. I've written six different openings to this particular piece and I've thought about it for weeks. If I'd approached this the same way I do advertising, I could have spared myself much unnecessary writing and deadline tension. But I started with this notion that writing copy was one thing and writing about writing copy was another. As always, I've come back to the realisation that communication is communication and the same rules apply. NEVER, go "Ready, Fire, Aim." If you do, you'll always shoot yourself in the foot.

Consider the familiar cycle of "Ready, Aim, Fire". "Ready" takes a second, "Fire" takes a fraction of a second, but it's the "Aim" part that's most crucial, that can seem interminable, what with the squinting, focusing, steadying, and just when you think you've drawn the exact right bead, you waver and have to begin all over again.

And so it is with the making of advertising. When I write, it's with explosive passion and bravado. With a tinge of insanity even. But before I write, I'm painstaking, plodding, disciplined – and uncommitted. Passion has no place in the planning.

When I think, I don't work. And when I work, I never think. When you are ready to write, it should be automatic, fuelled by knowledge so comprehensive that the advertising almost writes itself.

This is not just because it makes sense to be in full possession of all the facts, or to examine a problem from every possible angle and aspect. As a writer, one simply has no choice. Only with absolute knowledge of a subject can you hope to transcend the banality of mere facts and experience the freedom of insight.

I was once quoted as having said, "I can teach a monkey to

write an ad but I can't teach a monkey to think". I still believe that to be true.

Really, any fool can write an ad. With today's technology, you could even program a computer to write body copy. Just plug in all the product information, some consumer benefits, a few relevant behavioural hot buttons, the client mandatory, and presto. I'm convinced out would come a serviceable piece of copy. Truly, you could manufacture advertising. Equally true, it would look and sound and feel – phoney. It would lack some - thing sublimely ordinary, something human. It would seem as though a monkey, a fool or a machine had written it.

To me, all advertising that is truly great reeks of honest humanity. Between every word you can smell the hot breath of the writer. Whether a result of wit, intelligence, insight or artfulness, great advertising invariably transmits itself to the receiver on a fragile human frequency.

What I do, what we all do, is not about describing what a product or service does.

It's about making real how the products or services we write about bring improvement, comfort, even a bit of magic to a single human life.

TASTE THE BEEF THAT ESCAPED THE MEDDLESOME HAND OF MAN.

Once upon a time, all beef tasted pure and natural like the Coleman Natural brand. But that was a long time ago, back before science and technology reared their heads.

That was back when beef was untouched by humans who, being human, don't know how to leave well enough alone.

Today, most beef cattle are raised with man's unflinching eye turned more toward profit than palatability. From birth, many are shot with hormones to speed their growth. It is common practice to give cattle regular doses of antibiotics to ward off disease. There is no clinical proof that eating this kind of beef is bad for you. But plain common sense should tell you that, at the very least, it ain't natural.

Now we know "natural" is the most over-used and near meaningless word in advertising lingo today.

But when it comes to the Coleman family and the beef we raise, "natural" isn't a word, it's a mission. We Colemans have been involved in the rearing of natural beef since 1875. That's a long-term commitment.

In recent years, we've grown into a totally integrated beef producer that controls every aspect of product quality from conception to consumption, enforcing rigorous standards every step of the way.

No Coleman cattle are given hormone or steroid implants ever.

No Coleman cattle are treated with antibiotics, either by injection or through feeding, ever.

All feeds are regularly tested for chemical residues and rejected if any traces are found.

All Coleman beef cuts are trimmed of fat to tighter standards than conventional beef. Some cuts are as much as 40% lower in fat.

One of the results of this total dedication: Coleman has surged to become the largest selling brand of beef in America's natural food stores, where customers are fanatically finicky about the wholesomeness of the food they eat.

Another result is the taste of the beef itself.

Coleman beef is lean without any loss of tenderness, never stringy. It's juicy without tasting fatty.

In fact, it's so clean, unadulterated and honest-tasting that once you've tried it, there will be no going back to anything less.

Especially if your family is eating less beef than it used to. When it's Coleman, less is more.

For more information write to: Coleman Natural Meats, Inc., 5140 Race Court, Denver, Colorado 80216.

WHERE TO BUY COLEMAN NATURAL BEEF

A & P • Big D • Big Y • Bread & Circus • Demoulas • FINAST • Foodmart • Hannaford Brothers • Purity Supreme • Roche Brothers • Shaws • Star Markets • Stop & Shop • Victory •

MAN HASN'T MESSED WITH IT.

Written on cocktail napkin, 3 am, New York, 1974

PHOTOGRAPHED BY JOEL MEYEROWITZ

Tomorrow morning when you get up, take a nice deep breath. It'll make you feel rotten.

It is said that taking a deep breath of fresh air is one of life's most satisfying experiences.

It can also be said that taking a deep breath of New York air is one of life's most revolting, if not absolutely sickening, experiences.

Because the air around New York is the foulest of any American city.

Even on a clear day, a condition which is fast becoming extinct in our "fair city," the air is still contaminated with poisons.

On an average day, you breathe in carbon monoxide, which as you know is quite lethal; sulfur dioxide which is capable of eroding stone; acrolein, a chemical that was used in tear gas in World War I; benzopyrene, which has produced cancer on the skin of mice; and outrageous quantities of just plain soot and dirt, which make your lungs black, instead of

the healthy pink they're supposed to be.

At the very least, the unsavory elements in New York air can make you feel downright lousy. Polluted air makes your eyes smart, your chest hurt, your nose run, your head ache and your throat sore. It can make you wheeze, sneeze, cough and gasp. And because air pollution is responsible for many of those depressing "gray days," it may affect your mental well being. If you're a person who is easily depressed, prolonged exposure to polluted air certainly isn't doing you any good.

Of course, at its worst, air pollution can kill you. So far, the diseases believed to be caused, or worsened by polluted air are lung cancer, pulmonary emphysema, acute bronchitis, asthma and heart disease.

600 people are known to have died in

New York during two intense periods of air pollution in 1953 and 1963. How many others have died as a result of air pollution over the years is anybody's guess.

Who is responsible for New York's air pollution problem? Practically everybody. Dirt, smoke and chemicals belche from apartment buildings, industrial plants, cars, busses, garbage dumps, anywhere things are burned.

But the purpose of this advertisement is not to put the finger on who's causing the problem. It's to get you outraged enough to help put a stop to it.

What can you, yourself, do about air pollution? Not much. But a million people up in arms can create quite a stink.

We want the names and addresses of a million New Yorkers who have had their fill of

polluted air.

The names will be used as ammunition against those people who claim New Yorkers aren't concerned about air pollution.

If we can get a million names, no one can say New Yorkers won't pay the price for cleaner burning fuels, better enforcement of air pollution laws, and more efficient methods of waste disposal.

The cost of these things is low. A few dollars a year.

The cost of dirty air is higher. It can make you pay the ultimate price.

Box One Million
Citizens for Clean Air, Inc.
Grand Central Station, N.Y. 10017

IF YOU'D LIKE TO GET IN THE THICK OF THE FIGHT AGAINST AIR POLLUTION, SEND US A LETTER ALONG WITH YOUR CHECK FOR $2.00 (OR MORE) AND BECOME A MEMBER OF CITIZENS FOR CLEAN AIR, INC.

Written on shirt cardboard, 7 am, New York, 1966

VOLVOS LAST A LONG TIME. ISN'T THAT BAD FOR BUSINESS?

To some manufacturers, building a product that lasts is the height of foolishness.

But it's an idea that's highly respected among enlightened consumers.

So instead of designing our cars to fall apart so that you'll have to buy another one, we design our cars not to.

That way you'll want to buy another one.

How well our cars last is best summed up by this fact: 9 out of every 10 Volvos registered here in the last eleven years are still on the road.

And in a world where people are becoming increasingly disenchanted with the cars they drive, our customers are coming back for more. The car most often traded in on a new Volvo is an old Volvo.

How's business?

Well, Volvo is the largest selling imported compact in America today. And this will be our best year ever.

The Volvo policy of enlightened foolishness is paying off.

Written on tablecloth, 10 pm, New York, 1970

Written on shopping bag, 8.15 am, New York, 1965

MY CHICKENS EAT BETTER THAN YOU DO.

Frank Perdue

The problem with you is that you're allowed to eat whatever you want.

My Perdue chickens don't have the same freedom. They eat what I give them. And I only give them the best. Their diet consists mainly of pure yellow corn, soybean meal, marigold petals— you'd call it health food.

My chickens drink nothing but fresh, clear water from deep wells.

The reason I'm so finicky about what goes into my chickens is simple: a chicken is what it eats. And because they eat so well, Perdue chickens are always tender, juicy and delicious. And have a healthy golden-yellow glow that separates them from the rest.

If you want to start eating as good as my chickens, take a tip from me.

Eat my chickens.

FRESH YOUNG CHICKEN

PERDUE

QUALITY GUARANTEED OR MONEY BACK

KEEP REFRIGERATED

Perdue Farms Inc. P.O. Box 1537-S Salisbury, MD 21801

IT TAKES A TOUGH MAN TO MAKE A TENDER CHICKEN.

Written on yellow pad, 11 pm, New York, 1972

Maybe your second car shouldn't be a car.

Don't laugh.

It makes a lot more sense to hop on a Vespa than it does to climb into a 4000-lb. automobile to go half a mile for a 4-oz. pack of cigarettes.

To begin with, a Vespa can be parked.

It'll give you between 125 and 150 miles to a gallon. Depending on how you drive. And using regular gas.

The Vespa is a reliable piece of machinery. Its engine has only three moving parts. There's not much that can break. (People have driven Vespas over 100,000 miles without major repairs.) And it's so simple to work on, a complete tune-up costs six dollars.

It's air-cooled. There's no water, no anti-freeze.

The transmission is so well built that it's guaranteed for life.*

Vespa has unitized body construction. The whole thing is made from one piece. It's not bolted together. It can't rattle apart.

If you buy a Vespa your neighbors won't move out of the neighborhood. The Vespa is a motorscooter, not a motorcycle. There is no social stigma attached to driving one.

There are six Vespa models to choose from. You can buy one of them with the money you'd spend just to insure and fuel the average second car for a year. And you can count on getting most of that money back should you ever decide to sell your Vespa. It won't depreciate nearly as fast as a car.

You may laugh at the Vespa today. But tomorrow when you're stuck in traffic and one scoots by, remember this.

The laugh is on you.

Vescony, Inc., 949 Commonwealth Avenue, Boston, Massachusetts.
*Providing regular maintenance is performed in accordance with schedule outlined in the warranty. Warranty provides for replacement or repair (at importers' option) of all transmission parts at no cost for either parts or labor. Overseas delivery available. ©1964 Vescony, Inc.

Vespa

Written on tablecloth, 1 am, New York, 1965

Tim Mellors started out writing for magazines in the 60's. He then became a Copywriter working on famous campaigns like the orignal Dulux Dog, Captain and the Sure Deodorant "Tick". In the 80's he was Creative Director at Saatchi & Saatchi where he worked on the Conservative Party, British Airways and launched the Independent Newspaper.

He has worked in America and Australia, where he began directing commercials. In the early 90's he was

Creative Director at GGT where he worked on Paul Merton's Imperial Leather Soap, Ariston and on and on, Red Rock Cider with Leslie Nielsen, Holston Pils with Denis Leary and of course Cadbury's Flake. He is now Chairman and Executive Creative Director of Mellors Reay & Partners.

Tim is a member of D&AD, was President of the Jury at the Cannes Festival and is currently President of the Creative Circle.

This is the only good bit of copy I think I've ever written.

Why? Well I don't see myself as much of a writer kind of writer. I'm not a craftsman, I love words when I speak them, they come jumbling out in an amazing way, but when I write them it's like threading a needle with garden gloves on.

So this Alexon piece appealed to me. It just came straight out of my brain, down my arm onto the Pentel and ended up fully formed on the paper.

Avedon's photograph of Iman, in the days before the Thin White Duke, is mesmeric (look at the eyes). Add Arden's brave – some would say reckless – art direction wrapping Alexon's finest round her head. Even Max Bygraves would have been inspired to write something good by such a concoction.

I don't believe any piece of ad copy I've ever read comes anywhere near the wit and perspicacity of Zoe Heller, or the cranky wisdom of Bernard Levin. And when you get right down to it, that's what we're up against, right there in the next column.

Like all creatives I'm insecure, praise – driven and full of self – doubt. So how do I have the temerity to offer up this bit of writing in this august publication? Charles Saatchi told me he loved it.

A VEDON
LEXON
FRICA

Yee hoo!, the old woman cries, as she butts the dancer gently in the belly. The dancer has been approved. The dancer is outstanding. The eye popping, limb contorting swirl of magic and colour that is the tribal dance of the Nomads of the Niger has reached its mesmeric climax. In a great white egg of a studio somewhere on New York's East Side, Richard Avedon the photographer who Truman Capote has called "The man with gifted eyes," breathes the tingling magic of the Wodaabe tribe into Alexon's African collection. Colours and primitive pattern woven into cloth, woven into clothes bring Alexon screeching into the now.

Barbara has been Executive Creative Director of CME.KHBB since January 1993. Before that she was Deputy Creative Director and a founding partner of Bartle Bogle Hegarty during its first ten years. Other experience includes a year at Boase Massimi Pollitt, nine years at Doyle Dane Bernbach (when they were separate agencies) and a year at Collett Dickenson Pearce.

"They come in different ways, so many different ways," Mick Jagger declares with a melodramatic pleading in his voice, like he's being forced at knife-point to divulge some great private secret. Which, in a sense, he is — how he and Keith Richards write songs together. Not the old shopworn shorthand about the birth of Satisfaction or Honky Tonk Women, but how they really do it from genesis to revelation.

These words open an article on the Rolling Stones by David Fricke published in a recent *Rolling Stone* magazine.

They seem an extraordinarily appropriate way to begin my section of D&AD's book on copywriting.

The point is, I suspect nobody really knows how they do it. We all have our ways of putting off that awful moment when, in the good old days, Mont Blanc or biro met a virgin sheet of A4.

Now, of course, it's the moment when chewed fingers meet PC. Call me old-fashioned, but I can't help wondering if the nature of copy will change now that it's created directly onto a screen. The nature of art direction has certainly changed since a Mac started to mean something other than a hamburger to the art directors among us.

Before I start to write a piece of copy, I like to have a conversation with somebody who lives and breathes the product or service. For cars, that might be a client, it might be a motoring journalist. For nappies it could be with a mother, father or nanny. Or an expert in paper technology. For any manufactured article, the quality control people at the factory are usually good value.

The point is, in my view, a copywriter can't have too much information at his or her fingertips. Copywriting is, after all, the art of saying a great deal in as few words as possible. (And, in that way, can be closer to poetry than prose.)

So, I assemble my facts and figures. Then I might list the few ingredients instinct tells me will best make this particular cake. And then, and this is the important bit, I think myself under the skin and into the head of the person I'm addressing.

Empathy really is all. A child I know once demonstrated this brilliantly. He was a boy about eight and rather well-spoken. I overheard him playing in the next door garden in the mixed inner London street in which he lived. He was dropping his aitches and effing and blinding like there was no tomorrow. When asked why he was speaking this way he said, with devastating child's logic, "So David will understand me". Quite.

So, gather your facts and get under the skin of your target. Talk to them in their language, not the Queen's. What else? Be brief. I believe it was Pascal who added an apology to the bottom of a long letter, explaining that he hadn't had time to write a short one. Why take twenty words to say what you could say in five? Why decide on a long copy ad when a poster-in-the-press will do?

For most people, and particularly women who work outside as well as inside the home, money isn't the most precious commodity these days; time is. We copywriters would do well to respect that.

For that reason, I make no excuses for including completely copy-free ads in these pages. And, indeed, actual posters. For a copywriter, communicating a headful of ideas via a handful of words is, in many ways, the ultimate challenge.

If I could proffer just one piece of advice it would be this: edit, edit, edit.

HOW CAN I GO TO THE CUP FINAL WHEN MY HEAD'S THROBBING?

DON'T EXPECT ME TO SHAVE WITH THESE SPOTS ALL OVER MY CHIN.

IF YOU HAD SORE, SWOLLEN BREASTS, YOU WOULDN'T WANT TO BE CUDDLED EITHER.

I CAN'T POSSIBLY CLEAN THE CAR WITH THIS NAGGING BACKACHE.

MY STOMACH ACHES AND IT'S SO BLOATED MY BOSS ASKED IF I WAS PREGNANT.

I'LL NEVER CLIMB THE LADDER OF SUCCESS WITH LEGS THIS WOBBLY ONCE A MONTH.

Have you ever wondered how men would carry on if they had periods?

At the risk of sounding sexist, we must observe that men can be terrible babies when they're ill.

A cold so easily becomes 'flu.' A headache, 'migraine.' Indigestion, a 'suspected heart attack.'

If men had periods, the cry would go up for the 3-week month, never mind the 5-day week.

The fact is, it's women who have the periods. Month after month after month . . . for about 35 years.

And far from carrying on, women are busy, for the most part, soldiering on.

We like to think we're some help.

As the chart shows, there are Dr White's products designed to make your life a bit more bearable, whatever kind of periods you have to put up with.

And whatever your personal preferences might be.

Unlike most other sanitary protection manufacturers, we have no axe to grind in the tampons versus towels war: we make both. And we make both exceptionally well.

Dr White's Contour tampons have rounded end applicators, so insertion doesn't make you catch your breath…or anything.

Dr White's Panty Pads have a unique Tendasoft cover to keep you drier and more comfortable.

And Dr White's Maxi press-on has two widely-spaced adhesive strips running the length of the towel, so it stays securely put whether you're climbing a mountain or, indeed, the ladder of success.

After 104 years in the business, we aren't naive enough to imagine we could make your period a lot of laughs, exactly.

But we're certain we can make it less of a (dare we say it?) bl**dy nuisance.

WHICH DR. WHITE'S TOWELS AND TAMPONS WILL SUIT YOU BEST?				
IF YOUR PERIOD IS:	Light	Medium	Heavy	Very Heavy
Looped Towel	Dr White's No. 1	Dr White's No. 1 or 2	Dr White's No. 2	Dr White's No. 2 or 3
Press-on Towel	Dr White's Panty Pads Regular	Dr White's Maxi or Panty Pads Super	Dr White's Maxi or Panty Pads Super	Dr White's Maxi
Press-on Mini Towel	Dr White's Fastidia			
Applicator Tampon	Dr White's Contour Regular	Dr White's Contour Super or Regular	Dr White's Contour Super	

Dr White's Towels and Tampons.
Help make your period less of a problem.

IF YOU'RE FINDING YOUR PERIOD A PROBLEM, PLEASE FEEL FREE TO WRITE TO SISTER MARION AT LILIA WHITE LTD, ALUM ROCK ROAD, BIRMINGHAM B8 3DZ

Brief: contemporize the image of Dr White's while maintaining the brand's authority. Help make BBH famous. Recognition: D&AD Press Silver, D&AD Copywriting Silver. Art director: John Hegarty.

Claudine went to the Ladies to power her nose.

Brief: present Pernod as the authentic Parisian spirit. Interesting from a copywriting point of view in that it plays around with language. Recognition: short–listed in several award schemes. Illustrator: Graham Rawle. Art director: Peter Harold.

GOLDEN SHRED GETS ITS TANG
FROM SEVILLE ORANGES.

SOME MARMALADES DON'T.

Brief: emphasize the quality and heritage of Golden Shred. Help make BBH famous. Recognition: D&AD Poster Gold and Silver. Art director: John Hegarty.

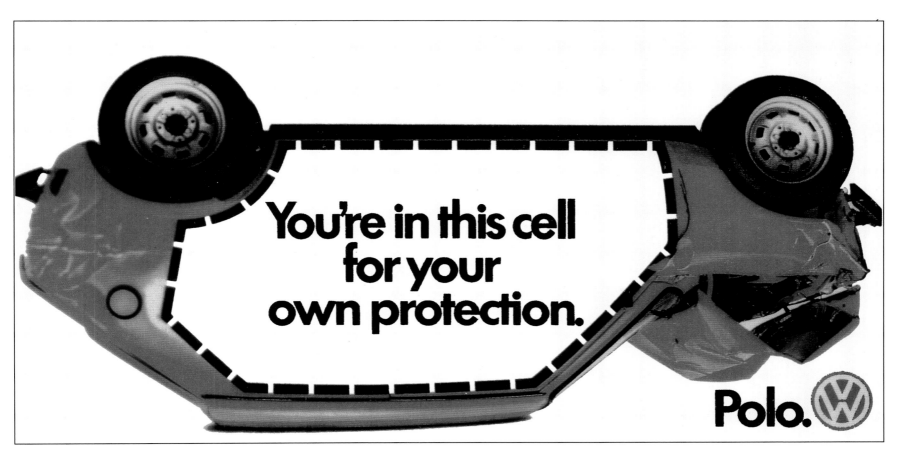

You're in this cell
for your
own protection.

Polo.

Brief: present the Polo as the best small hatchback in the world. Recognition: D&AD Poster Silver. Art director: Peter Harold.

Brief: communicate the build quality and advanced technology of Creda appliances. Recognition: D&AD entry. Campaign Poster Silver. Art director: Peter Harold.

Brief: impress art directors with the quality of Studio 10's retouching. Make David Taylor richer and more famous. Recognition: D&AD entry, Campaign Press Silver. Art director: Derek Hass.

"You can't, you're the boss."

Everybody has bad days. Even bosses.

But when you're the boss of a small business, a bad day can get out of proportion.

In a big company, you'd probably be surrounded by experts in finance, sales, personnel, marketing, production and so on.

People you could talk to, argue with, try your ideas on, blame, have lunch with, confide in and who would generally make you feel better.

But when you're the boss of a small business, you're on your own.

At ICFC we've learnt quite a lot about the growing pains of small businesses.

We've helped nearly 5,000 of them over the last 34 years.

And we've usually found that some friendly advice and somewhere between £5,000 and £2 million can brighten up the blackest day.

ICFC
The smaller business's biggest source of long-term money.

INDUSTRIAL AND COMMERCIAL FINANCE CORPORATION LIMITED. ABERDEEN 0224 53028. BIRMINGHAM 021-236 9531. BRIGHTON 0273 24391. BRISTOL 0272 292081. CAMBRIDGE 0223 62126. CARDIFF 0222 34021. EDINBURGH 031-226 3885. GLASGOW 041-221 4456. LEEDS 0532 30511. LEICESTER 0533 26854. LIVERPOOL 051-236 2944. LONDON 01-928 7822. MANCHESTER 061-833 9511. NEWCASTLE 0632 815221. NOTTINGHAM 0602 47691. READING 0734 861943. SHEFFIELD 0742 664561. SOUTHAMPTON 0703 32044.

Brief: offer owners of small businesses a loan to help them survive and prosper. Be sympathetic to current difficulties (not hard as I wrote this by candlelight during the 3–day week). Recognition: D&AD entries in press and copy sections. Art director: Peter Harold.

Chris O'Shea left school at 16 and went straight into advertising. His first agency of note was French Gold Abbott where he stayed for five years. Then he moved to the fledgling Abbott Mead Vickers. After five years he thought that there must be more to life than advertising, so he resigned and became a truck driver. After six months he realised there wasn't, and rejoined AMV for four more years. In 1984 he left to become copy chief at Lowe-Howard Spink and two years later became joint executive creative director with art director Ken Hoggins. In 1989 they moved to help Chiat Day set up their London office. In 1991 they left to found their own agency Banks Hoggins O'Shea.

This probably won't be the best piece of copy you've ever read. But then again if it helps you write the best piece of copy you've ever written, I'm sure you won't complain.

I'll start with where I start.

If it's an ad that has the faintest whiff of an award about it, I go into the bathroom at home with an HB pencil, an A3 pad, 2 old annuals and lock the door.

The pencil and pad are because mankind, for all its genius, still hasn't come up with a quicker way of transferring thoughts from the brain to paper.

The old annuals are because I always begin by reading through dozens of good ads in order to fill my mind with quality writing. (This is based on the principle that you'll do more for your tennis game by partnering Pete Sampras than the nerd in the next office.)

And the bathroom? Because I need solitude.

I begin by drawing a line from top to bottom of the pad two-thirds of the way across it.

The larger portion, on the left, is where I'll write the actual copy.

And the smaller is to serve as an 'ideas repository' for later use — pleasing phrases, thoughts for the ending, interesting stylistic touches — that will dart into my sieve-like brain as I'm writing and, unless noted down, be lost forever.

Then I think about structure.

If there is any secret to writing copy it is, to my mind, simply a matter of setting down information in the correct order. If I can get this right, the argument will flow smoothly, moving logically from one point to the next.

Then I start writing. And stop. And start. And stop.

Is it just me, or is the opening paragraph never, ever easy? (I'll often write four or five different ones before deciding on the best route into an ad.)

All the while I have fixed in my mind a mental picture of who will read what I'm writing.

I don't mean "AB males aged 35-44 with a promiscuous attitude to white spirits." I mean I think of an actual person, be it a friend, neighbour or relation who is in the target audience.

When I see that person in my mind, I know what will appeal to them.

That way I can write copy the way I believe all copy should be written: as a conversation between two human beings rather than an announcement from manufacturer to consumer.

As I'm writing I try to keep it simple.

This dictates that I write in 'spoken' rather than 'written' English.

(A fact which neatly avoids any criticism of this piece from all you eagle-eyed grammarians out there.)

The temptation is always to indulge in verbal gymnastics. It's taken me a long time to learn that, while they may impress your peers, they serve only to obscure communication. (An old but very good writer once told me "You're paid to make clients' products look clever, not yourself.")

I also try to remember that I have more than the 26 letters of the alphabet at my disposal. I have colons, semi-colons, italics, dashes, question marks, brackets, strokes, even (yes!) exclamation marks. Used sparingly, they can add richness and texture.

And now the vexed question of length.

I love long copy.

Holding someone's attention for three minutes has to be better than whizzing through six sales points in 30 seconds.

It allows me to build, layer by layer, a well-reasoned argument that hopefully leads the reader to the inescapable conclusion that the product I'm telling him or her about is better than anyone else's.

That said, however, if it comes out too long for what Ken Hoggins, my art director, has in mind, I cut it. (Cutting invariably improves copy.)

But if it comes out too short, I don't add to it. Padding always shows. (I just try to persuade Ken to set the type bigger.)

As I near the end of a piece I check the rhythm and cadence by reading it again and again. Out loud. In a phoney American accent.

(If you think that's crazy, don't call me, call David Abbott. He gave me this tip.)

What next?

Oh yes. The really inspired / poignant / rib-ticklingly funny last paragraph.

That's always a problem, isn't it?

WE'D LIKE TO TALK ABOUT SOMETHING GIN ADVERTISEMENTS SELDOM MENTION.

HAS it never struck you as strange that most gin advertisements make very little mention of the gin they are advertising?

You will see beautiful people in equally beautiful locations.

You will read witty and entertaining slogans.

You will see enticing photographs of bottles containing colourless liquid.

But what is actually *in* the bottle they wish you to buy?

PERHAPS the reason they tell you very little is because, in truth, there is very little to tell. One good quality gin is much the same as another.

In contrast, Bombay Sapphire stands apart from them all.

Indeed, its refined and gentle flavour can come as something of a revelation to the most discerning of gin drinkers.

THERE are two reasons for this. The ingredients we use. And the unique method of distillation we employ.

At this point we should perhaps introduce you to the man who, more than anyone else, has the responsibility of producing what is the world's finest gin.

His name is Mr Ian Hamilton and he is our Master Distiller.

Now aged 53, Mr Hamilton joined the distillery at the age of 16, and there can be few men on this earth who know more about gin.

Although he has in his time produced many gins, he regards Bombay Sapphire as his supreme achievement. And we need hardly add that it is also his favourite drink. (He takes it with ice and a little tonic, but *no* lemon, since he feels it is represented perfectly adequately in the original recipe.)

MR Hamilton, a master of understatement, will tell you that gin is basically nothing more than grain spirit flavoured with natural ingredients called 'botanicals.'

The cheaper gins use only Juniper and two or perhaps three other botanicals. (Hence the harshness of their flavour.)

The premium quality gins (including, probably, the one you drink) tend to use four or maybe even five botanicals. These will be *Juniper Berries, Coriander Seeds, Angelica* and *Lemon* or *Orange Peel*.

When Mr Hamilton distils Bombay Sapphire, he uses no less than ten.

He will also include *Orris Root* from Tuscany. *Liquorice* from China. *Almonds* from Spain. *Cassia Bark* from Indo-China. *Cubeb Berries* from Java. And, from West Africa, the exquisitely named *Grains of Paradise*.

Why so many?

Because, in the view of **GIN.** Mr Hamilton, if any fewer were used a single flavour would tend to dominate and the perfect balance of subtle flavours would be lost.

As important as the number of botanicals in our gin is the quality of each.

It is interesting to note that when Mr Hamilton examines samples he is unaware of their cost, lest financial considerations influence his thinking.

HE makes his choice by smelling, biting, chewing and rubbing. Only then, when a firm order has been placed, is he informed of their price.

(It will come as no surprise to learn that almost invariably he chooses the costliest.)

But botanicals, however many and however good, will not alone impart the delicateness of flavour that characterises Bombay Sapphire.

THE real secret is the manner in which it is distilled.

The normal method of producing quality London Dry Gin is to add the botanicals to grain spirit in a still, boil up the whole mixture and then condense the vapour.

However, Bombay Sapphire employs an altogether different method.

One that is, to the best of our knowledge, unique in the world.

Instead of boiling up the spirit with the botanicals, ours is distilled *alone*.

This difference is crucial.

It means that the spirit is already in *vapour* form when it first comes into contact with the botanicals, which are housed in a perforated copper basket above the still.

In this way the spirit vapour defuses slowly through them, absorbing the delicate aroma of each to create a balance of flavour unparalleled in any other gin.

SO much for the science of distilling Bombay Sapphire.

But what of the art of Mr Hamilton?

When a distillation is about to take place one of the first jobs of Mr Hamilton and his 3 Assistant Distillers is to pack the botanicals basket.

Like the still, the basket was fashioned from heavy gauge copper more than 130 years ago.

The exact proportions of each botanical are something that Mr Hamilton will not reveal. (It is something that is known to only 4 people in the world.)

When pressed all he will say is that the recipe is one that dates back to 1761.

When the botanicals basket has been packed to Mr Hamilton's satisfaction a valve is opened which allows steam to circulate around the jacket at the bottom of the still containing the grain spirit. (Incidentally, we use only 100% pure neutral spirit from Scotland.)

After an hour or so the spirit begins to vapourise and pass upward through the botanicals basket.

AT this point a heady alcoholic fragrance begins to permeate the distillery room.

(On one occasion, the staff were actually blood tested to ascertain whether inhalation of this pungent aroma rendered them ever so slightly incapacitated. All we can say is that nothing was proved.)

The Master Distiller must now perform his most crucial role.

As in the distillation of Scotland's finest malt whiskies the first and last stages of the process produce 'feints'. Basically, this is spirit of substandard strength or quality.

Periodically Mr Hamilton will draw off a little gin.

He must judge the precise moment when the 'feints' turn to the 'middle cut' which will be routed into a receiving tank and eventually become Bombay Sapphire.

To aid him, he has no computers, no chemical analysis printouts, no digital displays.

All he has is his nose, his palate and 37 years of experience.

After anything from six to six and a half hours (every distillation is different) Mr Hamilton will judge the moment when the botanicals have yielded the best of their flavour and declare any further distillate to be 'feints.'

THE next stage is for the 'middle cut' to be blended with water to reduce it to the correct alcoholic proof.

Even here Bombay Sapphire may differ from the gin you normally drink.

A certain best selling gin has recently reduced its proof to 37½% across Europe. We are delighted to report ours will never be less than 40%, because that is what the discerning customer wants.

Now one might imagine all that remains to be done is to put the gin into the translucent sapphire blue bottle that so distinguishes Bombay Sapphire. (If you were wondering, the gin itself is not blue.)

Well, not quite all.

EVERY single new production must first be tasted by a panel which includes the Master Distiller, the Quality Control Manager and the Managing Director.

And only when they have judged it to be the very finest London Dry Gin can it be released for sale around the world.

By now you will doubtless realise that the way we produce our gin is hardly the most cost efficient.

With this in mind, can we turn briefly to the ticklish subject of Bombay Sapphire's price?

To be blunt, it is somewhat more expensive than other premium gins.

But as with most things in this life, the very best quality invariably requires one to make a little extra outlay.

Finally we would like to thank you for taking the time to read such a lengthy advertisement.

Your reward, we promise, will be your first taste of Bombay Sapphire Gin.

ULTIMATELY, THERE IS BOMBAY SAPPHIRE.

May we recommend the liver and bacon to follow?

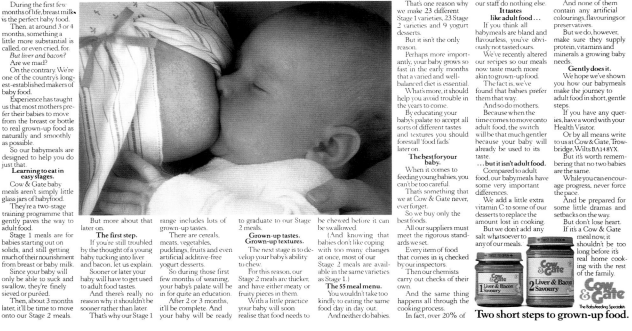

During the first few months of life, breast milk is the perfect baby food.

Then, at around 3 or 4 months, something a little more substantial is called, or even cried, for.

But liver and bacon? Are we mad?

On the contrary. We're one of the country's longest-established makers of baby food.

Experience has taught us that most mothers prefer their babies to move from the breast or bottle to real grown-up food as naturally and smoothly as possible.

So our babymeals are designed to help you do just that.

Learning to eat in easy stages.

Cow & Gate baby meals aren't simply little glass jars of babyfood.

They're a two-stage training programme that gently paves the way to adult food.

Stage 1 meals are for babies starting out on solids, and still getting much of their nourishment from breast or baby milk.

Since your baby will only be able to suck and swallow, they're finely sieved or puréed.

Then, about 3 months later, it'll be time to move onto our Stage 2 meals.

But more about that later on.

The first step.

If you're still troubled by the thought of a young baby tucking into liver and bacon, let us explain.

Sooner or later your baby will have to get used to adult food tastes.

And there's really no reason why it shouldn't be sooner rather than later.

That's why our Stage 1 range includes lots of grown-up tastes.

There are cereals, meats, vegetables, puddings, fruits and even artificial additive-free yogurt desserts.

So during those first few months of weaning, your baby's palate will be in for quite an education.

After 2 or 3 months, it'll be complete. And your baby will be ready to graduate to our Stage 2 meals.

Grown-up tastes. Grown-up textures.

The next stage is to develop your baby's ability to chew.

For this reason, our Stage 2 meals are thicker, and have either meaty or fruity pieces in them.

With a little practice your baby will soon realise that food needs to be chewed before it can be swallowed.

The 55 meal menu.

You wouldn't take too kindly to eating the same food day in day out.

And neither do babies.

That's one reason why we make 23 different Stage 1 varieties, 23 Stage 2 varieties and 9 yogurt desserts.

But it isn't the only reason.

Perhaps more importantly, your baby grows so fast in the early months that a varied and well-balanced diet is essential.

What's more, it should help you avoid trouble in the years to come.

By educating your baby's palate to accept all sorts of different tastes and textures you should forestall 'food fads' later on.

The best for your baby.

When it comes to feeding young babies, you can't be too careful.

That's something that we at Cow & Gate never, ever forget.

So we buy only the best foods.

All our suppliers must meet the rigorous standards we set.

Every item of food that comes in is checked by our inspectors.

Then our chemists carry out checks of their own.

And the same thing happens all through the cooking process.

In fact, over 20% of our staff do nothing else.

It tastes like adult food…

If you think all babymeals are bland and flavourless, you've obviously not tasted ours.

We've recently altered our recipes so our meals now taste much more akin to grown-up food.

The fact is, we've found that babies prefer them that way.

And so do mothers.

Because when the time comes to move onto adult food, the switch will be that much gentler because your baby will already be used to its taste.

…but it isn't adult food.

Compared to adult food, our babymeals have some very important differences.

We add a little extra vitamin C to some of our desserts to replace the amount lost in cooking.

But we don't add any salt whatsoever to any of our meals.

And none of them contain any artificial colourings, flavourings or preservatives.

But we do, however, make sure they supply protein, vitamins and minerals a growing baby needs.

Gently does it.

We hope we've shown you how our babymeals make the journey to adult food in short, gentle steps.

If you have any queries, have a word with your Health Visitor.

Or by all means write to us at Cow & Gate, Trowbridge, Wilts BA14 8YX.

But it's worth remembering that no two babies are the same.

While you can encourage progress, never force the pace.

And be prepared for some little dramas and setbacks on the way.

But don't lose heart.

If it's a Cow & Gate meal now, it shouldn't be too long before it's real home cooking with the rest of the family.

Cow & Gate The Babyfeeding Specialists

Two short steps to grown-up food.

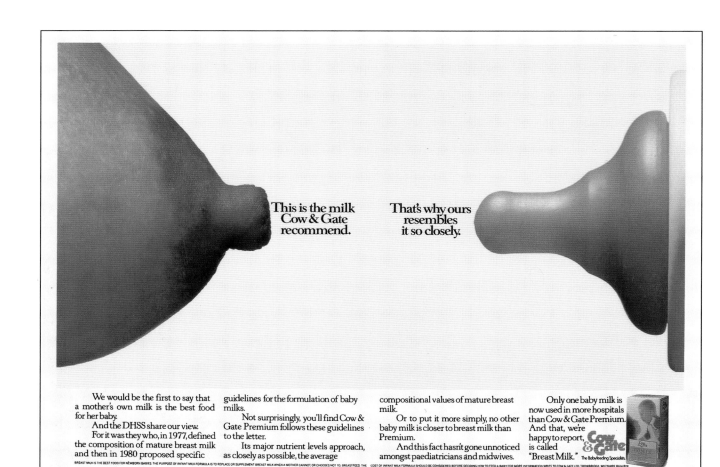

This is the milk Cow & Gate recommend.

That's why ours resembles it so closely.

We would be the first to say that a mother's own milk is the best food for her baby.

And the DHSS share our view.

For it was they who, in 1977, defined the composition of mature breast milk and then in 1980 proposed specific guidelines for the formulation of baby milks.

Not surprisingly, you'll find Cow & Gate Premium follows these guidelines to the letter.

Its major nutrient levels approach, as closely as possible, the average compositional values of mature breast milk.

Or to put it more simply, no other baby milk is closer to breast milk than Premium.

And this fact hasn't gone unnoticed amongst paediatricians and midwives.

Only one baby milk is now used in more hospitals than Cow & Gate Premium.

And that, we're happy to report, is called "Breast Milk." **Cow & Gate** The Babyfeeding Specialists

YES, BUT DID THEY GET PROMOTED?

"Don't rock the boat." "Why put your head above the trench?" "Play it safe." "Remember: an opportunity missed is a mistake avoided."

The argument for buying from one of the old-guard computer makers is, for many, as seductive as it is irrefutable.

They can justifiably argue that their systems will do a job that is adequate, acceptable and competent.

Adequate? Acceptable? Competent?

Come, come. Are these the words you would want on your annual performance review?

Will they single you out as one who's destined for the boardroom?

Of course they won't.

So let us look at an alternative plan of action.

When the talk turns to the purchase of new PCs, let slip to the powers that be that you've been burning the midnight oil.

Tell them your digging and delving has unearthed this extremely interesting computer manufacturer called Dell.

Tell them Dell operate a system called 'Direct Relationship Marketing'.

Tell them that, in English, this means Dell don't sell through dealers, but work directly with their customers.

Tell them this allows your company to have a direct working relationship with the people who actually design and build the PCs with no middleman muscling in to confuse matters.

Then deliver this little gem:

Tell them Dell's way of working will save substantial amounts of money. Not just in the initial purchase price or rental, but in total operating costs over the years.

Tell them Dell have systems, and everything that goes with them, from entry-level 286s to mighty networking 486 models.

Tell them you've already had a foretaste of the benefits working direct can bring.

Tell them you've spoken to Dell. You've discussed your company's business. You've outlined your objectives. And, together, you've devised a solution that'll cope more than admirably.

Tell them it can be in and working within days.

Promise them total peace of mind by announcing that with it comes a lifetime

of free technical advice and support.

Tell them that if ever a snag occurs it won't be a problem, since Dell solve 90% of them over the phone there and then.

(And if they can't, they will have an engineer on the job the next working day.)

Tell them this is doubtless one reason Dell was rated way above everyone else in the prestigious Computer Weekly/Datapro user-satisfaction poll.

Now at this point some bright spark may well say "Sounds good in theory. But I'm not sure we should work with a company we don't know from Adam."

So tell them that Dell is the 7th largest PC manufacturer in the States.

Tell them they've been phenomenally successful on this side of the Atlantic too.

Tell them over half Dell's sales now go to The Times Top 1000 companies such as BP and Thorn EMI.

But *don't* tell them about this advertisement.

And don't tell them all you really did was pick up the phone or fill in the coupon.

After all, you don't want to make it look too easy, do you?

Name _____ Position _____

Company _____ Address _____

_____ Postcode _____ Telephone _____

0800 414535

IT'S BEST TO BE DIRECT.

Tim Riley worked at BMP, Simons Palmer and Leagas Delaney before joining BBH in March 1993. He's | *won three D&AD silvers, several Campaign Press and Poster awards and a Gold at Cannes.*

I have a confession to make, and it's an unusual one for a copywriter.

I don't like writing copy.

This isn't as much of a problem as you might think, though.

Because the truth is, nobody likes reading copy either.

People buy magazines to read the articles, not the ads.

You're lucky if people notice your work at all.

So I always try to make the headlines tell as much of the story as possible.

(Consequently, I end up with some very long headlines.)

Occasionally though, there'll be ads where writing detailed copy is unavoidable.

What do you do then?

You get somebody to help you.

When I was a junior at BMP, there were three very good writers, Alan Tilby, Dave Watkinson and Alan Curson, who were patient enough to read through my copy and suggest improvements.

Never was this more eloquently done than when Al Tilby looked at what I'd written, carefully tore it in half, then in half again, and let the pieces flutter gently into his wastepaper bin.

"You can do better than this," he said.

I did.

The other way I learnt was by reading old ads, over and over again.

One I always admired was the Health Education poster, "This is what happens when a fly lands on your food".

I liked the way the writers, Charles Saatchi and Michael Coughlan, made the story so compelling with such a deadpan, factual style.

In 73 words of copy they use only one adjective.

(And the one they do use, 'runny', is a killer.)

When Peter Gausis and I did the ad you see here for The Guardian's serialisation of the H–Block hunger strike story, I tried to use the same approach.

We simply set down the bare facts.

There's also a limit to the number of words you can fit on a cigarette paper.

The Ian Rush DPS I did with Andy McKay was Simons Palmer's first press ad for Nike.

Nervous at following the likes of Dan Wieden and Jim Riswold, I read through a whole stack of their proofs to try to get the right tone of voice for the copy.

(Looking at it now though, I wonder if I was right to use such an American style to describe something as British as foot–ball.)

Old ads aren't the only things you can read for inspiration.

Given a poster to do about Michael Jordan, Andy and I found an article about him in an old copy of American Esquire.

At one point, the author described Jordan's game as "an ongoing dialectic with Isaac Newton".

Once we'd looked up 'dialectic' in the dictionary, it was a short step to "Michael Jordan 1 Isaac Newton 0".

But perhaps the best advice on actually writing copy comes from an ad.

It was written for VW in 1962 by, I think, John Withers.

Underneath the headline, "How to do a Volkswagen ad", the copy concludes:

Don't exaggerate.

Call a spade a spade. And a suspension a suspension. Not something like 'orbital cushioning'.

Talk to the reader, don't shout. He can hear you. Especially if you talk sense.

Pencil sharp?

You're on your own.

During the H-Block hunger strike, IRA prisoners wrote thousands of messages on cigarette papers like this one. Each message was screwed up into a ball, hidden in a prisoner's anus, slipped to a visitor, hidden again in the visitor's mouth, then taken to IRA headquarters. Now you can read these messages — the inside story of the hunger strike, 'Ten Men Dead' by David Beresford starts tomorrow in the Guardian

Agency: BMP. Art Director: Perer Gausis.

GOALKEEPERS. THE BAD NEWS IS HE WEARS NIKE. THERE IS NO GOOD NEWS.

You think Ian's pleased that Arsenal won the championship last season? You think he's happy that Alan Smith scored more goals than he did? So. He's going to take it out on someone, right? In his brand new Nike boots. What's that? You've heard Dukla Prague are looking for a keeper? Catch on pretty fast, don't you?

Agency: Simons Palmer. Art Director: Andy McKay.

Agency: Simons Palmer. Art Director: Andy McKay.

Agency: BMP. Art Director: Perer Gausis.

NOT ALL MARRIED MEN HAVE AFFAIRS WITH WOMEN.

According to the dictionary, a bisexual man is simply 'one who has sex with both men and women.'

As a way of life, however, bisexuality can prove to be anything but simple.

Yet few of the problems bisexual men have faced in the past can compare with the one that confronts them now.

HIV. The virus that leads to AIDS.

The Human Immunodeficiency Virus is transmitted when infected semen, blood or vaginal fluid enters the body.

And of all sexual activities, unprotected anal intercourse presents the highest risk.

Even using a condom won't make it completely safe.

If you'd like more information about what's safe and what isn't, ring 0800 838 575.

Lines are open from 4pm to 10pm daily. All calls are free of charge and completely confidential.

Agency: BMP. Art Director: Perer Gausis.

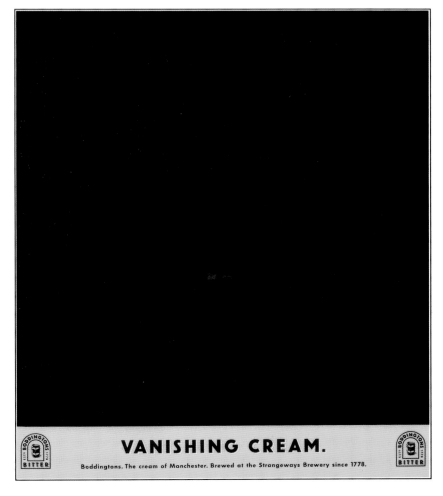

VANISHING CREAM.
Boddingtons. The cream of Manchester. Brewed at the Strangeways Brewery since 1778.

Agency: BBH. Art Director: Mike Wells.

In thirty-something years in the advertising business, I've worked in agencies of all shapes and sizes – from four people when we started Wight, Collins, Rutherford Scott in 1979 to 36, Saatchis when I joined, to several hundred, Saatchis when I left. On the way I worked for the Sunday Times (great fun) to Lintas (well, different), and others. I've been called everything from trainee copywriter to World Creative Great Panjandrum.

I've worked in Australia, the US, briefly, the Far East, even more briefly. I've sat on the D&AD Executive committee, and chaired The British Television Advertising awards jury. So it's been fun, and it still is. But in all that time and in all those places, in truth, I've just done one thing. Think up ads, and write them. (OK, two things.) Sometimes good, mostly so-so, sometimes crummy. But it's what I do best, and it's certainly given me the most joy and dismay and satisfaction.

He bashed a knife loudly against a tin tray. Bang! Bang! Bang!... The din cut through the rowdy street market, and heads swivelled towards it.

"Ever tried to cut yer 'froat with a blunt knife?", he shouted, sawing at his jugular with mock frustration. An interested crowd started to gather round him.

Hint 1. Get attention. An invisible ad is not an effective ad.

"Better still, ladies. Ever tried to cut yer old man's 'froat with a blunt knife?" The laughter attracted more people. What was going on here? This might be fun.

Hint 2. Intrigue your reader. But not irrelevantly. Lead him or her in the right direction.

"I'll tell you wot is murder ladies. Have you ever tried to cut the rind off a rasher, or fillet a fish or string runner beans with a knife like this?" I started to lose interest, and was about to move off when I noticed that several of the women were nodding in recollection. He'd struck a chord. I stuck around.

Hint 3. Single out your target. Understand their problems, hopes and needs. Ignore everyone else.

He scornfully flung aside the knife, and produced his "little miracle" as he called it. It looked just like a knife to me, but apparently it was like no other knife we'd ever seen. He told us it was as sharp after six months of non-stop demonstrations as the day he'd discovered it. "Watch this", he said.

And for the next few minutes with impressive dexterity, he sliced beans, sharpened a pencil, peeled an avocado, chopped a prawn...even shaved a slice from a stone.

Hint 4. Always demonstrate your product's superiority if you possibly can.

As he worked, he talked. He told us that the metal was discovered through space research, that micro-surgeons used specially fine scalpels made from it, and that this "little miracle" (he wouldn't call it a knife) was banned from general sale in some countries, because it was "too easy to cut yer old man's 'froat with it".

Hint 5. Facts are more persuasive than empty claims. (But a little humour can sugar the pill.)

He told us we were lucky to be standing there, because the only other place he knew where we'd find it "was at 'arrods, where it cost ten quid. No tell a lie, £9.99 – 'arrods give you back 1p back from a tenner".

Hint 6. Create a desire – a shortage perhaps.

Hint 7. Give the product credibility (Harrods, in this case).

However, he would save us the inconvenience of going all the way to Harrods. And better still he'd give us more than one penny back. In fact, he'd give us more than one pound back. How much? Five pound? No, he was daft, but it was his nipper's birthday party, he was in a hurry to get away... so just this once he'd give us eight pounds back from a ten pound note. Just £2 for this "little miracle", but he only had a few, so.......

A sea of hands shot towards him wildly waving banknotes to catch his eye.

Hint 8. Clinch the sale. Make the buyer want to do something, and make him do it.

As I walked away clutching my little miracle I began to sense that I had a lot to learn about persuasive selling, and that any aspiring copywriter could do a lot worse than go into the streets and watch a real pro like this at work.

That was some time ago, and I hope the ads I've chosen to show you incorporate at least some of the wiles and wisdom I heard that day.

What are your chances of getting pregnant tonight?

120,000 unwanted babies are born in Britain every year. The more you know about contraception, the less chance you've got of having an unwanted baby. How much do you know?

Questions

1. How many children can a woman have?
2. If 'withdrawal' has been good enough for hundreds of years, what's wrong with it now?
3. Does swallowing a whole packet of the Pill bring on an abortion?
4. Do spermicides offer protection against VD?
5. How can one woman make another pregnant?
6. What does family planning advice in a clinic cost?
7. Which is the odd one out? The Margulies Spiral, Hall Stone Ring, Golden Square, Lippés Loop.

8. Would these be safe in June?
9. Can a virgin wear a loop?
10. Does a woman need to worry about contraception after she's had the menopause?
11. Who first practised birth control? The Ancient Egyptians, The Greeks, The Romans, The Elizabethans or The Victorians?
12. What's wrong with douching to prevent pregnancy?
13. How long should you leave a cap in place after intercourse?
14. What can a family planning clinic tell you that a friend can't?

15. How can this help stop a baby?
16. Will the loop make your periods more painful?
17. Is it safer to make love before a period or after a period?
18. Are the cheap forms of contraception always the least effective?
19. Does it help to stop babies if you stand during intercourse?
20. How long do you have to wait in a family planning clinic?

21. How can alcohol make you pregnant?
22. Do you become unusually fertile when you stop taking the Pill?
23. Do all the family planning clinics welcome single girls?

24. How would you feel with this inside you?
25. Can a man have a climax after a vasectomy?
26. Is there a special method of contraception for young girls?
27. Where is your nearest family planning clinic?

Answers

1. A healthy woman could bear a baby every year. Perhaps 20 or 25 children. Could you bear the thought?
2. The Victorians practised 'withdrawal.' In those 60 years the population of Britain rose from 18,000,000 to 37,000,000. 'Withdrawal' is chancey because a man can release sperm before he reaches orgasm. So all the willpower needed and frustration caused by withdrawing can be wasted.
3. No.
4. Not at the moment. Spermicides kill sperms, not VD germs. However scientists are working on it.
5. Just by talking to her, and giving her bad advice. Too many women would rather listen to friends about contraception than go to a family planning clinic where help is friendly, private and, above all, accurate.
6. Before April 1st it will be free in some clinics, about a couple of pounds in others. After April 1st all advice, examinations and fitting will be free at National Health Clinics. And the contraceptives, themselves will be available on prescription (20p). Much cheaper than an unwanted baby.
7. They're all names of intra-uterine devices, except, Golden Square— a famous place in London.
8. Probably. The dates stamped on French Letter packets allow a certain margin of error—but you wouldn't be wise to bank on it.
9. No. The loop is for the woman who has already had intercourse—or, better still, had a baby. And very effective, too. But a virgin can't be fitted with a loop.
10. A woman can still have a baby two years after her last period. The more recently she's had children the greater the risk.
11. Even the Ancient Egyptians, 3000 years ago, concocted strange contraceptive creams. Obviously they weren't too keen to become mummies, either.
12. It doesn't work, and it can cause infection.
13. Six hours, at least. You can leave it in longer, but not less.
14. Your friend may tell you what's best for your friend. A doctor or clinic will tell you what's best for you. Women differ both emotionally and physically, and need different contraceptives.

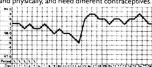

15. After a woman has ovulated (that's when she's most fertile) her temperature rises. And three days after ovulation she's 'safe' to make love. So a thermometer can help discover the 'safe' period. Unfortunately a touch of 'flu, say, can also put your temperature up, which is confusing.
16. If you have comfortable periods before you have a loop fitted, you are unlikely to develop painful periods afterwards. If you do you should consult your clinic or doctor.
17. The so-called 'safe' period is the eight or nine days before a period. Unfortunately while you know when one period ends, it is impossible to be sure when the next will start. Periods can be regular for months and then suddenly vary. So to use the 'safe' period with security could restrict your lovemaking drastically.
18. Not necessarily. The loop and sterilisation are both inexpensive, and very effective. However, the very cheapest methods, 'withdrawal' and the 'safe' period are much less safe.

19. No. Nor does holding your breath during orgasm. Or jumping up and down after, or sneezing before, intercourse. There's more super-stitious nonsense talked about birth control than anything else.
20. You might have to wait a little while. But seldom more than 20 or 30 minutes—and never as long as nine months.
21. It can make you slapdash about your contraceptive. And it can lower a girl's resistance. A few large tots on a Saturday night can mean a tiny tot nine months later.
22. No. Nor are you more likely to have twins.
23. No one, single or married, man or woman, should think they will be frowned on at a family planning clinic. These clinics are there to stop unwanted babies, and single girls seldom want babies.
24. You would feel very secure. This is an IUD, one of the safest contraceptives of all. It may not look very comfortable, but if you've already had a baby, you probably wouldn't feel it at all.
25. Yes. And he does. Sperms are only a tiny proportion of the fluid when a man has a climax. A vasectomy just stops the sperms reaching the fluid.
26. It's tragic to see the number of girls in their early teens who become pregnant every year. The most effective form of contraception for these young girls (or anyone else) is not to have sex. Failing that, one can only say the more a young person knows about contraception the better.
27. If you don't know, contact your local health department, your family doctor, look under 'Family Planning' in the telephone directory or Yellow Pages—or write to, The Health Education Council, 78 New Oxford Street, WC1A 1AH.

The Health Education Council

I knew I'd written a pretty fair ad when I went into my office one lunch hour to find half a dozen secretaries gathered round my pin board engrossed. I think my street trader would approve. A headline to catch attention – and especially of the young people it was aimed at. Masses of information (but not, I think, too much). And a call to action.

You can tell a melon's perfect by squeezing it.

You can tell a pear's perfect by sniffing it.

You can tell a banana's perfect by peeling it.

You can tell a plum's perfect by pinching it.

You can tell an apple's perfect by shaking it.

JAFFA

You can tell a grapefruit's perfect just by reading it.

If it doesn't say Jaffa it's not a Jaffa.

WHAT MAKES THIS SUCH A GOOD ADVERTISEMENT?

1. You noticed it.
This is, after all, the First Rule of Advertising, isn't it? (See page 2 of the book).

2. You're reading it.
And, presumably, you're doing so because it may offer something useful, even if it's only information. (See page 3 of the book).
What book? Wait.

3. It's offering you something you've always wanted.
At this stage, you're finding out that, not only is it offering you an intangible morsel of useful information, but a book as well.
A book full of tips that could save you fortunes, or help you make millions.
Maybe.

4. It tells you how to get it.
The book is free
You'll notice we didn't put that piece of information in the headline. Neither did we print it in red, or in a starburst, or even in big letters.
This is because the fact that it is free is not the most important thing about it.
And also because we really only want to give it away to people who are serious about good advertisements. (See headline).
To get your free book, call Hong Kong 762 878, or Kuala Lumpur 298 4611, or Singapore 225 8088, or Bangkok 223 6848, or, in Australia, Sydney 957 4132.
And just ask.

5. It does not have a logo.
So, when you first glanced at the ad, you couldn't tell who placed it. So you had to read it. (See page 10 of the Book).
That's why this is such a good ad.

Sadly, I've lost my favourite Jaffa ad. Under the headline: "A word on grapefruit to help you choose the perfect one" was a long copy ad, with sub-heads and exploded diagrams with captions. But every single word of the copy was "Jaffa". The argument that a single word can be more persuasive than a hundred is as worth remembering when writing copy as when buying grapefruits. By the way, I like the Jaffa ad, above, as well.

I wrote this with Neil French in Singapore. I've put it in because, well, I like it, and because it reiterates in print, the techniques the market trader uses so effectively hawking his knife.

"I bet he drinks Carling Black Label."

This isn't an ad, of course, but I'm proud of it because all my son's friends think it's great, and everyone knows it, and that can't be bad. Incidentally it started life as "I bet he drinks a lot of milk", but we didn't win the pitch so it changed drinks. Never throw away a good idea. Never throw away any idea, period.

When Ron Collins and I did this ad in 1980, £4 was a King's ransom to pay for a suntan oil. Better to make a virtue of the price, than slide it in apologetically, later. There was a good story too, about the oil of the Bergamot, later to become such a dirty word in beauty products. This often–imitated ad owes much to Ron's classic art direction. Which brings me to my final piece of advice. Listen to everyone around you. Yes, even account handlers.

How can I defend this poster? I who have gone on record deploring the endless and often mindless use of puns and wordplay in headlines? I said, and I still believe, that such tricks are the first resort (and usually the last) of the lazy. In my defence I would say that just occasionally a word play works a treat. Also it's short. Three words is about right for a poster. Five at most.

John Salmon started his career in advertising as a typographer at Erwin Wasey. He left England in 1957 to gain copywriting experience in Canada and New York, returning eight years later to join Doyle Dane's newly opened office in London. John joined CDP in 1967 and became Creative Director two years later. Since that time, he has been closely involved with the agency's creative output; he is now Group Chairman, responsible for overall creative standards in London and the European network.

Clearly, there are limits to the amount of copy anybody can be expected to read about anything. It varies according to the level of their interest in the subject and the amount that can usefully be said about whatever you're flogging. I believe it was Howard Gossage who first said, "People don't read copy, they read what interests them". Furthermore, I agree with David Ogilvy who said, "The more you tell, the more you sell."

However, first of all you have to attract attention and arouse interest. This is the job of the headline and picture rather than the body copy, and there is a good deal of research which shows that only a small proportion of those who are stopped by an advertisement go on to read more than half of the copy. The copywriter's job is to increase the proportion as much as possible.

Conventional wisdom suggests that the headline and picture should communicate the main message of the ad. But sometimes a curiosity headline (like 'Lemon') will stop an extraordinarily large number of people and provoke an unusual level of interest in the copy.

Those who get engrossed in the copy are the readers most likely to be sold by the ad. It follows that the more people you can encourage to get into the copy and the more you can make them read, the more successful your ad is likely to be.

Writing the first sentence is as difficult as writing the headline. It has to expand the headline idea and lure the reader on to the next sentence. The first line of the Lemon ad is, 'This Volkswagen missed the boat.' According to anecdote, this was the original headline. True or not, there is a lesson here. Save all those headlines you write as you are struggling to come up with the greatest line of your career. Some may find a place in your copy.

You should write from the stand-point of the reader's self interest and base your copy on the benefits, tangible or emotional, offered by your product or service. Develop a tone of voice that will resonate with the particular people you are hoping to nobble. You'll find this easier if you go and talk to some of your potential or actual customers. They will become flesh and blood human beings, rather than anonymous 'consumers'.

One of my reservations about group discussions is that they provide digests of what the respondents say inflected by the researcher which tend to make personal contact with customers seem superfluous.

In direct conversation you will be able to discover how they relate to your product. You'll hear the language they use when they talk about it and the value they place on it. This is likely to be quite different from the terms used by the brand manager to whom the product is the most important thing in the world.

The ability to communicate product benefits to customers in language they find credible and sympathetic is one of the major values an agency offers its clients. Copy should read like a letter from a friend.

The look of the copy is important, too. A uniform mass of grey type may provide the rectangle of texture that your art director wants but it will deter many potential readers. Regardless of the length of your copy, there is no plausible reason for making it uninviting or hard to read.

Generally, use short words, short paragraphs. This will automatically break up the copy into bite-sized portions and make it impossible for the reader to stop.

On the other hand, short paragraphs can result in a lot of widows and this can make copy look bitty and uninviting. So co-operate with your art director and be ready to adjust your words in the interests of getting an attractive setting.

Sometimes the fear of making copy formidably long leads

writers to condense their material too much. Impacted language with a lot of meaning packed into too few words is hard to digest and can be another reason for readers to give up.

Publications vary in the demands they make on readers, both typographically and in the difficulty of their prose. This is because they are addressed to groups with different levels of education and different levels of reading skill. Make your copy slightly less demanding than the editorial matter in both respects.

I always hang on to my copy until I have forgotten the act of writing it. When I look again I invariably want to alter or cut something. I go on doing this until the traffic man snatches it out of my hand.

Copy is the core of advertising. Content matters more than form and an idea isn't an idea unless it can be expressed in words. That is not to say that the visual aspects of advertising aren't vitally important.

To my mind a synthesis of image and words which leaves the reader just enough to do is the ideal to aim for. For example, a picture of a Volkswagen and the word 'Lemon'. Here the reader is virtually compelled to solve the enigma of a paid advertisement which shows a picture of a product and describes it in a totally deprecating manner. The act of solving it makes him a participant before he has read a word of copy. By reading it he becomes involved.

It becomes his.

In this wild, trendy, irresponsible world, Dunn and Company manage to preserve an island of calm.

With men's clothing working itself into a frenzy all about us, we're under pressure to change.

By resisting, we risk being thought stick-in-the muds. Reactionaries even.

But it's a chance we're willing to take.

We prefer to go on building our business as we have been doing for the past 80 years.

After all, we can't grumble. There are 180 Dunn's shops up and down the country.

And right now they're selling our spring range of ready-made suits; thornproofs, twists, tweeds, saxonies and worsteds. Weekend suits that will raise nobody's eyebrows if worn to the office.

Our prices start at 11 gns and go up, a pound or so at a time to £27. At each price we manage to give excellent value.

And here our size is an advantage. We buy fabrics in very large quantities. So we can get them at very keen prices.

It's no exaggeration to say that you could pay half as much again as we charge, to have a suit made-to-measure, and not get cloth as good as we use.

But good value isn't the only thing to recommend our ready-made suits.

With a Dunn's suit you can see exactly what you're buying.

We don't ask you to stand with a length of cloth over your shoulder trying to visualise the finished suit.

And you don't have to wait weeks to find out if you were right.

You can see immediately whether a Dunn's suit fits you. And whether the style suits you.

If it does, you can take it with you. In this respect, we're really rather modern. **Dunn & Co**

In spite of ourselves.

How to beat the Army Officer Selection Board.

It's a fact that only about 20% of the candidates applying to the Army Officer Selection Board pass. In spite of what some disgruntled applicants may tell you however, the Board isn't bent on keeping people out.

Quite the opposite. While setting a necessarily high standard, the Board goes out of its way to help applicants show their stuff.

So we're only going an inch or two further by giving you a few tips that could improve your chances.

Are you a fit person?

First off, don't be in a hurry to present yourself to the Board if you can't run up stairs without blowing like a geyser. Get fit first.

While none of the tests used by the Board demand Olympic standards, they all call for considerable mental effort. And you can't think at your best if you're exhausted by the previous obstacle.

Take the task illustrated for instance. Study it now while you're calm and collected and doubtless a number of possible solutions will occur to you. You can probably imagine yourself giving crisp, explicit orders to your team and them moving across the obstacle with their equipment in a smooth flow of action.

It won't be like that if you're jack-knifed on the grass wheezing for breath. The Board will not have the chance to see how good you really are.

Another thing that will help you over the obstacles is an understanding of levers, pendulums and inclined planes. So if you're rusty brush up.

You don't need a plum in your mouth.

We'd hate anybody who has been to a public school to get the idea that the Board is prejudiced against them.

So if you went to Eton don't waste time hanging around the East End trying to pick up the accent. It will do you no good. And the converse is equally true if you happen to come from the East End.

The Board isn't interested in your style of speech. But it will be keenly interested in what you have to say.

During the time that you spend with the Selection Board you will be interviewed by a Major, a Lieutenant-Colonel, and a Brigadier: possibly by a Major-General and certainly by an Education Officer.

You had better have plenty of material.

Like most people, they enjoy chatting to somebody who has had a bit of experience.

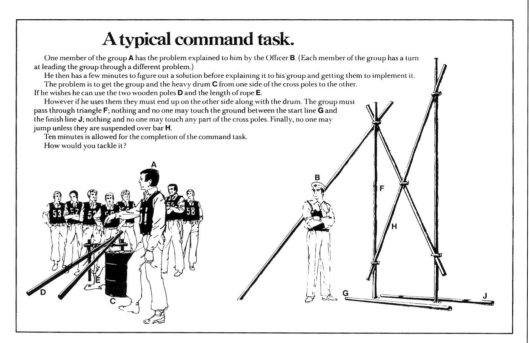

A typical command task.

One member of the group **A** has the problem explained to him by the Officer **B**. (Each member of the group has a turn at leading the group through a different problem.)

He then has a few minutes to figure out a solution before explaining it to his group and getting them to implement it.

The problem is to get the group and the heavy drum **C** from one side of the cross poles to the other.

If he wishes he can use the two wooden poles **D** and the length of rope **E**.

However if he uses them they must end up on the other side along with the drum. The group must pass through triangle **F**; nothing and no one may touch the ground between the start line **G** and the finish line **J**; nothing and no one may touch any part of the cross poles. Finally, no one may jump unless they are suspended over bar **H**.

Ten minutes is allowed for the completion of the command task.

How would you tackle it?

Somebody who has been around and who has met different sorts of people.

They don't want to hear a rundown of the week's television programmes. And if this is the limit of your experience hold off your application until you've branched out a bit.

Buy a rucksack and start working your way around the country. Talk to the crew on your father's yacht. Anything to broaden your contacts.

Understandably, officers like talking to candidates about the Army. So it's worth considering joining the Cadet Force or the University Officer Training Corps. These outfits can give you access to the regiment or corps that interests you. All grist to the mill. You might even consider reading a few books on military subjects.

All the interviewers will be looking for evidence of a keen interest in the Army. And they are not easy to fool. If you aren't interested, really interested, please don't bother them.

One of their favourite questions is 'What will you do if you get turned down by the Board?' Think about it. What are you going to say?

If you can impress your fellow candidates you'll impress the Board.

Besides talking to members of the Board, you'll be talking to your fellow candidates. There will be a group discussion on current affairs which will be led by the group leader and watched by other members of the Board.

So start reading the papers a bit more avidly than you do at the moment.

Later you'll be given a choice of subjects and a quarter of an hour to prepare a lecturette.

You'll also have to present persuasive arguments in favour of your solution to a variety of problems.

So, if you have trouble talking to groups of people, take steps right away. Join a debating society or a drama club. Take a soap box to Speaker's Corner. It won't take you long to overcome the communication problem.

And if you haven't had any experience of organizing groups of people at school you should try your hand with a youth group.

Don't think from all this that the Board expects you to appear before them ready and prepared to take command of a regiment. It's just that we felt that you'll make a better showing if you have some idea of what you're in for.

Remember, the Board want to pass you. But to be worth training at Sandhurst you have to display the qualities (however latent) required of an Army Officer.

If you think you're ready to face the Army Officer Selection Board, and you're under 29, write to: Major K. S. Robson, Army Officer Entry, Dept. F1, Lansdowne House, Berkeley Square, London, W1X 6AA. Tell him about your educational qualifications and your life in general so far.

Army Officer

WHAT WOULD YOU DO IN THESE SITUATIONS?

You answer a call from a neighbour who is disturbed by a domestic shouting match. When you get there the flat is wrecked, a woman is stretched out on the floor and the neighbours are crowding in. What's your first move?

You answer a call to the scene of an accident. A car has run into a petrol tanker at a junction. The driver and passenger of the car are covered in blood and are very still. The tanker driver is in a state of shock. A heavy flow of traffic is moving past at a good clip. Petrol is spreading over the road. A man is lighting a cigarette. Over to you.

PANIC VOMIT COPE RUN ☐
TICK HERE TICK HERE TICK HERE TICK HERE

RIGHT now you may be hesitant to claim that you know how to cope with situations like these.

But after only six months with us in the Metropolitan Police you could be handling even trickier problems with confidence.

How can we be so sure?

We're careful who we take on.

You have to be British, at least 5′8″ tall, intelligent and fit before we'll consider you.

You also have to have a "good character", which means we can't take a chance on you if you've been in serious trouble with the police.

We will bring out the worst in you.

Then you go to Hendon for 16 weeks of intensive training.

Quite a bit of the time is spent in classrooms, learning about law; about police procedures and about the powers of a Police Constable.

You'll do social studies. And you'll learn how to give evidence in court.

And you get practical police training from instructors who are all very experienced police officers. They set up crime and traffic incidents that would make Chief Superintendent Barlow think twice. And then they act the part of awkward members of the public. If you've got a quick temper or a sarcastic tongue they'll find it.

You'll learn how to control yourself under stress. And you'll learn where the pitfalls are for a young Police Constable, and how to avoid them.

You'll go for one week on street duty with an experienced policeman.

Then if you pass your exam, you'll be posted to one of the Metropolitan Police divisions.

During the first few weeks at a police station, you'll go out on patrol with an experienced police officer.

Then you learn what it's really all about.

Very quickly you'll realise the difference between being at Hendon and being on the ground in London.

An instructor pretending to bleed to death isn't the same as someone actually doing so outside the local bank.

On the other hand, the criminals you meet may not be quite as awkward as some of the instructors acting the part.

Just like in any other occupation, you get to know when to apply the rules and when to use your common sense.

And then, all of a sudden you're on your own. And we guarantee that by then you won't panic, run, or vomit whatever you encounter. (Well, you won't vomit where anybody can see you anyway.)

But you are still on probation until you've been in the force for two years.

During which time you'll go on various courses. You'll learn the basics of criminal investigation and you'll probably learn to drive.

And you'll learn more every day you're on street duty.

When the two years are nearly up and you're through your exam, you're all set to apply for promotion or specialisation if that's what you've decided you want.

How far you go is up to you.

The never-ending variety of things that you have to deal with as a Police Constable will keep you involved and interested for years.

A lot of constables spend their whole time in the police on street duty. They feel, quite rightly, that this is where the main police work is done.

In fact, everybody who is in the police who isn't a constable on street duty is helping the constables on street duty, to do their job.

You help prevent people injuring one another and robbing one another.

You help them overcome all kinds of difficulties that they can't, won't or don't know how to overcome themselves.

And you can only do so if you're there on the ground, in contact with the people. You can't do it from an office.

Nobody does it just for the money.

The pay isn't sensational. But its a lot better than it looks at first glance. You start at a minimum of £1,433 a year for a 42 hour week during your probation. Then you get a rise every year for the first six years. Besides which police pay is reviewed regularly to keep it in line with the cost of living.

If you are married you get a free house or flat or a tax paid rent allowance of up to £15.53 per week to pay for your own accommodation. Obviously if you are single you get less.

Promotion is by examination.

Once you've proved yourself as a Police Officer, there's nothing to stop you going for promotion if you want to.

You simply have to pass the promotion exam. After five years service (less in some cases) you become a Sergeant.

After another four years you may move up to Inspector.

If you do exceptionally well in your exam for Sergeant, you can apply to go to the National Police College, Bramshill, for a one year course.

A year after successfully finishing the course you'll almost certainly be an Inspector. (And this is possible before your 25th birthday.)

From an Inspector upwards promotion is by selection.

Along the way, you may decide you want to specialise. You may apply to go into the CID or the Traffic Division, the Mounted Branch or become a Dog Handler. You might fancy the River Police.

As a member of the Metropolitan Police you are automatically a member of all the many sports and social clubs run by the force. No matter what your favourite sports or hobbies are we cater for them. And our facilities are probably as good or better than you'll find anywhere.

Now, here's a challenge you've got to face right now.

The dreaded coupon.

Have you got what it takes to fill it in and send it to us?

We'd like to think we can depend on you.

LONDON'S 8,000,000 PEOPLE TAKE A LOT OF LOOKING AFTER. COME AND GIVE US A HAND.

Paul Silverman is the Chief Creative Officer of Mullen, Wenham, Mass. He was a published fiction writer and journalist before joining Mullen in the mid-1970's when it was a three-person shop. The agency now employs over 160 people and has a client list that includes Timberland, Rolls-Royce, Campari and J&B Scotch. Over the years Paul's work has won at Cannes and all the major American shows. Recently, the Wall Street Journal gave him the full-page spotlight in its Legends of Advertising series.

All written advertising derives from an ancient myth about an Arabian prince. In every piece of copywriting the consumer is Aladdin. The product is the genie in the lamp.

This is the first of many pontifications about copywriting I'll try to cram into this short piece. Only after reading them all will you understand that success cannot be assured unless you learn, not Arabic, but Chinese.

What, after all, is a copywriter? An advocate, rather like a lawyer.

Like lawyers, copywriters build persuasive cases for clients by selecting truths that are positive and omitting truths that are negative. This is different than lying. Lying is inelegant and foolish. It is not professionally challenging.

Being challenged is important, and this is why, if you want to perform at your copywriting best, you must let the clock tick until it sounds like a time bomb. In other words, insist on a deadline and wait until it gets pretty close. Deadlines are the legal amphetamines of professional writers.

In my opinion, a deadline breathing down your neck will be a far more effective stimulus than a jog around the park or an hour on the treadmill. A maxim of the Age is that physical exercise clears your mind and generates energy. I find it makes me calm and, therefore, stupid. The absurd conceptual fusions required in copywriting can best be achieved under tension and anxiety.

For related reasons I would urge that you avoid the so-called 'brainstorming' session, in which a dozen people gather in a room, loudly free-associate ideas and paper the walls with meaningless truisms scrawled in magic marker. This is a 1950's advertising cliché and the refuge of mediocre minds. Good stuff usually comes out of two people who are so plugged into each other conceptually they can be a thousand miles apart and still complete each other's sentences.

To get an honest shot at the gold, make sure you find employment at one of the agencies (there are only a handful) skilled at consistently selling bold creative work. A lifetime of creating great copy at a timid agency will win you the reputation of being a timid copywriter, because all that will reach the public are your tenth-draft compromises.

Be sure to remember that clients are not literary critics. Usually they buy your passion, not your prose. Look them in the eye. Don't rely on the fax machine to sell your stuff.

Copywriting requires different skills than novel-writing. A good analogy is baseball, where you have two kinds of pitchers. Starting pitchers, who pace themselves to go the whole game. And relief pitchers, who jump in when there's a crisis and throw brilliantly for short bursts. A relief pitcher can't waste a pitch. And a copywriter can't waste a word.

It follows that effective ad writing must move at higher speeds than normal writing. To make your writing move fast always assume a passive reader. Not someone leaning forward at his desk to devour every word, as if his job depended on it. But someone sitting back on a toilet seat, riffling and browsing, his mental engine at idle.

To break through such torpor will require a sledgehammer or a hell of a headline. Once you have it, avoid second starts. Consider the headline your first sentence.

Object to everything as you write it. Keep rewriting until you say yes. Build your ad on a series of yes responses.

Develop the ability to split your personality. Role-play, just like actors do. Visualise one reader and write to that one person. Stay on this track.

Pay attention to paragraph transitions. They are the corners of your race track. Avoid the natural impulse to brake and hesitate.

Puns, these days, are risky business. But brilliant puns work. Anything brilliant can break any rule.

Alas, we live in such a visual age that even the word 'copywriter' sounds old–fashioned. Shaping copy on a Mac to fit a visual makes you feel less like an author than a designer of words. Which brings us to the role of the art director and/or type designer.

These days, even the Shakespeare of Madison Avenue would be defeated by lousy typography. Typography supplies colour and mood, much as the voice does in spoken language.

This is old news in China, where the written language consists of thousands of characters, each of which was originally a picture. In this fact there is inscrutable guidance for copywriters of all nations, even those of the barbarian West.

Modern copywriting is cinematic, meaning that the double page spread has evolved into a movie screen. Like an ancient chinese scribe, your job is to write pictures. Use words as though they were frames of film in a camera, and shoot fast.

Verbs, of course, always make faster pictures than adjectives. a) A sharp, jagged cut in the paper was made by the knife. b) The knife ripped through the paper.

Of course, scenes on film (moving or still) communicate faster than any words, even verbs. And since the best ad writing involves compression (cut, cut, cut), one could argue that a copywriter's greatest act is to conceive of an unforgettable scene in which no words occur whatsoever.

As my allotted space runs out, I envision you, the reader, some years from now. You are in a red booth under a dragon–festooned lantern. You dine on bird's nest soup and Peking duck. The meal ends. The waiter brings you a fortune cookie. You crack it open and dig out the ancient message. "Wealth awaits the writer who truly values the art director over the dictionary."

When you have a picture that wants to be the star it's often better to flatten the headline language and give it a supporting role.

HAUTE COUTURE IN PARIS, TEXAS.

We don't know what the latest look is on the runways of Paris, France.

But we do know what they're showing this year in Paris, Texas, and Paris, Maine.

The same thing they show every year. Original, authentic Timberlands. Boots that, somehow, get more beautiful with every mudbath. Just like a fancy Parisienne couture model.

That's where the similarity ends. Nobody kicks around a French model the way they kick around our boots. We set the meanest example ourselves — right in our own testing lab.

In one particularly grueling ordeal, we put a mass of water behind several pieces of our best Timberland boot leather.

We then flex the leather again and again, simulating the movements the human foot might make were it slogging through a similar mass of water deep in no man's land.

After flexing each piece sixteen thousand times, we accept only one result. No leakage whatsoever. A single drop and the leather is rejected. No appeals, no second chances.

Another torture test involves our so-called "boot within

a boot," your ultimate insurance of dry, comfortable feet under the worst, wettest, coldest conditions.

The boot within a boot is actually a sock constructed of waterproof Gore-Tex fabric, warm Thinsulate® insulation and smooth Cambrelle.

We take this innocent-looking sock and give it the infamous bubble test. We fill it with air, submerge it in a glass water tank, and we patiently watch. One air bubble and the sock is sacked. Period.

Besides these and a multitude of other trials, we construct our boots by impermeably bonding the upper to the midsole, creating a water-tight cradle around your foot. We keep seams to a minimum, and sew each stress point with no fewer than four rows of waterproof nylon lock stitching.

So, when a size 12 guide boot says Timberland® on it, you know you can put it through anything on earth. From Paris, France, to Paris, Texas.

Because it's already been there.

The Arch of Triumph

The arch of Paris, France, is a stone monument to victory. The arch of Paris, Texas, is the midsole support system in a Timberland boot. Voila!

Timberland
**BOOTS, SHOES, CLOTHING,
WIND, WATER, EARTH AND SKY.**

They're also found in the canyons of Wall Street.

What could a canyon dweller have in common with a condo dweller? As far as the weather goes, probably more than you think.

For who would say that a Northeast gale howling down the corridors of Wall Street is any easier to endure than a Southwest windstorm thundering through a ravine?

Since both of these explosions of wind, water, earth and

sky play a role in shaping the American landscape, it is our view that both should play a role in the design of clothing for the American landscape.

Which is why you will see your canyon dweller hit the trail in Timberland Ultralight chukkas, mountain shorts, denim shirt and windproof field coat. While three thousand miles to the

east at sea level, your condo dweller hits the streets in our dress casuals and weatherbucks — classic city footwear whose tough tap sole construction and waterproofing give them longevity unheard of in the annals of urban fashion. So if you think Timberland only means the rugged outdoors, think again. Because the rugged outdoors is right outside your window.

Timberland
Boots, shoes, clothing, wind, water, earth and sky.

These three Timberland campaigns, all from the same writer, show how different visual treatments and typography alter the brand personality and "take-away", even when the core copy message is basically the same throughout.

This shoe has 342 holes.
How do you make it waterproof?

Wherever you look in our footwear line, you find holes.

You find wingtips with scores of stylishly arranged perforations.

You find handsewns with scores of needle holes. Moccasins. Canoe moccasins. Boat shoes. Ultralights for easy walking. Lightweight comfort casuals for weightless walking.

Built by a lesser waterproofer, each of these styles has enough openings to admit a deluge.

But we're the Timberland company, and you have to understand where we got our start. Over twenty years ago, we were exclusively a boot manufacturer, and we were the first people to successfully produce fine leather sporting boots that were totally waterproof.

The lessons we learned then are why we're able, today, to build wingtips and handsewns you could go wading in.

Lesson one. Select only the cream of the world's leather crop, then spend the money to impregnate every pore with silicone at the same time the leather is being tanned in the drum. (We leave the shortcuts to our competitors, the ones who merely brush the surface with silicone after the leather is tanned. And the consequences, unfortunately, we leave to their customers.)

Lesson two. Be inventive. It takes more than one technology to stop water.

For example, to build a waterproof wingtip, we take a page right out of the old Timberland bootmaker's manual. We bond the upper directly to the midsole, creating an impermeable seal around your foot.

Then we build a special umbrella under those stylish wing perforations. It's actually a "shoe within a shoe."

A bootie lining of our softest saddle glove leather, fully waterproofed with silicone. Guaranteed to stop a monsoon.

Handsewns require a different solution, but one that also harks back to our boot days, when we became an early collaborator of the W.L. Gore

Company, creators of waterproof, breathable Gore-Tex™ fabric.

To waterproof the needle holes of a handsewn moc, we use an exclusive technique in which Timberland saddle glove leather is laminated to a Gore-Tex bootie. Once we place this inside the moc, you have a shoe that's an open and shut success. Open to air and shut tight to water. Climate-controlled, in other words, both inside and out.

So even if it never leaves the canyons of Wall Street, every Timberland waterproof shoe owes its character to a world that will never see a sidewalk. The canyons, tundras and marshlands where our boots were born.

Which makes Timberland shoes more than waterproof.

They're water proven.

Boots, shoes, clothing, wind, water, earth and sky.

I'm a ❏ red hot mama,
but I'm ❏ blue for you.
I get ❏ purple with anger
at the things you do.
And I'm ❏ green with envy
when you meet a dame.
But you burn my heart up
with an ❏ orange flame.
I'm a ❏ red hot mama,
but you're ❏ white and cold.
Don't you know your mama
has a heart of ❏ gold.
Though we're in those ❏ grey
clouds, some day you'll spy
that terrific ❏ rainbow
over you and I.

Rodgers and Hart, *Pal Joey*

Unigraphic
Color Separations that Sing

Sometimes the writer's best contribution is to think of something that involves almost no writing of his own.

Sometimes you write a headline and look for a picture. In this ad, the picture suggested the headline.

In this case the horses function as body copy. Their bodies are more expressive than words.

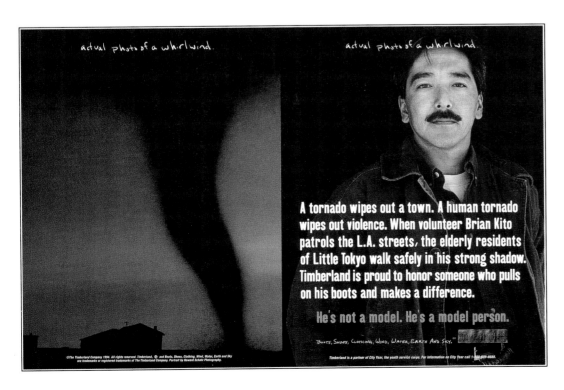

Words are like cameras. Use them to create vivid pictures in the reader's mind.

I was born in 1950 in a newly independent India – the era chronicled so vividly by Salman Rushdie in Midnight's Children – and attended the same Bombay school as he did. Had a happily grubby childhood running wild in the rain forests of India's Western Ghats.

At Mayo College, a white marble mirage in the Rajasthan desert, improbably topped with an onion–dome clock tower – wizened brahmins attempted to teach me Sanskrit and sitar. Somehow I ended up studying girls, guitar, beer and Eng. Lit. at Pembroke College, Cambridge.

I wanted to make documentaries, but after a spell as an itinerant, penniless scriptwriter, was hired in 1976 by David Bernstein to do ads instead. In 1979 I spent a year in India working on a new English translation of Vatsyayana's Kama Sutra – the first published in the West since Richard Burton's 1888 edition.

In 1980 I joined O&M to work with Garry Horner, unwittingly following once again in the footsteps of Salman Rushdie, who had also been a copywriter at O&M and also worked with Garry.

Joined Collett Dickenson Pearce in 1984. Won first of six D&AD Silver pencils in 1986. Copy awards include the Campaign Silver for the Best–Written Ad four times. Awards are nice, but more satisfying was lifting Amnesty's response figures to a peak of 14 times the industry average. I've been lucky enough to work with some of the best art directors in the world, notably Neil Godfrey, my partner for six happy years at CDP.

In 1991 I co-founded Antennae, a combination of advertising, multimedia, environmental, legal and programming talents. Created and launched the Bhopal Medical Appeal. In 1995, in the spirit of truth, we renamed the company Chaos.

Of all the ads I've written, my favourite is 'In Praise of Bowel Nosodes', composed in Indian English for a roguish friend who runs an Indian bookshop. It never won an award or got into any annual, but I love it like a brother.

This friend, the bookseller Shreeram Vidyarthi, is famous for tormenting his customers. 'Ohé, janaab,' he will say to a man who is mishandling a book, 'Treat it like your mistress, not your wife.' When I was translating the Kama Sutra, I'd ordered some old Sanskrit erotic texts from Shreeram. Imagine my horror when he bawled out across the crowded shop, 'Ohé, Sinha sahib! your sex books have arrived.' 'Nosodes' is really a sort of gonzo performance, in which the ad itself becomes an undiluted blast of Books from India.

Shreeram has always taken a professional interest in my advertising work. No-one was more disgusted than he when a cretinous junior Minister at the MOD turned down the Army Officer ad about Mahatma Gandhi on the grounds that it was insulting to Indians. With heavy irony, we pointed out that it

had been written by an Indian. Shreeram even rang the Ministry of Defence, pretending to be the Secretary of the Gandhi Society, and gave the civil servant who answered a stern lecture about relics of cultural imperialism. His motives, needless to say, had little to do with non–violence, love of country and Bande Mataram. No, the ovoid shyster simply wanted the ad to run in his ghastly Indian Bookworm's Journal, total circulation, 3,000, all articles penned by himself under a variety of names.

'Yaar, one juicy advert can finance the whole damn issue. Doesn't the British Army owe us something? Didn't we fight for bally blighters in two world wars?'

For the same reasons, he wanted to run the Imperial War Museum ad. On a visit there, I had been moved by a letter that Lieutenant Eric Heaton wrote to his parents on the eve of the Battle of the Somme. Later, looking through the archives, I came across a photograph of his unit in action at the precise moment he was hit, and could not escape the terrifying thought that Eric Heaton was in there somewhere, bleeding to death. Unusually, with this ad the copy was written before the headline. After rejecting dozens of lines, I finally wrote down the thought that had obsessed me from the instant I first saw the picture.

An ad that did run in Shreeram's journal was the spitting skinhead for the Metropolitan Police. We'd actually planned to use an ad I'd written in Hindi: a picture of an Asian PC, with 1,000 heartfelt words under the banner 'Dóst ya Dróhi?' ('Hero or Traitor?'). Shreeram promised a whole issue focused on police and racial tensions – special print run of 30,000, dished out free in Southall and Brick Lane, copies airlifted to New Delhi – elite effort, no expense spared, I swear. Trouble was, the Met, willing to spend money running our 'Prejudice' ad in glossy middle class magazines, jibbed at the prospect of talking to real live ethnic people. So it never happened. Pity. I had planned to enter it for a copy award as my revenge on D&AD's bovine jurors.

When Neil Godfrey and I took over the Metropolitan Police campaign, we made a decision to probe deeply and write honestly about what we found. I'm told this led to someone on a D&AD jury saying the ads should be debarred from the judging because 'they're not ads, they're journalism'. Thanks, whoever you were. With an accolade like that, who needs awards?

Advertising people often say my ads don't read like ads, which I take as a compliment. The Guinness ad was an attempt to wrap a Sherlock Holmes miniature around a pint of Guinness. In this yarn the dark ruby hue of the mother-of-stouts inspired the plot. In another, Holmes identified the murderer by the imprint his moustache left in the creamy head. The campaign was kiboshed by the Ernest Saunders scandal.

It's not easy to avoid sounding like an advertisement. I can spend hours on a single sentence and have sometimes done twenty drafts of a long ad, creeping downstairs in the middle of the night to call the thing back on the screen. In the bright light of 3am, every flaw glares at you. The bits you cherish most seem horribly contrived. At this point I generally chuck the whole lot out and write something new off the top of my head.

When a piece works it feels obviously right. Good writing flows like music. It has a logic that is part technical, part rational, part emotional. It's also easy to tell where it's not working. A useful short cut is to hold typed copy at arm's length and scan it with half-closed eyes. Writing that makes ugly shapes on the page usually flows like a blocked drain.

Two favourite writers of mine are Tony Brignull and Neil French. I love their work because it is never merely clever, it's intelligent. Every line contains a fresh idea.

Sometimes, the right ideas for a piece are hard to find. Writing about Kurds bombed with chemical weapons, I got into a blind rage and accused Margaret Thatcher, George Bush and the readers of The Guardian of having done nothing to help. The first draft stopped there. I showed it to my wife, who said it sounded like a hysterical rant. It was, but I was desperate to find a way to keep it in. It was two days before the answer occurred. To justify the rage, Amnesty must take the blame on itself. Had

its attempts to alert the world worked, public opinion would have stopped the genocide. People must join to make Amnesty strong enough to be heard next time. A brave client swallowed hard, and the ad brought in a record response.

Shreeram became my client one afternoon at his French chateau, a romantic ruin whose last known use was by gypsy horsetraders as a stable. Much of our visit was spent forking hay out of the front rooms and stuffing holes in the roof with sodden copies of Paris Match. Nonetheless the lilacs were in bloom and Shreeram's shiny new ride-on mower was something to behold. His problem was that he had somehow to pay for all this. Hence our conversation. 'You are a professional huckster,' he said. 'Make me rich. Sell my bookshop with snappy slogans.'

'Bhai sahib,' I told him, 'you don't need slogans. An ad shouldn't be a list of boasts, yoked together with puns and tawdry wordplay. It's a chat. There's as much listening as talking in a good piece of copy. Never write things you'd rather die than say in person. You must accept that the reader has a right to reject your message and should be given the chance to do so. Good writing is subtle. It derives its deepest meaning not from what is said, but from what is left unsaid. Deciding what not to say and how not to say it can take a long time and be very frustrating.'

'Shabaash!' said Shreeram, 'Let us employ these too-elite stratagems to launch a frank appeal to the readers of the Literary Review asking them to save us from the bailiffs.' (We did, and many of Auberon Waugh's people sent donations.)

Over the years I've worked for all sorts of clients, from Shreeram's bookshop to huge corporations, and come finally to these conclusions. Life is too short to work for people you don't really like, or products and causes you can't believe in. As a writer, your words go out into the world to millions of people and change things. It's a big responsibility. If all you care about are awards and money, you are playing for the smallest available stakes. Me? Because I know how powerful words are, I want to play for the highest stakes. I want to help shape the future.

"When our children were dying you did nothing to help. Now God help your children."

Iraqi Kurdish refugee

The Kurdish district of Garmiyan in the mountains of north-eastern Iraq used to be a pretty place.

There were wheat fields and apricot orchards. The gardens grew melons and pomegranates and grapes. Most houses had a cow tethered outside.

One April morning in 1988, the mountainsides echoed to the drone of Iraqi bombers and the flat thud of chemical bombs.

A white cloud drifted among the apricot blossom. Whoever breathed it, died.

Later that day, a group of Kurdish guerillas came across a procession of people, blistered and burned, stumbling silently from a stricken village.

Azad Abdulla was one of the guerillas. "Can you imagine," he asks, "what it's like to die this way? If it's cyanide you get dizzy and choke. If it's mustard gas your skin blisters and your lungs begin to bleed and you drown in your own blood."

Abdulla laughed when we showed him a leaflet which tells Americans in Saudi Arabia how to survive a chemical attack.

(It's reproduced here.)

It advises turning off the air-conditioning and standing under a running shower.

But the Kurdish villagers had no such luxuries.

Instead, they had to evolve their own crude methods of coping with poison gas attacks.

They would retreat into a cave after having lit a fire at its mouth. They would climb to the tops of mountains. They would wet turbans and wrap them round their faces.

On that April morning there had been no time to take even these crude measures.

Azad Abdulla and his companions found a small boy and girl clinging to each other. While running away through a wheat field they had come under attack from an Iraqi helicopter and become separated from their parents. The parents had died but the children did not know this.

They kept saying that when it grew

light they would go and look for them. They thought it was night. They did not realise that they were blind.

Almost to the day (on April 12th 1988), Junior Foreign Office Minister David Mellor was forecasting that British industry would soon find "a large market in Iraq."

Was he unaware that Saddam Hussein was systematically gassing Iraq's Kurdish minority? Hardly.

Only three weeks earlier, more than 5,000 men, women and children had died horribly in an Iraqi poison gas attack on the Kurdish town of Halabja. The atrocity received world-wide TV and newspaper coverage.

"Bodies lie in the dirt streets or sprawled in rooms and courtyards of the deserted villas, preserved at the moment of death in a modern version of the disaster that struck Pompeii. A father died in the dust trying to protect his child from the white clouds of cyanide vapour. A mother lies

by side. In a cellar a family crouches together." (Washington Times, March 23rd 1988).

The world was shocked. But not shocked enough to do anything effective. While the USA condemned Iraq's use of chemical weapons, calls for sterner action were resisted.

According to James Adams, Defence Correspondent of the Sunday Times, such western impotence must have acted as an incentive to President Saddam Hussein.

The world's inaction is a subject about which we at Amnesty International find it difficult to remain polite.

For years we have been exposing atrocities committed by the Iraqi government. Nothing effective has ever been done.

On 8th September 1988, five months after Halabja, Amnesty appealed directly to the United Nations Security Council to stop the

(After expressions of concern from another UN body in August 1990, we are still awaiting effective action.)

Saddam Hussein's annexation of

You, Margaret Thatcher, did nothing effective. You, George Bush, did nothing effective. You – yes you – reading this advertisement, did nothing effective.

Right now you have a choice. Get offended, or get involved.

This advertisement is an appeal for more members and more money. But we must tell you frankly that there is now little Amnesty can do for the people trapped in Iraq and Kuwait, be they Kuwaitis, Westerners, Asians or the 4 million Iraqi Kurds who are also living in fear.

So why should you join us?

Because we failed with Iraq. Failed to make any impact on Saddam Hussein. Failed to stir the United Nations into doing anything effective. Failed to reach enough ordinary people, like you, who were willing to channel their outrage into constructive action.

God knows how many lives this failure will yet cost.

We have got to make it impossible in future for governments to ignore the genocide of helpless women and children. It must become morally unacceptable for governments to look at photographs of dead children from places like Halabja and then carry on 'business as usual' with their murderers.

That's why you should join us and, if you can afford it, make a donation to our campaign funds. (Small donations gratefully received, business-people please think big.)

"We were screaming till we could not speak," says Azad Abdulla, "and yet no-one listened." It's you he's talking to. If you can hear what he's saying, clip the coupon.

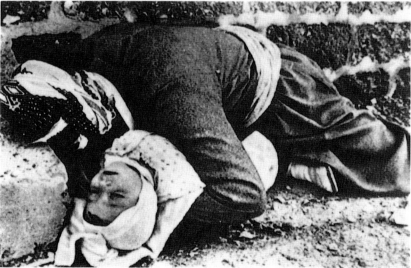

cradling her baby alongside a minibus that lies sideways across the road, hit while trying to flee. Yards away, a mother, father and daughter lie side

massacre of Kurdish civilians by Iraq. Nothing effective was done.

A year after Halabja, we published a report detailing how an eyewitness saw a baby seized as a hostage and deliberately deprived of milk to force its parents to divulge information.

How children as young as 5 years old had been tortured in front of their families.

We revealed that at least thirty different forms of torture were in use in Iraqi prisons, ranging from beatings to burning, electric shocks and mutilation. Torturers had gouged out the eyes of their victims, cut off their noses, ears, breasts and penises, and axed limbs. Objects were inserted into the vaginas of young women, causing the hymen to break. Some of these methods had been used on children.

The report failed to move the United Nations Commission on Human Rights which, days after its publication, voted *not* to investigate human rights violations in Iraq.

Kuwait seems to have taken many people by surprise. Why?

Why be surprised by the savagery of the Iraqi regime that daily tortures and kills Kuwaiti citizens?

Why be surprised that westerners trapped by the invasion are now helpless hostages?

Why be surprised that it is now young Britons who face the chemical weapons that wiped out thousands of defenceless Kurdish villagers?

Yes, we told you so. In '80, '81, '82, '83, '84, '85, '86, '87, '88 and '89. And you did nothing effective to help.

The opening of this ad is too mannered and should have been cut. It works when the anger starts to show, but took a great deal of thought to resolve.

COULD YOU TURN THE OTHER CHEEK?

As a police officer, sooner or later you're bound to encounter abuse, threats, provocation, even physical violence. Be careful how you respond. Lose your temper and you could lose your job. Photograph by Don McCullin

COOL CUSTOMER, are you? Okay, let's see how far you can get before you blow your stack.

You are walking down a street. Some youths start jeering at you: "'Ello, 'ello, 'ello." Smile. You've heard it all before, every name a copper can be called: rozzer, old bill, pig, fuzz, peeler, flatfoot, the filth. And some less complimentary. Shrug it off.

You're out in the patrol car when you see a car without lights weaving through the traffic. You flash your headlights at him to stop. Instead, he accelerates away.

Siren on. Ahead your target, still without lights, narrowly misses a woman on a pedestrian crossing and then goes the wrong way round a roundabout, while a youth leaning out of the passenger window showers you with empty beer cans and two-finger salutes.

The car skids round another corner

and slides into a brick wall, but the youths inside are out and running. You chase, abandoning your car with its engine still on and door left wide open. As you grab the driver, he mouths obscenities at you.

"You can't go on the attack, whatever the provocation."

Still in control of your temper? Okay, try this.

A demonstration is turning into a riot. You're bussed in, nervous and not sure what to expect. It's frightening. The crowd, in ugly mood, surges against the frail police line.

Suddenly a lone voice calls your number "EF203, EF203." The others take

it up. "EF203, EF203." They're all staring at you, trying to psyche you out. Why you?

It gets worse. Bottles arc down and burst in showers of flame. Stones and half bricks drop out of the air and threaten to brain you. You cannot leave the line.

At last the crowd starts drifting away. As the tension ebbs, you see a man step forward and deliberately stub out his cigarette on the flank of a police horse.

This all sounds a bit melodramatic, but we've made none of it up. Each of the details we've described really happened.

How would you have reacted?

Strangely, people often find that in a real emergency they stay calm. But stress builds up in the body like static and can earth itself without warning.

Three days after a riot like the one

above you may arrest a well dressed drunk. "Look here," he drawls, "do you realise who you're talking to?" And jabs you in the chest.

Careful. This trivial annoyance may become the lightning rod for all that pent up stress and rage.

If, in any of the situations we have described above, you were to lose your temper, you might also lose your job.

It doesn't seem fair, does it? But then being a police officer is no ordinary job. As someone sworn to uphold the law, you of all people cannot break it.

And the law says that you may use no more than reasonable force. You can't go on the attack. No matter what the provocation.

So what should you do? Should you say: "Are you going to come quietly or do

I have to use earplugs?" In fact, a bit of humour can often defuse a potentially ugly situation. As can tact, restraint and good common sense.

Of course, it's a strain being on best behaviour 24 hours a day. Never switching off. With the very highest standards to set and live up to. Sometimes, all that bottled up stress can make us difficult to live with.

An officer on motorway patrol raced to an accident. A car was on fire. The heat was ferocious. He had to watch, helpless, as a child the same age as his own daughter burned to death before his eyes.

When he got home, his wife produced supper. Without a word, he picked up his plate of food and flung it through the window. Until then he had kept control of his emotions. But that night of all nights he could not face a cooked meal.

As a police officer you will inevitably endure your share of unpleasantness and you'll have to evolve your own way of dealing with it.

But why are we dwelling on these

traumatic subjects? Isn't this supposed to be a recruitment advertisement? Are we trying to put you off?

Actually, yes.

If you're put off by an advertisement, you'd never be able to cope with the reality.

"It gets worse. Bottles arc down and burst in showers of flame."

And we need people who can cope. People who are tough, tender, sensitive, strong and disciplined, all at the same time. They aren't easy to find. At present we take only one in five applicants. We'd rather look at fewer, better candidates.

Seeing you've got this far, we'll now admit that a career in the Met isn't all grief. Few jobs are as rewarding.

Ask the much loved Streatham home beat officer who, helmet under arm, cigar stuck firmly in mouth in flagrant disregard

of regulations, can tell you the name of every child in his manor.

Ask the constable who, while patiently unravelling the intricacies of gang warfare in, of all places, Southall, has been invited to six Indian weddings in the last year.

Ask the sergeant who now runs what is virtually a Bengali advice centre in Whitechapel.

We can offer 28,000 more examples. If you don't believe us, stop any police officer in the street and ask.

When you've learned what they get out of the job, ask how they got in.

They'll tell you about our twenty week

basic training course at Hendon. And life on the beat at one of London's 187 police stations where, under the tutelage of a sergeant, you will learn the art of handling people. And yourself.

Right now, your next step is to fill in and post the coupon below.

We're looking for mature, fit people aged between 18½ and 45, especially from the ethnic minorities. You should be at least 172cms tall if you're a man, 162cms if you're a woman.

Ideally, you'll have some 'O' level passes or their equivalents, but we value your personal qualities more.

Top: Before writing these ads, Neil Godfrey and I spent two months with the Metropolitan Police. We interviewed dozens of officers, were called out to knife–fights, taught to drive at Hendon Police Driving School, crouched terrified in the back of speeding patrol cars, spent days at Scotland Yard's Black Museum, helped home beat officers calm battered wives, took in the sights of Streatham with the Vice Squad, chased a burglar across a row of back gardens in Southall and spent a memorable day walking round the ruins of Whitechapel with Don McCullin, dogged by a small soiled man who insisted that in a half demolished building, he had unearthed a cache of papers which revealed the identity of Jack the Ripper.

Left: One of several ads I wrote for Shreeram Vidyarthi. They became a well known fixture in 'The Bookseller' and used to bring him letters from as far afield as Chile and Saudi Arabia. The ads cost about £30 each to produce on an old Atari ST in the days before I had a Mac.

Mahatma Gandhi on the threshold of 10 Downing Street. Nothing Gandhiji did, no protest he began, no movement he inspired, ever embarrassed the British Government so much as his turning up to meet the Prime Minister and the King wearing a dhoti. Fifty years later, it seems he still has the power to embarrass ministers, as this ad was turned down on the grounds of being 'insulting to Indians', despite having been written by one.

HE'S A SHINING EXAMPLE OF WHAT EVERY ARMY OFFICER SHOULD BE.

Someone once asked Mahatma Gandhi for his views of Western civilisation. After a moment's thought he replied: "It would be a very good idea."

If you are considering a career in the Army, we would like you to think carefully about this remark.

At the time it was made, memories of Ypres, Verdun, the Somme, Passchendaele and Vimy Ridge were still fresh in people's minds.

The 'Great War for Civilisation' had been the worst slaughter humanity had ever known.

On the first day of the Somme, British casualties alone numbered 57,470 dead, wounded and missing.

By 1918, several million young Britons, Indians, French, Germans, Canadians, Anzacs and Americans lay beneath the chalky soil of Picardy.

No wonder Gandhiji was bitter. He hated war.

Which, you may think, makes him an odd choice of role model for aspiring Army Officers.

Well, consider this: a new European war would make the battles of 1914-18 look like Sunday school outings.

Even one relatively low-yield nuclear weapon would be worse than a hundred Sommes.

So if the modern Army has one overriding purpose, it is to prevent conflict.

In trouble spots throughout the world we act as peacekeepers, a task which calls for strength, yet restraint.

This attitude, strange though it may seem, has a great deal in common with Gandhiji's philosophy of non-violence.

"A non-violent person," he said, "will lay down his life in preventing quarrels."

In Europe as part of NATO, we help to keep a peace which has now lasted for nearly five decades.

But, you may ask, what credibility would our deterrent have if we sought to avoid conflict at all costs?

The answer is that if pushed to it we will fight. (Even Gandhiji told his followers, "If the only choice is between cowardice and violence, choose violence.")

We have to be prepared for war yet work for peace.

This isn't as contradictory as it sounds. "Non-violence is a weapon of the strong," Gandhi said. "A child who has not the strength to wield the club does not practise non-violence."

Nor is it ever a safe or easy option.

If you were regularly pelted with filth and insults while on peace-keeping duty, would you have the strength to grin and bear it?

If one of your men had his leg blown off by a terrorist bomb and passing civilians laughed to see his death agonies, would you be able to control your anger?

Would you be able to continue to act coolly, clearly, decisively, fairly, under circumstances which would drive most men mad with fear and rage?

To exercise such restraint takes a special kind of person.

Such a one, wrote Gandhiji, "must cultivate a habit of unremitting toil, sleepless vigilance, ceaseless self-control."

"Incorruptible, fair and square in his dealings, truthful, straightforward and utterly selfless, he must also have true humility."

Of course he himself was the most outstanding example of what he preached.

He was a man of great physical and moral courage. An inspiring leader and a brilliant tactician.

He had immense integrity, discipline, a powerful sense of service and in his personal life was a warm and loyal friend.

All of which are qualities we would be delighted to recognise in any young Army Officer.

For more information about a career as an Army Officer please telephone 0800 555 555 at any time (call free of charge).

Or post this coupon to Major John Floyd, Army Officer Entry, Freepost 4335, Dept. 0112, Bristol BS1 3YX.

Full name _____

Address _____

_____ Postcode _____

Date of birth _____ Nationality _____

My attempt to write a 'real' Sherlock Holmes miniature. Before writing this and six other stories, I took myself to Conan Doyle's house in Crowborough in Sussex, a few miles from where I live, and tried to visualise the countryside through the eyes of a century ago. Guide books containing old photographs of the area gave me many clues and I did not forget that Conan Doyle had been a spiritualist. I doubt if it is his voice speaking through me here, but the exercise was great fun while it lasted.

The ILLUSTRATED ADVENTURES of

SHERLOCK HOLMES

I. The MYSTERY of the

FRAMFIELD RUBY

"You will recall, my dear Watson," Sherlock Holmes said to me one day, "how the dreadful business of the Abernetty family was first brought to my attention by the depth to which the parsley had sunk into the butter on a hot day."

Upon my nodding agreement he produced with a flourish some yellowing sheets of paper. "These then may interest you," he said. "My notes on the singular affair of the Framfield Ruby. It is, if I say so myself, the most perfect miniature of its kind in the science of detection.

I SHOULD LIKE A GLASS OF GUINNESS.

"It was at a dinner at Lord Furnival's, that the young Duchess of Framfield lost a valuable ruby ring. Or rather, lost the ruby - which was the size of a pigeon's egg - it had once adorned the forehead of a Hindoo idol. Upon glancing down she uttered a cry and fainted dead away. It was then discovered that of the ring all that remained was an empty gold setting - the ruby had vanished.

"Of course, dinner was abandoned as all present hunted high and low for the missing stone. But to no avail. It had utterly disappeared. Lord Furnival's house being no great distance from Baker Street, I was called and found the distraught host and his guests assembled in the Chinese drawing room.

"'We are anxious to avoid a scandal,' he said, 'and would rather not call in the police if you can help us to locate the missing stone.'

"I examined the dining table which was just as the company had left it, the places still set for an intimate dinner of eight people. A dish of oysters had been served, and to judge from the plates, the meal had not been completed when the tragedy was discovered.

"'I shall be happy to oblige,' I said. 'But I perceive that you have been enjoying Guinness with your oysters and I should like if I may to take a glass while I consider the matter.' As you know, Watson, it is widely believed that Guinness nourishes the reflective faculties.

"'You may have all the Guinness you wish,' said his Lordship, 'only do please address yourself to the question of the missing gem.'

"The butler now appeared with a glass and a jug of the admirable beverage. Of course, Watson, you realise that the pouring of a Guinness is an art which takes time. One must allow the first wild surges to subside and then continue pouring gently until a thick, creamy head forms on the—"

"Yes, yes, Holmes," I said. "I am as fond of the stout as you are, but do get on with the tale."

"Your impatience," said Holmes, "is no more than that of Lord Furnival and his friends was. It was an agony for them to watch as slowly I sipped.

"Gradually, the level in the glass was lowered. The head, you know, is possessed of the most remarkable cohesive powers and remains intact to the bottom of the glass - it is one of the chief beauties of the dark stout. When at last I had finished, there was a sigh of relief, which turned to annoyance as I called for the glass to be replenished. The Duchess moaned and was again overcome with nerves.

"'Mr Holmes,' said his Lordship, 'I must ask you to curtail your enjoyment until you have enquired into this matter.'

"'Indeed,' I replied, 'there is nothing further to investigate. The case is solved.'

"'But this is astonishing, Holmes,' I cried. 'You had done nothing but drink Guinness.'

"'Precisely,' he replied. 'And if, Watson, you would be so kind as to pour us each a glass of that excellent beer, I shall soon furnish the solution to the mystery.'

"I was kept in considerable suspense as the dark liquid frothed into the glasses and we drank in silence before my friend spoke again.

"'Upon examination of the table, I had noticed that of the four gentlemen present, three had drained their glasses before they were refilled. It is easy to see that the descending head leaves rings around the glass. In the case of the fourth, the Guinness had not been finished before the glass was refilled.

"Now such is the charm of the beer, that it is inconceivable that a man who enjoys it should not have drained his glass. It could only be because the glass contained something that did not wish to be uncovered..."

"'The ruby!' I cried.

"'Exactly so,' replied my friend. 'When the stone became loose and rolled from the lady's hand, it was unnoticed by any save one gentleman who, finding himself in possession of it, and, needing to conceal it quickly, saw that he had the perfect hiding place to hand.'

"'If you will raise your glass, Watson, and hold it up to the light you will see that, dark though it is, the beer contains a brilliant ruby highlight. Indeed, it is one way the connoisseur can tell Guinness from inferior stouts.

"'No doubt this was in the mind of Colonel Sebastian Moran as, in those desperate seconds, he wrestled with his conscience and failed to resist temptation.'

"'Moran!' I cried. 'that rascal!'

"'It was the beginning of our enmity,' Holmes replied gravely. 'Of course, there was no need to accuse him, since I was able to return the jewel to its grateful owner without further delay. I said that I had found it beneath a napkin. And now, Watson, there is just time for another glass before breakfast.'"

"Bravo Holmes," I cried, "this is pure genius." He made no reply, but I could see that he was deeply moved.

THE FRAMFIELD RUBY

{ One of a series of stories commissioned by Arthur Guinness & Son, to commemorate the Sherlock Holmes Centenary, 1887-1987. }

16th Middlesex retreating with heavy losses from Hawthorn Ridge, 7.45am.

SOMEWHERE IN THIS PICTURE, 2nd Lt. ERIC HEATON LIES DYING.

By 4am, there was enough light to see the German lines.

Near the rivers, mist still lingered, but the wooded ridges were clear.

A light rain began to fall and the men in the trenches held out their helmets to catch the water. Their throats were dry.

The rain gave way to a cloudless blue sky, without a breath of wind. It was going to be hot: a perfect summer's day.

Tangles of yellow weed marked the enemy trenches and the grassy fields of No Man's Land were covered in scarlet poppies.

At 6.25am, the British guns opened fire on the German positions.

It was July 1st 1916. The Battle of the Somme was about to begin.

A walk-over

All along the 18 mile front, British infantrymen were preparing for the coming action.

They did not expect a tough fight. Their generals had promised them that the German trenches would be empty, wiped out by the British artillery.

One Brigadier-General assured his troops they would not need rifles. They could go over the top with walking sticks.

During the previous week, the German lines had been hit by 1,508,652 British shells and mortar bombs.

People in the south of England heard the bombardment and wondered if a naval battle was being fought in the Channel.

Few realised that the far off thunder was the beginning of the Big Push which would win The War To End Wars.

Fix bayonets

Not every soldier believed it would be a walk-over.

Some men, peering out across their parapets, could see that the barbed wire entanglements opposite them were still intact.

One sergeant in the Middlesex could not stop the shaking in his body growing worse and worse as Zero Hour approached.

Others were in high spirits. Captain Neville, of the 8th East Surreys, gave each of his platoons a football to kick off towards the German trenches.

A rum ration was served and some men became tipsy. "Fix Bayonets" was carried out with much laughter.

A letter home

In his front line trench in the Beaumont-Hamel sector, 2nd Lt. Eric Heaton of the 16th Middlesex was nerving himself up for his first action.

He was 20 years old and had been in France four months. On the eve of battle he had written to his parents:

"I cannot quite express my feelings on this night . . . My greatest concern is that I may have the courage and determination necessary to lead my platoon well".

Eric Heaton had a crucial task.

At 7.20am, ten minutes before Zero Hour, a gigantic mine: a tunnel packed with explosives, would detonate beneath the German redoubt at Hawthorn Ridge.

His men were to cross 500 yards of No Man's Land and quickly occupy the newly formed crater.

Zero hour

At 7.20, the mine at Hawthorn Ridge blew, spewing a huge column of chalk and earth thousands of feet into the air.

Seconds later, shock waves rocked the trench where Eric Heaton and his platoon waited, throwing men to the ground.

German artillery immediately opened fire on the nearest British trenches and shrapnel rattled like hail above the heads of the 16th Middlesex.

The men could not understand where the enemy fire was coming from – weren't the Germans all supposed to be dead?

When the last seconds had ticked away, Lt. Heaton blew his whistle and started up the ladder to No Man's Land.

The 9th Platoon of the 16th Middlesex scrambled up after him, weighed down by their heavy packs.

Slowly, they fanned out into a long line and began to move towards the smoking Hawthorn Ridge crater.

The new tactics

Because the generals expected little German resistance, they had altered the normal rules of an infantry attack.

The British soldiers were to advance slowly in waves.

Each wave was to walk forward at a steady pace, covering no more than 100 yards in two minutes. (A speed of rather less than two miles an hour.)

As the leading waves paced farther into No Man's Land, they started hares that were still living there among the long grasses and wild summer flowers.

Then the German machine-gunners opened up.

'Tac-Tac-Tac'

Too late, it became clear that their deep shelters and dugouts had preserved the Germans from the British artillery.

The waves of soldiers, following orders, came walking slowly forward and toppled like dominoes as the machine guns swept their lines.

The dead lay in long rows where they had fallen. As the few survivors continued to advance, German howitzers began to pound No Man's Land.

A man in Eric Heaton's battalion described what it was like:

"Imagine stumbling over a ploughed field in a thunderstorm, the incessant roar of the guns and flashes as the shells exploded. Multiply all this and you have some idea of the Hell into which we were heading."

The fate of the 16th Middlesex

Eric Heaton's men were unlucky. In the ten minutes between the blowing of the Hawthorn Ridge mine and the start of the attack, the Germans had already occupied the newly formed crater.

The 16th Middlesex were swept by machine gun fire and blown apart by artillery shells. The leading wave had almost disappeared, but individual survivors kept to their steady, disciplined pace.

The following waves met the same fate, yet always a few men survived and kept going.

2nd Lt. Eric Heaton was last seen alive in the maelstrom of exploding metal near the German front line.

"I saw him in No Man's Land not far from the German lines and at that time he was quite alright in company with Mr Tuck." (Pte. A.J. Bird) The two officers were exhorting their men to push on through the German barbed wire.

Oranges and lemons

The enemy's barbed wire entanglements, like his trenches and his troops, were supposed to have been utterly destroyed by the British artillery bombardment.

Yet all along the front, men who had survived the holocaust of No Man's Land reached the German wire to find it still intact.

At Gommecourt, five miles to the north of Eric Heaton's sector, the reason for this was plain to see.

Unexploded British mortar bombs, large and round as footballs and painted bright orange, lay in drifts against the wire.

They were, in the soldiers' slang, 'napoo'. No good. Duds.

Most of those who tried to cut or thread their way through the German wire got caught on the long barbs.

One by one, as they struggled there, they were shot.

Missing believed Killed

No-one knows for certain what happened to 2nd Lt. Eric Heaton.

One report stated that he had been wounded by a machine gun and later killed by a shell. But one of his platoon said that he saw him hit in the knee – it was almost blown off – and thought that he had bled to death.

Eric Heaton was one of 57,470 men listed killed, wounded or missing on that first day of the Somme.

Unmentioned in despatches

You will not find 2nd Lt. Eric Heaton in the history books. His moment of glory went unrecorded. His last remains are a bundle of letters and photographs kept in a cardboard box in our vaults.

From them, we have pieced together his story.

Our Museum contains thousands of such stories. Not just from the Somme, but every battle of the First and Second World Wars.

Not just the stories of soldiers, airmen and sailors, but of civilians who found themselves caught up in war. We would like to tell their stories. But without your help, many of our cardboard boxes will never be opened.

Will you help us?

The Imperial War Museum is in urgent need of help.

Our building leaks. Plumbing, wiring, heating and drains must all be completely replaced. The glass roofs above our main galleries are beyond repair.

Facilities for visitors, particularly the disabled, are poor.

Worst of all, the Museum is simply too small to display its collections properly.

We have very little money. In fact, we could not have published this advertisement but for the generosity of the newspapers in which it appears.

The first phase of our redevelopment scheme will cost £9,000,000. If we can raise £2,500,000, the Government have said that they will give us the rest.

You can help us by making a donation or a covenant. Every £10 covenanted will produce £14.30. Please address donations and enquiries about covenants to the Director, Imperial War Museum, Lambeth Rd, London SE1 6HZ. Cheques should be made payable to 'The Imperial War Museum Trust (Redevelopment Appeal)'. Thank you.

IMPERIAL WAR MUSEUM APPEAL

GIVE YOUR PAST A FUTURE

Inspired by a letter in the Museum. The copy was complete before I looked for a headline.

John graduated from the University of Missouri School of Journalism. His early career included stints at BBDO-Minneapolis where he worked primarily on Hormel products including SPAM, and Martin/Williams-Minneapolis where much of his work was for 3M products including Post-it Notes and Scotch tape. After Martin/Williams, John began a nearly eight-year stint at Fallon McElligott where he created advertising for a number of the agency's blue-chip clients including Prince spaghetti sauce, Scotts lawn products and Windsor Canadian Whiskey to name a few and, most predominantly, spent his final four years at Fallon creating the US work for Porsche. In 1993, John moved to Chiat/Day-Los Angeles as Creative Director focusing on Infiniti, Nissan's US luxury car division.

I like to say that my work has spanned the gamut from SPAM to Porsche. The ultimate expression of range, almost anyone would agree.

As with acting, range is the most important characteristic for an advertising writer if one is to be prolific. This is assuming raw talent. But many writers with raw talent have created one or two good campaigns for products that are near and dear to them, then disappeared. The art of the business comes in being able to understand the problems and opportunities of any product, and then understand how to create a bond between that company or product and those people they are trying to reach.

In many ways, creating advertising is the same discipline as acting. You must start by mentally discarding your own identity. You have to become the people you are communicating with. Internalise their interests, joys, fears, tastes, even biases. Often it means mentally and emotionally becoming someone you would never in a million years be like yourself.

I think that's why virtually every great advertising creative I've met is a student of humanity; interested in every different trend or personality type or culture they've ever been exposed to. They are fascinated by the 'human condition'. They are incessant people watchers. They are also, and many business types will be shocked to read this, among the most tolerant people you will ever find. They often get a reputation for being intolerant; for being spoiled prima donnas who refuse to bend or compromise.

But that is usually because they are defending this very need for uniqueness; the need to break through the homogeneity of modern life and speak in a powerful and distinct way to one pocket of humanity, creating a powerful and distinct identity for a brand by doing so.

This need is often shunned or even resisted by clients who want to be everything to everybody. After all, it's the nature of the corporate world with all its hierarchy to breed fear and caution; the propensity to try and fit in. In a Porsche commercial, I once likened the committee thinking of the corporate world to a flock of small birds, huddling in a tree 'seeking safety in numbers'.

This leads to another key aspect of the creative process. And, while not literally a step in the actual creation of great advertising, it is equally important. Just as you must 'become' your prospect in order to create a message that will be meaningful to them, you must 'become' your client if you expect to sell them on the idea. This is the process many creatives fail at. They feel cheap if they attempt to 'play the corporate game'. In reality, your client is a consumer just like those for whom you created the advertising. You must understand their beliefs, fears and prejudices if you expect to get them to do as you wish. This doesn't mean that you become political; it simply means that just as you must learn to speak the language of your prospect, you must learn to speak the language of your client to make them understand your thinking. Of course, you can't do great advertising for a bad client. Some companies are so overwrought with fear and the desire for safety that they will never buy a truly breakthrough way of presenting their product. At the same time, a lot of the greatest advertising ever written is collecting dust in file cabinets because the creatives didn't think through how to communicate the idea to their client in a fashion that would overcome any reservations with the excitement of the idea's potential.

This is what makes advertising so tricky to practice, yet at the same time so rewarding. Advertising is a bridge between the worlds of art and business. It must entertain, intrigue and emotionally move people if you are going to get their attention, yet it must fulfil very basic marketing needs. Those creatives who learn how to cross back and forth between these two worlds, invisibly, unnoticed by either consumer or client, are the ones who not only create good work but see it produced.

With these basic tenets for preparing to create great advertising, and preparing to sell it, in mind, some of the functioning caveats or practices I have found valuable would be:

– Pay careful attention to your first ideas. They are formed with the same innocence, naiveté and lack of jadedness that consumers have when first exposed to your advertising. There is value in that innocence and simplicity.

– On the other hand, don't stop too soon. Even if the essence of your first ideas is correct, explore every possible expression of that essence. Write every headline 100 different ways. Advertising is art, and like poetry, every comma will affect the balance of meaning.

– Understand what the perceptions of your product are now. The current attitude of the consumer is the starting point, and the desired attitude is the finish line. Often, clients are reticent to admit what the current attitude toward them is. You have to make them understand. You can't start the race in the middle.

– Once you have placed yourself in the mind-set of the consumer, relax and be human. Don't be afraid to think cynical thoughts or joke about the product as you work. I've found that a lot of great ideas started as jokes which, when explored, could be turned around to make a powerful, positive statement. Ideas that start this way have an honesty the consumer appreciates.

– Don't just accept cultural change, embrace it and try to understand what leads to it. Advertising is a living chronicle of the evolution of society.

– Resist developing a style. You're trying to speak with people on their own terms, not preach at them with your own beliefs.

The basic motivations of people never really change. That's why Shakespeare is still relevant today. Human history pretty much boils down to the influence of love, sex, greed, hunger and insecurity. If you want to write great advertising, once you get through all the complexities, always go back to the basics.

Frequently, our writers are people who lost their previous job.

On the eve of the 1988 presidential election two former presidents, Carter and Ford, penned letters of advice and counsel to be delivered to the winner.

But they didn't mail them. They gave them to us.

That's because they wrote the letters in response to a request from World Monitor magazine. A request to share their vision of what the new leader could expect. A vision that could come only from having held the job.

At World Monitor, we believe that to truly understand today's complex global issues, you go to the people who have been involved behind closed doors. And let them explain things in their own words.

That's why whatever the story, we search for an expert to write it. From an insider's perspective. And go wherever in the world we have to in order to find them.

Be it a Chinese government official, a former KGB officer or an American schoolteacher.

It's a search for insights no journalist could ever uncover in a newsroom.

For instance, Gerald Ford foresaw that the Berlin Wall could come down in the upcoming presidency. (Remember, this was in October of 1988, even before the election.)

And that's why the people you find reading World Monitor, like the people who write for it, are leaders. Individuals trying to understand the dynamics at play; to survive and prosper in the global village we all now share.

World Monitor. Where those who have been there, and those on their way, come together. To write. To read. And to think. Bound by the notion that there is still no substitute for experience.

WORLD MONITOR
THE CHRISTIAN SCIENCE MONITOR · MONTHLY
Where the people in the news report the news.

Fortunately, every day comes with an evening.

There are some things in life that simply defy explanation to those who have not shared the experience. Such has always been our dilemma at Porsche.

In 1948, in the image of his own dream, Professor F. Porsche created a sports car so responsive and with such an individualistic personality it was almost alive; an extension of the driver's own thoughts and feelings; childlike in its unbridled spirit. For two generations we have sought to explain the sensation. And have always found ourselves saying, simply, you have to try it.

The 1991 Porsche 911 Carrera 4 is part of the current generation in this legendary, mystical family.

To test-drive the Carrera 4 is to discover a relationship between yourself and a car we can but feebly try to express here. Race-bred components are intricately matched to make it seem almost as if it were an extension of your own limbs.

It is this tactile sense of direct contact and control that has been the hallmark of every Porsche. Today, the Carrera 4 uses electronically controlled all-wheel drive to bring the feeling to an unprecedented peak.

Combining sensors and a sophisticated computer, the Carrera 4 monitors traction at each wheel with every revolution. Upon detecting any spin, within 25 thousandths of a second it directs power to the wheels having more grip, correcting slip usually before the driver is even aware of it. Not only does it put more of the car's incredible potential to the ground, but it makes it more useable and predictable.

The all-wheel drive system works together with a new suspension, including a self-correcting design in the rear, to make cornering a startling display of synergy between car and driver.

Every facet of the car contributes to this character. Porsche engineers, for example, say the ideal brakes should make it feel as if you are squeezing the brake discs between your fingertips. Engage the massive, internally vented ABS disc brakes in the Carrera 4, and you'll sense time momentarily freeze as you are hauled to a rock-solid, straight-line standstill.

The fact is, it's ludicrous of us to try and explain the experience further. In over 40 years, we have yet to find a way to do so. All we can say is, if you are the type who looks for joy and stimulation where others see only one of life's necessities, you will no doubt visit your authorized Porsche dealer for a test-drive. Then we'll be able to talk.

The 1991 Porsche 911 Carrera 4

It's like children.
You can't understand until you've had one.

Fortunately, every day comes with an evening.

WINDSOR CANADIAN
Supreme

Luke Sullivan began his career in advertising at Bozell & Jacobs in Minneapolis in 1979. He spent five years | *in Richmond, Virginia, working at The Martin Agency, and has been at Fallon McElligott since 1989*

In *Walden*, Henry David Thoreau exhorted his readers to "Simplify, simplify, simplify." And while it's a little scary to take a blue pencil to Hank's copy, here is my rewrite: "Simplify."

That is my lesson for this book on copywriting: simplify. Everything else after the period in this sentence is repetition of that point, like the last two-thirds of Thoreau's maxim.

Go to the airport and observe somebody reading a magazine. By my watch, it's about two seconds per page. This is the milieu in which your next ad will be read. To succeed, an ad has to be as simple as a stop sign.

In fact, the metaphor of a stop sign applies on several levels. It is relevant. It is one word. There is no introductory copy and no explanation is needed.

Let your next ad be so. Let it be a headline, and nothing else. A visual, and nothing else. Or just two lines of body copy.

(It is fair to ask here, why aren't the ads I've done, the ones included on these pages, why aren't they this simple? My answer is: I wish they were. This simplicity is something I strive for; it is what I want.)

Let simplicity be your byword in all the phases of producing an ad. Let the strategy be simple. Let it be one adjective. Saturns are honest cars. Volvos, safe. Porsches, fast. People live in broad strokes. Write in broad strokes.

Let the goal of the ad be simple. A famous general named Karl von Clausewitz warned: "Attack on as narrow a front as possible." The way I put it: "You can't pound a nail in sideways."

And let your layout be simple. I heard an excellent designer say "Elegance is refusal." Three words that say so well what I have tried so clumsily to say in 300.

An ad borne of a simple strategy, built on one adjective, rendered in one brush stroke, such an ad is usually the kind we see later in awards annuals that make us grind with envy; that make us gasp and say "I could have done that. It's so simple." Yet it's this very simplicity that fools us into believing the ad was done with ease.

To take a common thing, a car, a shoe, a fish stick, and to simultaneously reduce and amplify it in such a way as to stop a distracted magazine reader in some airport dead bang in his tracks, *that* is the art of this business.

The artist Cezanne said this: "With an apple, I will astonish Paris."

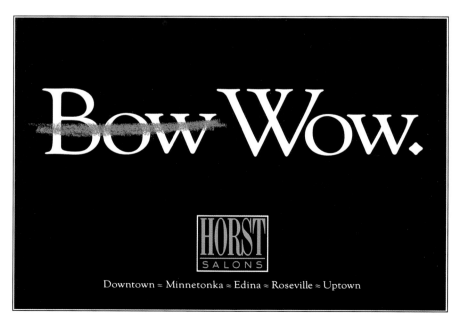

Horst Salons Art Director: Carol Henderson.

Imagine having your body left to science while you're still in it.

Three animals die every second in U.S. laboratories.

The monkey pictured here was surgically crippled and then forced to use his deadened arm.

Other animals, including rabbits, dogs, and cats are routinely blinded, shocked, mutilated, decapitated and force-fed poisons in tests which could easily be replaced with modern and more reliable alternative tests.

These sadistic animal tests are being conducted by the government, universities, medical associations, and profit-making corporations.

And always behind closed, locked doors. Pigs, rats, chickens, horses and other laboratory animals suffer by the millions.

The cost to U.S. taxpayers, however, is in the billions.

If you think these kinds of cruel experiments have no place in the 20th century, please join us: People for the Ethical Treatment of Animals.

PETA is America's leading animal rights organization. By working with medical and legal professionals, the media, members of Congress, and people like you, PETA has been able to stop some of the most horrifying animal experiments, including the one pictured here.

Even as you read this ad, there are thousands more lab experiments being conducted without your knowledge, *but with your tax dollars.*

So please join us today.

Yes, I want to help stop the abuse of animals in experiments.

Name _____

Address _____

City _____ State _____ Zip _____

Please accept my tax-deductible contribution of: $15 _____

$25 _____ $50 _____ $100 _____ other _____

Contributors of $15 or more receive a free copy of the book *Animal Liberation.*

People For The Ethical Treatment Of Animals

P.O. Box 42516 Washington, D.C. 20015 (202) 726-0156

People for the Ethical Treatment Of Animals, Art Director: Wayne Gibson.

For those of you who think Maseratis are just low-slung, high-priced sports cars made only for a handful of racing fanatics, we have some refreshing news.

You're only partially right.

Yes, it's true Maseratis are crafted for only a handful of people who are fanatical about owning special cars.

And, yes, they can be very quick and impressive automobiles.

But, no, the Maserati is not outrageously priced, and it's not the temperamental race car you think it is.

In fact, Maserati is a comparably priced, perfectly sane alternative to the Mercedes, Jaguar or BMW.

So while the Maserati has a well-deserved, larger-than-life image, it's a car for the real world, a car you can actually own.

The main reason there aren't many on the road, of course, is that there couldn't be.

Italian craftsmen painstakingly assemble each car, doing much of the work by hand. Every part of every car is made slowly.

Except, of course, the engine. Which is made fast.

How fast? Well, the muscle under the hood of the 1989 Maserati 228 pictured here is capable of rocketing its driver to 60 mph in 6.3 seconds on its way to a top speed of 140 mph.

The 2.8 litre, electronically fuel-injected, twin-turbocharged V-6 engine can actually deliver 225 horsepower at 5500 rpm.

But this power is never reckless: it's guided by power-assisted rack and pinion steering. And the power-assisted four-wheel disc brakes hold everything in check.

What's under the hood is, however, no more remarkable than what you find behind the door of the new 228.

Inside every Maserati are seats covered

There are two reasons you don't pass many Maseratis on the road. There aren't many on the road. And they are, after all, Maseratis.

with Italian glove leather that's hand-sewn by old world craftsmen, not machine-sewn by robots.

The paneling, the gearshift lever and even the parking brake handle are burled walnut or burnished rosewood.

And on the dashboard of every Maserati, just above the controls for the automatic climate control system, is a Swiss-made, jewelled clock to help you appreciate every

second you spend in these plush surroundings.

While we're on the subject of time, we'd like to point out that every 1989 Maserati owner in America is now protected 24 hours a day, 365 days a year.

They're protected both by our roadside assistance program and by our 3-year/36,000 mile Maserati buyer protection plan.*

These are, of course, merely the logical reasons

for owning one of our exhilarating automobiles.

The best reason might be the little voice inside your head that's been beckoning you to a Maserati ever since you were a kid.

See your dealer. And do it soon. After all, only an exclusive group will be able to buy Maseratis this year.

And, as we said, they're going fast.

You only live once. Do it in a Maserati.

© 1988 Maserati Automobiles Incorporated. *See dealer for details of written warranties. Maserati does not condone exceeding posted speed limits.

Maserati automobiles. Art Director: Wayne Gibson.

Get paid to think up stuff like this.

Some ad agency actually paid a writer and an art director to think up this crazy visual idea for an ad. But coming up with wildly creative solutions to real marketing problems is what advertising is all about. And, after 8 semesters at Art Center, you'll have a good portfolio and a good shot at landing a job in a field that's financially as well as creatively rewarding. Call us at 818-584-5035. Or write to Admissions, Art Center College of Design, 1700 Lida St., Pasadena, CA, 91103.

ArtCenter

Art Center. Art Director: Joe Paprocki.

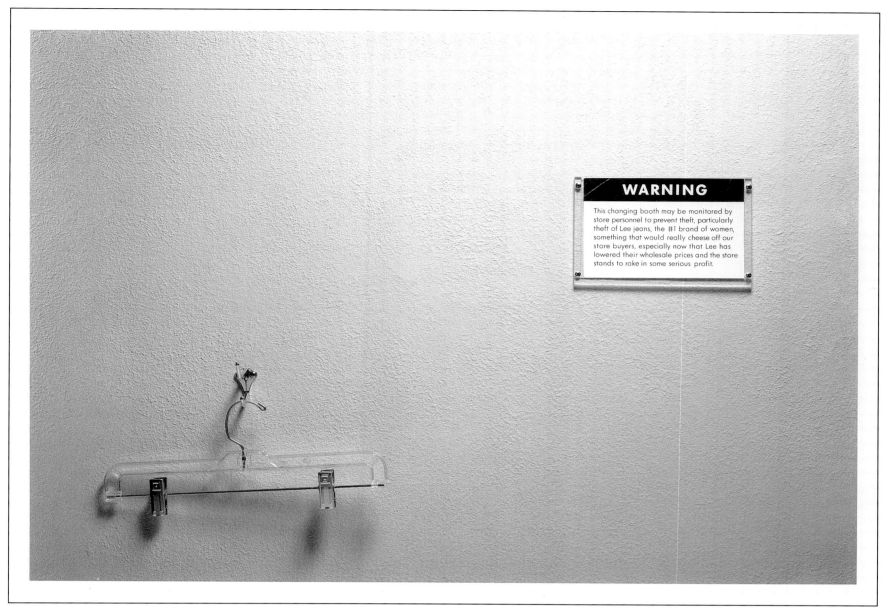

Lee jeans . Art Director: Arty Tan.

Everyone knows, yellow and blue make green.

The best-selling tennis ball plus the best-selling racquetball equals money. It's so simple, it's elementary.

Penn Tennis Balls. Art Director: Arty Tan.

I was born and grew up in the borough of Manhattan in NYC, the only person currently living and working there who did so (everyone else came from Brooklyn or places even more distant). I began my career writing biographies of businessmen for a company that ran instructional seminars and went from there to writing promotional materials for America's leading maker of toilets.

After that apprenticeship I got a job at Ogilvy & Mather. In the years following I worked at Scali McCabe Sloves; Young & Rubicam; Needham Harper & Steers and Ammirati & Puris, causing at least one bank loan officer to wonder why people in advertising change jobs so often.

In 1985, with the backing of the UK's Boase Massimi Pollitt, I opened my own agency, Angotti, Thomas, Hedge, which grew from a standing start to $100 million in billings in seven years.

I left in 1992 and served as a creative consultant at a variety of agencies before settling in at Lowe and Partners/SMS. I've won the awards that people asked to contribute to books such as this have won, including 27 One Show pencils. I'm currently Vice President of The One Club for Art & Copy in New York, and I've written about creativity for Advertising Age and other publications. I'm still looking for a decent apartment in Manhattan.

Except for the client, the agency and the copywriter's significant other, no one is under any obligation to read anyone's ad (and don't be too sure about the significant other, either).

So it's not surprising that much advertising is driven by this modest insight, which is true as far as it goes. The problem is that it doesn't go far enough. The hurdle every ad faces isn't simply getting noticed but getting believed. An ad enters a reader's life like a sullen, shifty-eyed suspect in a police line-up, and there's no presumption of innocence to protect it. The presumption is more likely to be that it's lying, and it will be led off in handcuffs unless it can prove otherwise.

What can an ad do to overcome that bias? Some thoughts:

1. Demonstrate greater insight into the needs of the audience.

People who better understand your needs (a category that includes spouses and shrinks) are seen as better able to meet them. The same for ads. *This ad knows me*, the reader feels, *I can trust it a little bit.* That helps dispel the wariness that buyers feel towards sellers, who often can't be trusted even a little bit. An ad for Xerox information retrieval systems used an obscure provision of Murphy's Law to show an understanding of the problem its target audience faced. It pictured someone in an

office with a phone planted in his ear, hearing the bad news: "We've tracked down the information you've been looking for, sir. It's definitely lost."

2. Attack conventional wisdom.

It's one of advertising's happier paradoxes that ideas that run counter to widespread belief are often more believable. They can startle the reader into fresh perceptions, and they have the quality of new truths replacing older, outworn ones. In the media world there's a truism that a magazine is best measured by its cost-per-thousand numbers, how many readers reached for how many ad dollars. *Barron's*, an investment publication whose readers typically sit on seven-figure nest eggs, challenged the truth of that truism. It argued that quality of readership not quantity was what mattered most. "Lowest cost per millionaire", the headline read.

3. Since facts are more believable than claims, it's better to express claims as facts.

In advertising, *claim* is often a euphemism for *lie*. Many of these euphemised lies are specially constructed to wiggle past lawyers and network censors. You can't say your peanut butter has more peanuts, not without a notarised peanut count, but you can say someone will be a better mother if she serves it. At your arraignment all you have to do is plead Puffery. All charges are dropped. Puffery forgives everything. To lawyers and censors, it's okay to lie as long as you lie on a grand enough scale. To everyone else, a lie is still a lie, and it's almost always transparent. That's why, instead of just asserting that BMW was a good investment, a BMW ad used the car's high resale value to prove the point. And it did so, not by comparing the car to other cars but to other investments people in that target audience might make: "Last year a car outperformed 318 stocks on the New York Stock Exchange."

4. Give the reader permission to believe.

Despite universal cynicism towards salesmen in general and ads in particular, there's a part of us that really wants to believe we'll have more and better sex if we use a certain after-shave or hair conditioner. Unfortunately that part is patrolled by a beefy armed guard who can easily wrestle inanities like this to the ground. What our beefy armed guard needs is enough supporting logic to accept your premise and not look like an idiot. DDB's advertising for Avis didn't just say Avis tried harder; it said when you're only number two you have to – or else.

5. Make it illogical for the reader not to believe.

A collorary to point four. There's a line from Coleridge that goes: "Nothing can permanently please which does not contain within itself the reason why it is so, and not otherwise." The Avis premise, evoking a world where little fish swim faster or get swallowed by bigger fish, met that standard. So did a Volkswagen billboard that showed the car's hood opened onto its rear, air-cooled engine. "No radiator problems. No radiator," read the irrefutable headline.

6. Be the smartest choice in your category.

This notion crops up on every other creative brief these days. It's your basic 'nineties' strategy, although it's lying about its age; advertisers were using it when buyers paid in seashells. It works because everyone wants to be seen as having done some-thing intelligent when he buys a product, or at least not having done something dumb, buyer's remorse being timeless and universal. That's why the Saab 9000 was positioned as "The sports sedan for people who inherited brains instead of wealth."

7. Create an aspiration to buy.

If you have a pulse, you have aspirations. And if a product embodies your aspirations, its advertising doesn't need to be a salesman any more. It can be an alluring inner voice whispering encouragement to act on those urges. For Wild Turkey, the premium entry in the bourbon category, that meant reminding its audience that anything less was foolish economy and self-denial: "There are less expensive bourbons. There are also thin-ner steaks and smaller cars."

In short, an ad is, by definition, a half-truth; it only argues the case *for* the product. The case *against* will cheerfully be pro-vided by the competition, and will be helped along by the healthy cynicism a reader brings to every ad. Which means if he only believes half of what you say your half-truth is reduced to something like a quarter-truth, and you've come perilously close to the point where it's not worth bothering anymore.

If there's a simple principle that sums all this up – and there isn't, but here goes anyway – it's that people who write ads should assume readers are at least as bright as they are. This has the advantage of being true much, maybe most, of the time. It also makes for honest writers – and credible ads.

Somewhere at this moment a jet aircraft carrying several hundred passengers is touching down at triple-digit speeds.

On runways whose surfaces could be perfectly dry, or dotted with icy patches, or glazed with rainwater.

It is about to perform the single most important act any moving vehicle ever performs: the act of stopping.

That feat is no less important when performed on behalf of one to five passengers in a BMW, which, besides roads and weather, must also contend with the treacheries of traffic.

That's why both vehicles use "what is considered by many to be the biggest advance in braking since the disc." (AutoWeek)—the anti-lock braking system (ABS).

STEER AND STOP AT THE SAME TIME.

On the BMW, as on the aircraft, electronic sensors measure the rotational speed of the wheels, feeding this data to a computer. (The computer is well fed; we use four sensors as against a competitor's three.)

Then, operating on the computer's command, a hydraulic control unit applies braking pressure as it should be applied: in the rapid pumping movements that prevent the brakes from locking.

And it does so faster than humanly possible, even if the human in question is a Grand Prix driver. An experienced race driver might be able to pump four times a second; our ABS system, ten.

Should any wheel begin to lock, the computer instantaneously reduces braking pressure until control is regained. A vital factor in panic stops, where both wheels and driver freeze, placing the car at the mercy of its own momentum. ABS permits you to steer and stop at the same time.

ABS is new, and standard, on the BMW 735i, 635CSi and 535i. But in the ways that matter most, it isn't new at all, having proven itself not just on airborne vehicles, but their landborne equivalents: BMW race cars dating back over a decade.

A SYSTEM, NOT AN AFTERTHOUGHT.

ABS arrives not as an addendum or afterthought but as part of a larger system devoted to maximizing your control over the vehicle.

For example, ABS matches, and is fully justified by, BMW's new 3.5-liter fuel-injected engine—a zealous power plant whose talents for acceleration are ideally counterbalanced by ABS's skills in deceleration.

It is also a perfectly compatible mate to BMW's fully-independent suspension systems, with which it shares a common birthplace: high-speed racecourses, where issues of agility and precision take on a special urgency.

All that sets the BMW apart from every other luxury car in the world—but also gives it some vital common ground with the other high-performance vehicle shown (in part) here:

The recognition that true performance isn't measured just by how fast a vehicle goes, but by how well it stops—and how well it does everything in between.

THE ULTIMATE DRIVING MACHINE.

© 1984 BMW of North America, Inc. The BMW trademark and logo are registered.

THE HIGH-PERFORMANCE VEHICLE ON THE LEFT NOW USES THE SAME KIND OF BRAKING SYSTEM AS THE ONE ON THE RIGHT.

LAST YEAR, A CAR OUT-PERFORMED 318 STOCKS ON THE NEW YORK STOCK EXCHANGE.

If you'd bought a new BMW 320i in the beginning of 1980, and sold it at the end, your investment would have retained 92.9% of its original value.
If you'd done the same with any of 318 NYSE stocks, you'd have done less well.
And you'd have forfeited an important daily dividend:
The unfluctuating joy of driving one of the world's great performance sedans.

THE ULTIMATE DRIVING MACHINE.

THE SPORTS SEDAN FOR PEOPLE WHO INHERITED BRAINS INSTEAD OF WEALTH.

There are basically two ways to approach the purchase of a sports sedan. You can spend your way into one, or you can think your way there.

For those who'd rather think than spend, there's the Saab 9000S.

The 9000S is the sports sedan that brings something rare to the category: a complete car.

First, it's a driver's car, engineered for those who take driving seriously

The Saab 900 Series:
*From $18,295 to $33,295.**
The Saab 9000 Series:
*From $22,895 to $33,995.**
For more information,
call 1-800-582-SAAB.

and do it well. It's propelled by the largest engine Saab ever built and a highly tactile steering system.

But unlike some driver's cars, the 9000S doesn't shortchange passengers. It's the only import roomy enough to be rated a "Large" car by the EPA.

Nor does it yield to a station wagon in its practicality. Fold down the split rear seats, and there's enough cargo space (56.5 cubic feet) to fit a six-foot sofa, with a hatchback for easy loading.

In fact, you could buy a 9000S for its utility alone, but then you'd have to ignore its full complement of standard amenities. Including leather upholstery, electric sunroof, heated seats, a driver's-side air bag and anti-lock brakes.

All this comes in a car that, according to studies by the Highway Loss Data Institute (HLDI), ranks among the safest cars in its class. And is backed by one of the longest warranties

in its class: 6 years or 80,000 miles.**

No $26,995* sports sedan can offer all that.

So if you've in fact inherited brains instead of wealth, the best place to spend that inheritance is at your Saab dealer, where the 9000S awaits your test drive.

SAAB
WE DON'T MAKE COMPROMISES. WE MAKE SAABS.™

*MSRP excluding taxes, license, freight, dealer charges and options. Prices subject to change. **Limited warranty covers major components of engines, transmissions and other systems. See your Saab dealer for complete details. ©1991 Saab Cars USA, Inc.

XEROX® is a trademark of XEROX CORPORATION.

"We've tracked down the information you've been looking for, sir. It's definitely lost."

Of all the pieces of information that might get lost, the one that does will probably be the one you need.

Of all the times it might turn up missing, the time it does will be the worst possible time.

These Axioms of Business Life are brought to you by Xerox. For the purpose of adding our own:

Of all the ways to deal with the problem of lost information, the best

is to prevent it from getting lost in the first place.

Which is why we offer electronic typing systems that let you store and retrieve documents as they're typed.

Computer services that let you retrieve information with the efficiency of a computer, but without having to own the computer.

Even telecopier transceivers that let you send copies of documents

cross-country without ever having the original leave the office.

At Xerox, our interest in all this is simple. Our business is helping businesses manage information.

Which brings us to our final axiom: You have to find it before you can manage it.

XEROX

Lowest cost per millionaire.

Ads like this usually congratulate themselves on their alluring cost-per-thousand figures.

And ours are more alluring than most: Barron's has a lower overall CPM than Business Week, Forbes or Fortune. Period.

But we point you now to a more revealing set of numbers— the sort that show up not on media plans but on personal statements of net worth.

Almost one third (31%) of Barron's readers come from households with a net worth of $1 million or more.* Which is substantially more than the competition.

That works out to a little more than two and a half cents a millionaire. Which is substantially *less* than the competition.

So if you're looking to reach an upscale audience, no one will take you to the top of that scale as effectively as Barron's.

And no one charges as little for the trip.

BARRON'S
HOW THE SMART MONEY GETS THAT WAY.

*Source: Survey of Adults and Markets of Affluence, 1985, Mendelsohn Media Research, Inc.
CPM's are based on 7" x 10" black and white units for all publications
1986 DOW JONES & COMPANY, INC.

When you spend 2,922 days mellowing in an oak barrel, you're very, very sociable once you get out.

WILD TURKEY
8 years old, 101 proof, pure Kentucky.

There are less expensive bourbons. There are also thinner steaks and smaller cars.

WILD TURKEY
8 years old, 101 proof, pure Kentucky.

British Design and Art Direction (D&AD) is a professional association and charity working on behalf of the advertising and design communities. It was formed in 1962 to establish and support standards of creative excellence in the business arena as well as to educate and inspire the next creative generation.

D&AD's activities include the largest and most internationally respected awards scheme in the industry, familiarly known as the 'Yellow Pencils', which attracts over 14,000 entries from around the world each year. Associated with the awards is the D&AD Awards Annual which sells a further 13,000 copies and provides the basis of an exhibition which travels the world from New York to Melbourne.

High priority is given to education with a range of activities focusing on students of advertising and design. The Student Awards, since their initiation in 1979, have formed the centrepiece of the education programme, attracting over 1,000 entries from colleges across Europe. D&AD's college membership scheme is highly regarded for its excellent resources and the Guardian Student Expo provides member colleges with the opportunity to show their best work. Particularly popular are the quarterly Masterclass workshops which attract hundreds of applicants for 20 places. Successful candidates are invited to meet and work with young creative teams from leading agencies.

The Festival of Excellence is organised annually by D&AD to celebrate the best creative work of the year. The exhibitions, conferencing and events are well attended by many thousands of visitors and provide an important forum for client companies and practitioners in advertising and design. The Festival receives support from organisations such as the Confederation of British Industry, the Design Council and the Institute of Practitioners in Advertising.

Another popular aspect of D&AD's work is the President's Lecture series. These lectures are open to everyone and have proved to be enormously successful. Some of the most respected creative people in the world have spoken at these, including Saul Bass, Peter Blake, Tony Brignull, Tibor Kalman, Frank Lowe and Dan Wieden.

D&AD is supported by individuals and companies and has a membership of over 1,300 leading professionals.

For further information please contact:

D&AD
9 Graphite Square
Vauxhall Walk
London SE11 5EE
Tel: 0171 582 6487
Fax: 0171 582 7784

The Newspaper Publishers Association (NPA) is the national newspapers' trade association and provides the forum for members to come together to promote and further the interests of the UK national press.

One of the NPA's primary aims is to promote an independent and pluralistic press with the freedom to publish that which is decent, legal, honest and true in editorial and advertisement.

The NPA promotes the use of the press as an advertising medium and has run some dramatic and provocative advertising campaigns in all national newspaper titles, which have demonstrated the value and effectiveness of press advertising. Furthermore, the National Newspaper Campaign Advertising Awards, which were established to reward agencies for their brilliantly crafted press ads, now provide a benchmark for creativity in press advertising.

Advertising in the national press is further strengthened by the work which the NPA does with the advertising community – the different industry bodies and advertising agencies – to encourage good practice and ensure that business between national newspapers and agencies is transacted on a sound basis.

Environmental issues are considered particularly important by the newspaper industry and, through the NPA, initiatives are being formulated to protect the environment. These include promoting and encouraging the recycling of newsprint and supporting research activities to look into different uses for waste newsprint.

The NPA closely monitors legislation, both domestic and European, which may affect publishing or advertising, and supports the industry in representing its interests to government and other opinion formers in the UK and overseas.

The NPA also supports and participates in the production of high quality industry research to assist its members and the advertising industry.

Britain's national press is a uniquely effective medium. It plays a key political, social, commercial and cultural role in the UK – making newspaper readership part of everyday life for some 40 million people. With eleven national dailies and nine Sunday titles – a selection not matched by any other country – it presents great opportunities for readers and advertisers alike.

National newspapers, through the NPA, will continue to work closely on new initiatives and activities to ensure that the national press is a formidable communications medium in the future.

For further information about the NPA contact:

The Newspaper Publishers Association
34 Southwark Bridge Road
London
SE1 9EU
Tel: 0171 928 6928
Fax: 0171 928 2067